I0426069

# 2013 CONSUMER ACTION HANDBOOK

*Be a Smarter Consumer*

USA.gov/consumer

# CONTRIBUTORS

 GSA Office of Citizen Services and Innovative Technologies

January 2013

On behalf of the General Services Administration's (GSA) Office of Citizen Services and Innovative Technologies, I welcome you to the 2013 Consumer Action Handbook. First released in 1979 by the White House Office of Consumer Affairs, and transferred by Congress to GSA in 1997, the Handbook has long been one of the most helpful and popular consumer publications of the federal government.

Whether this is the first time you've seen the Handbook or you get a copy annually, I am confident that it will be a valuable tool to help you make smarter consumer decisions.

I know how important it is to have access to reliable information to make the best choices for you and your family. The Handbook simplifies your search, by compiling information from across government into one comprehensive guide. The Handbook addresses the consumer challenges and opportunities we all face. Some of the more popular topics include buying a car, getting your credit report, choosing a health insurance provider, and writing a social media will. As in past years, the Handbook also includes a template for writing a complaint letter that gets results and a robust consumer assistance directory, with contact information for corporate and governmental consumer protection offices.

The Consumer Action Handbook is just one way you can stay informed with free, trusted government information. You don't have to wait an entire year to get answers to your government questions. Visit USA.gov and GobiernoUSA.gov (in Spanish) or call 1-800-FED-INFO (333-4636) for practical government information. You can order or download electronic versions of this Handbook and hundreds of other government publications at Publications.USA.gov.

We also want to hear from you. Let us know what you think of the Consumer Action Handbook or if you have ideas for ways to improve it. Please email us at action.handbook@gsa.gov or on Facebook (www.facebook.com/USAgov) or Twitter (twitter.com/USAgov).

Sincerely,

Marietta Jelks
Editor-in-Chief, Consumer Action Handbook

---

The Federal Citizen Information Center would like to express its gratitude to the partners listed below who helped make possible the publication of the *2013 Consumer Action Handbook*.

American Cleaning Institute

American Express Company

American Financial Services Association Education Foundation

The Colgate-Palmolive Company

Consumer Product Safety Commission

Department of Veterans Affairs

FanFreedom.org

Federal Deposit Insurance Corporation

Federal Trade Commission

Financial Industry Regulatory Authority

Kellogg Company

Money Management International

National Futures Association

The Procter & Gamble Company

Securities and Exchange Commission

Society of Consumer Affairs Professionals International

THE WHITE HOUSE
WASHINGTON

December 14, 2012

Welcome to the Consumer Action Handbook.

Millions of Americans use financial products, including credit cards, mortgages, and student loans, to lay the foundation for a better tomorrow for themselves and their families. These tools help bring shared aspirations within reach and empower countless individuals to earn an education, afford a home, or raise children. Yet, irresponsible lending and deceptive practices pose serious risks to consumers, and my Administration remains committed to ensuring every American has access to the information and resources that allow them to operate safely and smartly in the marketplace.

This annual handbook is one of those resources, providing consumers with information essential to making financial decisions on everything from purchasing a home and paying for college to securing health care and protecting one's privacy when shopping online. This book is a practical guide for both the complex and the routine issues consumers encounter, and I encourage all Americans to take advantage of this valuable tool.

GSA Administrator

January 2013

Welcome to the 2013 edition of the Consumer Action Handbook. Each year, the U.S. General Services Administration's (GSA) Office of Citizen Services and Innovative Technologies updates this resource with consumer tips to help you in your daily life.

As the dedicated purchasing agency for the Government, GSA understands the importance of maximizing your budget and getting the best value on purchases. The practical information in the Consumer Action Handbook can help you to do the same when you are out shopping. With topics ranging from credit, mobile payments, and the latest frauds, the Handbook addresses topics that can protect your wallet.

The Handbook is also available online with interactive features at usa.gov/consumer. I hope that you take advantage of this Handbook and the information it provides.

Sincerely,

Dan Tangherlini
Acting Administrator

## USING THIS HANDBOOK

This everyday guide to being a smart shopper is full of helpful tips about preventing identity theft, understanding credit, filing a consumer complaint, and more. The information and resources you'll need are arranged as follows:

### PART I—BE A SAVVY CONSUMER

Read this section for advice before you make a purchase. To quickly locate specific topics and information, look in the Table of Contents (p. 1) and Index (p. 147).

### PART II—FILING A COMPLAINT

Turn to this section for suggestions on resolving consumer problems. The sample complaint letter on page 57 will help you present your case.

### PART III—KEY INFORMATION RESOURCES

Look here for a list of public resources and contact information.

### PART IV—CONSUMER ASSISTANCE DIRECTORY

Here you'll find contact information for corporate offices, consumer organizations, trade groups, government agencies, and more.

### VISIT US ONLINE

A searchable version of this *Handbook* is available online at www.USA.gov and in Spanish at www.GobiernoUSA. gov. You can also order or download an electronic version of the *Handbook* and hundreds of other consumer publications at Publications.USA.gov.

## QUICK CONSUMER TIPS

As a savvy consumer, you should always be on the alert for shady deals and scams. To avoid becoming a victim, keep these things in mind:

1. A deal that sounds too good to be true usually is! Be wary of promises to fix you credit problems, low-interest credit card offers, deals that let you skip credit card payments, work-at-home job opportunities, risk-free investments, and free travel.

2. Don't share personal information with someone you don't trust. Learn how to recognize fraud.

3. Beware of payday and tax refund loans. Interest rates on these loans are usually excessive. A cash advance on a credit card may be a better option.

4. Read and understand any contract or legal document you are asked to sign. Do not sign a contract with blank spaces or where the terms are incomplete. Some contracts include a clause that prohibits you from taking legal action and require you to engage in mandatory arbitration with a company in the case of a dispute.

5. Get estimates from several contractors for home or car repairs. Make sure the estimates are for the exact same repairs for a fair comparison.

6. Before you buy, make sure you understand and accept the store's refund and return policies, especially for services and facilities that charge monthly fees.

7. When paying for your purchases, double-check the final price. If you think the price that has been charged is incorrect, speak up. Remember, when shopping online, your purchase may include additional fees, such as shipping, handling, and convenience fees that are not calculated until you check out.

7. When shopping online, look for the padlock icon in the bottom corner of your screen or a URL that begins with "https" to ensure that your payment information is transmitted securely.

9. Don't buy under stress. Avoid making big-ticket purchases during times of duress (e.g., coping with a death or debt).

10. If you are having difficulty making payments on loans, notify your lender immediately so that you can work out a payment plan.

# TABLE OF CONTENTS

## BUYER BEWARE

### BEFORE YOU BUY

To avoid problems and make better decisions, use this checklist BEFORE you make a purchase:

- Decide in advance exactly what you want and what you can afford.
- Do your research. Ask family, friends, and others you trust for advice based on their experience. Gather information about the seller and the item or service you are purchasing.
- Review product test results and other information from consumer experts. See Key Information Resources (p. 59) or check the *Handbook* index (p. 147) for specific information.
- Get advice and price quotes from several sellers.
- Make sure the seller has all appropriate licenses. Doctors, lawyers, contractors, and other service providers must register with a state or local licensing agency.

## DRIP PRICING

Have you ever planned to make a purchase, only to find out that there are additional, sometimes mandatory, fees that weren't included in the advertised price? The total cost is not revealed until the end of the purchasing process. If so, you have been the victim of drip pricing. This practice makes it difficult for consumers to determine the full cost and compare similar options, when all the fees aren't disclosed up front. You can protect yourself by reading the policies before completing the sale and asking questions of sales personnel. Also, if you have charged your purchase on your credit card, you may be able to dispute the extra fees if they are more than you had agreed to with the seller.

- Check out a company's complaint record with your local consumer affairs office (p. 112) and Better Business Bureau (p. 67).
- Get a written copy of guarantees and warranties.
- Get the seller's refund, return, and cancellation policies.

## QUICK TIPS FOR AVOIDING FRAUD

There are many varieties of consumer fraud, but the most common ones are variations of fake check scams, credit repair, free trip offers, and sweepstakes. Here are some tips to help you avoid being a victim:

- **Don't give out personal information**. Be suspicious of anyone you don't know who asks for your Social Security number, birthdate, credit card number, bank account number, password, or other personal data.
- **Don't be intimidated**. Be suspicious of calls or e-mails that want you to provide or verify personal information immediately. Answer that you're not interested and hang up or don't reply to the e-mail.
- **Monitor your accounts**. Review bank and credit card statements carefully, and report unauthorized transactions to your financial institution immediately.
- **Use a shredder.** Tear or shred credit offers, bank statements, insurance forms, and other papers with personal information.

- Ask whom to contact if you have a question or problem.
- Read and understand any contract or legal document you are asked to sign. Make sure there are no blank spaces. Insist that any extras you are promised be put in writing.
- Consider paying by credit card. If you have a problem, you can dispute a charge made on your credit card (p. 13).
- Don't buy on impulse or under pressure; this includes donating to charity.

## SERVICE CONTRACTS AND EXTENDED WARRANTIES

Service contracts or "extended warranties" can add hundreds of dollars to your purchase price, but they are rarely worth the cost. Some duplicate warranty coverage you get automatically from a manufacturer or dealer. Ask these questions before you agree to one of these contracts:

- Does the dealer, the manufacturer, or an independent company back the service contract?
- How are claims handled? Who will do the work, and where will it be done?
- What happens to your coverage if the dealer or administrator goes out of business?
- Do you need prior authorization for repair work?
- Are there any situations when coverage can be denied? You may not have protection from common wear and tear, or if you fail to follow recommendations for routine maintenance.

## PRODUCT SAFETY RECALLS

Before you buy a used vehicle or other second-hand product, check to be sure that it hasn't been recalled for safety reasons. Some recalls ban the sale of an item, while others ask consumers to return the item for replacement or repair. Sometimes, a seller will provide a part that reduces the danger of using the product.

If you're buying a product for a child, be especially careful. Each year, there are approximately 100 recalls of children's products such as toys, clothing, cribs, and costume jewelry. Visit the websites in the "Check Here for Recalls" box to find the latest safety recalls. You can also sign up for free e-mail notifications at www.cpsc.gov/cpsclist.aspx or download the app from www.Recalls.gov on your mobile phone.

## IDENTIFYING AND STOPPING FRAUD

Look for these warning signs to avoid fraud:

- You are asked for your bank account or credit card number.
- Someone you don't know offers you the chance to receive a credit card, loan, prize, lottery, or other valuable item, but asks you for personal data to claim it.
- The solicitation looks like a government document and suggests that contest winnings or unclaimed assets are yours for a small fee. (The government doesn't solicit money from citizens.)
- Someone you don't know asks you to send money or money orders to claim a prize, lottery, credit card, loan, or other valuable offer.
- An unknown caller claiming to be a lawyer or in law enforcement offers to help you get your money back (for a fee).
- The deal is only good "for today" or a short time.
- A "repair person" suddenly finds a dangerous defect in your car or home.
- You are given little or no time to read a contract.
- A sale item is suddenly unavailable, but a "much better item" is available for slightly more money.
- Someone is trying to scare you into making a purchase.

To learn more about avoiding identity theft and fraud, go to page 38.

## SHOPPING FROM HOME

Late delivery, shipment of wrong or damaged items, and hidden costs are common complaints when consumers shop from home. To avoid problems and resolve them more easily, follow the advice in the Before You Buy checklist (p. 2). In addition, here are some general tips:

- **Be wary of post office boxes** and sellers in other countries. It may be difficult to find the seller to resolve a problem later.
- **Know the total price.** Make sure it includes all charges, shipping, handling, insurance, and taxes.

## CHECK HERE FOR RECALLS

- www.recalls.gov lists government-initiated recalls from federal agencies.
- www.nhtsa.gov publishes safety information on vehicles and equipment such as children's car seats.
- www.fsis.usda.gov lists recalls that involve meat, poultry, or processed egg products.
- www.fda.gov lists recalls that involve food, medicines, medical devices, cosmetics, biologics, and pet food.
- Report incidents and safety concerns with consumer products, search for incidents, reported by others at www.Saferproducts.gov

Coupons and other discounts should be deducted properly.

- **Make sure you are clear on what you are buying.** Watch for words such as "refurbished," "reconditioned," "closeout," or "discontinued."
- **The security code** on the back of your credit card offers you extra protections on online purchases.
- **Keep a record of your purchase.** Save any information the seller gives you, such as order confirmation number, product description, delivery date, cancellation policy, privacy policy, warranties, and order confirmation numbers.
- **Keep track of your order.** If it's late, you have the right to cancel and demand a refund.

**Your Rights**

When you order something by mail, phone, or online, the Federal Trade Commission (FTC) requires the company to:

- Ship the merchandise within the time promised, or if no specific delivery time was stated, within 30 days of receiving your order.
- Notify you if the shipment cannot be made on time and give you the option of waiting longer or getting a refund.
- Cancel your order and return your payment if the new shipping date cannot be met, unless you agree to another delay.

If you cancel your order, your money must be refunded within seven days (or your account must be credited within one billing cycle if you charged the order). The company can't substitute a store credit. If you applied for a charge account with the merchant at the same time that you placed your order, the company has an extra 20 days to ship the merchandise to allow time for processing your application.

These FTC rules only apply to the first shipment of magazine subscriptions or other merchandise you receive repeatedly. Orders for services (for example, photo finishing), sale of seeds and growing plants, and

## ONLINE AND GROUP COUPONS

In addition to the traditional coupons found in newspapers, coupons can be found online. They may be found on manufacturers', companies', dedicated coupon, or social media websites.

Group coupons are another online saving tool. Local companies offer reduced prices for things like spa services, gourmet meals, and outdoor adventures through a third-party company; then you pay the third-party company to take advantage of the deal. Group coupons allow you to try new experiences by reducing the trial cost. Before you purchase a group coupon, ask yourself, "Am I really going to use this?" If the answer is no, don't buy it.

Read the terms and conditions of all coupons for expiration dates or use limitations.

collect-on-delivery (C.O.D.) orders, are covered by a different FTC rule. Your state may also have rules that apply. Report suspected violations to your state or local consumer protection agency (p. 112) and to the FTC (p. 107).

### 3-Day Cooling-Off Rule

This federal law, which dates back to 1972, protects consumers in their homes during door-to-door sales pitches or at sales in temporary business locations. According to the FTC, the 3-Day Cooling-Off Rule does NOT apply to the purchase of new automobiles or items sold online. It only applies when a company is selling something that costs $25 or more at a location other than its regular place of business.

To comply with the 3-Day Cooling-Off Rule, a seller must inform buyers of their right to cancel the sale and receive a full refund within three business days.

Be aware that there are situations in which the Cooling-Off Rule does not apply:

- You made the purchase entirely by mail, online, or telephone.
- The sale was the result of prior contact you had at the seller's permanent business location.
- You signed a document waiving your right to cancel.
- Your purchase is not primarily for personal, family, or household use.
- You were buying real estate, insurance, securities, or a motor vehicle.
- You can't return the item in a condition similar to how you received it.
- You bought arts or crafts at a fair, shopping mall, civic center, or school.

Remember, if you paid by credit card and are having difficulty getting your refund, you may also be able to dispute the charge with your credit card company

under the Fair Credit Billing Act. See Credit Card Billing Disputes (p. 13).

### Online shopping

Online shopping websites often offer great deals, variety, and convenience. However, consumers need to be careful and make informed decisions about their purchases. Some tips for shopping safely online:

- Stick to websites that are known or recommended.
- Compare prices and deals, including free shipping, extended service contracts, or other offers.
- Search for online coupons, known as promo codes, which may offer discounts or free shipping. Some sites offer promo codes for coupons to be used in bricks-and-mortar stores.
- Get a complete description of the item and parts included, and the price, including shipping, delivery time, warranty information, return policy, and complaint procedure.
- Before you finalize the order, double check the quantity and total price are correct.
- Pay with a credit card. Federal law protects you if you need to dispute charges, but it doesn't apply to debit cards, checks, cash, money orders, or other forms of payment.
- Use a secure browser. Look for an address that starts with "https" rather than "http." Also look for a closed padlock icon, usually in the lower right-hand corner of the screen.
- Avoid making online purchases on public WiFi hotspots; these may not be secure, and your payment information could be stolen over the network. See WiFi (p. 41) for more information.
- Print your purchase order with details of the product and your confirmation number.

For more information, go to www.onguardonline.gov.

### Online Auctions and Sellers

Many people sell items on the Internet through auctions, classified ads, news groups, and chat rooms. Review the Internet section (p. 41) for safe shopping online as well as the general tips on shopping from home (p. 3). When participating in an online auction, remember to:

- Check how the auction works. Can you cancel a bid? Don't assume that the rules one auction site uses apply to another. Some sites offer step-by-step instructions that will take you through the bidding process.
- Find out what protections you have. Does the site provide free insurance or guarantees for items that are not delivered or are not what the seller claimed?
- Follow the strategies used in any auction. Learn the value of the item before you begin bidding, then establish your top price and stick to it.

- Read past customers' ratings to determine if the seller is reputable and delivered quality products, as promised.

- Only bid on an item if you intend to buy. If you're the highest bidder, you have bought it. Auction companies often bar those who back out of a deal from future bidding.

- If the seller can't accept payment by credit card, use an escrow service. A third party holds your money until you get your purchase and approve release of your payment to the seller. There is a small fee, but the peace of mind is worth it.

For more tips, contact the Federal Trade Commission at www.ftc.gov.

## AFTER YOU BUY

Even careful buyers can run into unforeseen problems later on. To minimize them, follow these steps after you buy:

- Save all papers that come with your purchase. Keep all contracts, sales receipts, canceled checks, owner's manuals, and warranty documents.

- Read and follow product and service instructions. The way you use or take care of a product might affect your warranty rights.

If you have a problem with the item you purchased, file a complaint (p. 55)

# BANKING

Choosing a bank is a major decision, and there is no one right choice for all consumers. When you shop for a bank, you have to consider the actual products and services it provides as well as the location of branches, size of the bank, fees, and interest rates. Even if you conduct most transactions online or at automated teller machines, you want to choose a bank with quality customer service. Also, consider the variety of products that the bank provides; some banks may specialize in checking and savings accounts, while others are full-service banks, offering loans and CDs. You don't have to maintain all of your accounts at one bank; you can have relationships with several to get the best rates on different services.

## PROTECT YOUR PIN

Beware of "shoulder surfers." Be suspicious of anyone lurking around an ATM or watching over your shoulder while you use your card. Some thieves even put a device over the card slot of an ATM to read the magnetic strip and record your PIN; this is known as "skimming." If you suspect criminal activity, walk away and use a different ATM.

## ATM/DEBIT CARDS

With a debit card and personal identification number (PIN), you can use an Automated Teller Machine (ATM) to withdraw cash, make deposits, or transfer funds between accounts. Some ATMs charge a fee if you are not a member of the ATM network or are making a transaction at a remote location.

Retail purchases can also be made with a debit card. You enter your PIN or sign for the purchase. Although a debit card looks like a credit card, the money for the purchase is transferred immediately from your bank account to the store's account. When you use a debit card, federal law does not give you the right to stop payment; you must resolve problems directly with the seller.

If you suspect your debit card has been lost or stolen, call the card issuer immediately. While federal law limits your liability for a lost or stolen credit card to $50, your liability for unauthorized use of your ATM or debit card can be much greater, depending on how quickly you report the loss.

- If you report a debit card missing before it is used, you are not responsible for any unauthorized withdrawals.

- Your liability is limited to $50 if you report the loss within two business days after you realize your debit card is missing and increases to $500 if you report the loss between two and 60 days.

- If you have not reported an unauthorized use of a debit or ATM card within 60 days after your bank mails the statement documenting the unauthorized use, you could lose all of the money in your bank account as well as the unused portion of your line of credit established for overdrafts.

Check the policies of your card issuer; some offer more generous limits on a voluntary basis.

Generally, banks may cover your overdrafts under their overdraft service and impose a fee on your account, or they may offer you a separate line of credit that includes interest charges. If your bank offers an overdraft service, you must opt into this service for most ATM and debit card transactions before the bank may impose any fees. Banks must disclose this option, the amount of the overdraft coverage fee, and the customer's right to cancel this service. For more information, go to www.consumerfinance.gov.

## BEFORE YOU SWIPE YOUR DEBIT CARD

Although both credit cards and debit cards are easy ways to pay for your purchases, debit cards have some different levels of consumer protection and potential for consumer fees.

Debit cards are directly connected to your bank account, so when you swipe your card, make sure you have the money in your account to pay immediately. If you don't have enough money in your account, your bank may "lend" you the money and pay the overage. However, it may charge you up to $35 for this courtesy, even if the dollar amount the bank covered was small. Determine whether you can opt out of overdraft protection. Some banks also charge you a monthly fee for making purchases with your debit card. Since new fees can be added without warning, be sure to check periodically for changes to your account fees for using your debit card.

Debit cards don't offer as much protection against fraudulent use or if your card is lost or stolen. Also, if you need to dispute a purchase, you are in a weaker position because the merchant already has the money and will only return it if you win the dispute.

Also, when you use your debit card to make reservations for hotels or rental cars, a hold is placed on your card (and your checking account), which can affect your other pending transactions. Even if the hold is removed, it may take as long as a week until the funds are available to you again.

### SAVINGS AND CHECKING

When it comes to finding a safe place to put your money, there are a lot of options. Savings accounts, checking accounts, certificates of deposit (CD), and money market accounts are popular choices. Each has different rules and benefits that fit different needs. The bank must provide you with the account terms and conditions when you open your account. When choosing the one that is right for you, consider:

**Minimum deposit requirements.** Some accounts can only be set up with a minimum dollar amount. If your account goes below the minimum, the bank may not pay you interest on the money you deposited and you may be charged extra fees.

**Limits on withdrawals.** Can you take money out whenever you want? Are there any penalties for doing so?

**Interest.** How much (if anything) is paid and when? Daily, monthly, quarterly, yearly? To compare rates offered by local and national financial institutions, visit www.bankrate.com.

**Deposit insurance.** Make sure your bank is a member of the Federal Deposit Insurance Corporation (FDIC). This agency protects the money in your checking and savings accounts, certificates of deposit (CDs), and Individual Retirement Accounts (IRAs) up to $250,000. For more information, see page 106 or visit www.fdic.gov.

**Credit unions.** A credit union is a nonprofit, cooperative financial institution owned and run by its members. Like the FDIC does for banks, the National Credit Union Share Insurance Fund (NCUSIF) insures a person's savings up to $250,000.

**Convenience.** How easy is it to put money in and take it out? Are there branches or ATMs close to where you work and live? Can you bank by phone or Internet?

If you are considering a checking account or another type of account with check-writing privileges, add these items to your list of things to think about:

**Number of checks.** Is there a maximum number of checks you can write per month without incurring a charge?

**Check fees.** Is there a monthly fee for the account or a charge for each check you write?

**Holds on checks.** Is there a waiting period for checks to clear before you can withdraw the money from your account?

**Overdrafts.** If you write a check for more money than you have in your account, what happens? You may be able to link your checking account to a savings account to protect yourself.

**Debit card fees.** Are there fees for using your debit card?

**Account fees.** Banks can charge fees on your checking or savings account to cover things like maintenance, withdrawals, or minimum balance rules. However, the bank must inform you of the fees up front as part of your account agreement and notify you when changes occur. Practices vary from bank to bank, but each must inform you of the fee change on your statement, in a separate letter, or in a pamphlet. For more information, visit www.federalreserveconsumerhelp.gov/findananswer/can-a-bank-really.cfm.

**Bounced checks.** It's your responsibility to have sufficient funds in your account to cover the checks you write. If you try to cash a check, withdraw money, or use your debit card for an amount greater than the amount of money in your account, you can face a bounced check or overdraft fee. Your bank may pay for the item, but charge you a fee or deny the purchase and still charge you a fee. In addition, the business to which you wrote the check may charge you an additional returned check fee. Bounced checks can also blemish your credit record, so you may want to talk to your bank about overdraft protection. For more information, visit www.federalreserve.gov/pubs/bounce.

6    www.USA.gov

To contact an organization, use the directory beginning on page 63.

## UNSOLICITED CHECKS AND CREDIT OFFERS

If you cash an unsolicited check, you could be agreeing to pay for products or services you don't want or need. In addition, those "guarantees" for credit cards or loans, without consideration of credit history, are probably a scam. Legitimate lenders never guarantee credit. For more information on how to identify fraudulent solicitations, visit www.ftc.gov.

### PHISHING SCAMS

"Phishing" is the use of fraudulent e-mail designed to steal identities as well as vital personal information such as credit card numbers, bank account PINs, and passwords. Phishing e-mails often ask you to verify this type of information. Scammers also go "SMishing," or phishing using text messages, by asking you to verify or confirm sensitive information. Legitimate companies never ask for your password or account number via e-mail. If you're not sure whether the e-mail is trustworthy, call the company directly and forward the email to spam@uce.gov. If you believe you've received a phishing e-mail, don't hit reply! The e-mail may even threaten to disable your account. Don't believe it!

Legitimate offers of credit often come in the form of "convenience checks," which credit card companies enclose with your monthly statement. However, convenience checks may carry higher fees, a higher interest rate, and other restrictions. If you don't want the checks, be sure to shred them to protect yourself from "dumpster divers" and identity thieves.

Watch out for checks from someone in a foreign country claiming that you won a lottery, for an investment, or to pay for an item you sold online. This could be a scam. Even if you deposit the check, the check may not be legal. Don't rely on money from a check, especially foreign or unsolicited, until your bank says the check has cleared or if you know and trust the person who sent it to you.

## PREPAID CARDS

Prepaid cards, also known as prepaid debit, stored value, or gift cards, are convenient ways to pay for your purchases. Banks and retailers issue them to offer consumers a way to make payments and conduct other financial transactions. You do not need to have a bank account or a credit history to use a prepaid card. There are plenty of situations where a prepaid card might be the most convenient choice, but be sure you understand the key terms and conditions BEFORE you buy.

Many cards carry protections similar to credit and debit cards. To obtain these benefits, you must follow the instructions for registering and activating your card. Be sure to record your card information, including the customer service telephone number listed on the back of the card in a separate place, so you can get a replacement if yours is lost or stolen. Some prepaid card issuers may charge fees for card activation, maintenance, and cash withdrawals.

If you have a problem with a prepaid card, first contact the customer service number. If the problem still isn't resolved, you may want to file a complaint with the proper authorities:

- For cards issued by retailers, contact the FTC (p. 107). You may also file a complaint with your local consumer protection office (p. 112).
- For cards issued by national banks, contact the Office of the Comptroller of the Currency (p. 105).
- For cards issued by state banks, contact the FDIC (p. 106) or state banking authority (p. 126).

For more information, visit www.nbpca.com.

### Government Benefits on Prepaid Cards

Many government agencies deliver financial benefits using prepaid cards. All Supplemental Nutrition Assistance Program (SNAP) benefits are paid via electronic benefit cards. Beginning in March 2013, all Social Security benefits must be paid via direct deposit or a prepaid debit card, which comes with federal consumer protections. Visit www.godirect.gov for more information.

**Contact the proper regulatory agency below:**

| Type of Institution | Regulatory Agency |
| --- | --- |
| State-chartered banks and trust companies | Federal Deposit Insurance Corporation (p. 106) and state banking authorities (p. 126) |
| Banks with National in their name or N.A. after their name | Office of the Comptroller of the Currency, U.S. Department of the Treasury (p. 105) |
| Federal savings and loans and federal savings banks | Office of the Comptroller of the Currency, Department of the Treasury (p. 105) |
| Federally chartered credit unions | National Credit Union Administration (p. 107) |
| State-chartered banks that are members of the Federal Reserve System | Federal Reserve System (p. 106) |

Whether you are buying or leasing a vehicle, these tips will help you get the best deal and avoid problems:

- Decide what kind of vehicle best suits your needs and budget.
- Check out the seller. For car dealers, check with your state or local consumer protection agency (p. 112) and Better Business Bureau (p. 67). If you're buying from an individual, check the title to make sure you're dealing with the vehicle's owner.
- Take a test drive. Drive at different speeds and check for smooth right and left turns. On a straight stretch, make sure the vehicle doesn't pull to one side.
- Handle trade-ins and financing separately from your purchase to get the best deal on each. Get a written price quote before you talk about a trade-in or dealer financing.
- Shop in advance and compare financing options at your credit union, bank, or finance company. Look at the total finance charges and the Annual Percentage Rate (APR), not just the monthly payment.
- Read and understand every document you are asked to sign.
- Don't take possession of the car until all paperwork is final.
- Choose an auto insurance policy that is right for you (p. 32).

## BUYING A NEW CAR

Do your research first and compare vehicles. Four key resources that offer vehicle performance, service, and safety information are: *Consumer Reports* (www.consumerreports.org), *Motor Trend* (www.motortrend.com), *Car and Driver* (www.caranddriver.com), and Edmunds automotive books and network (www.edmunds.com).

- Research the dealer's price for the car and options. It's easier to get the best price when you know what the dealer paid for a vehicle. The dealer invoice price is available on a number of websites and in printed pricing guides. *Consumer Reports* offers the wholesale price; this figure factors in dealer incentives from a manufacturer and is a more accurate estimate of what a dealer is paying for a vehicle.
- Find out whether the manufacturer is offering rebates that will lower the cost. For more information, visit www.autopedia.com/html/Rebate.html.
- Get price quotes from several dealers. Find out if the amounts quoted are the prices before or after rebates are deducted.
- Avoid low-value extras such as credit insurance, extended warranties, auto club memberships, rustproofing, and upholstery finishes. You do not have to purchase credit insurance to get a loan. See Service Contracts and Extended Warranties (p. 2).
- Hybrid cars are popular among consumers interested in fuel economy and reducing their negative impact on the environment. These cars combine the benefits of gasoline engines and electric motors and can be configured to achieve different objectives, such as improved fuel economy, increased power, or additional auxiliary power. For more information about hybrids, electric vehicles, and alternative fuels, visit www.fueleconomy.gov.

### GOVERNMENT FUEL ECONOMY WEB PAGES

- www.epa.gov/emissweb is a green vehicle guide that can help you identify vehicles that are fuel-efficient and have clean-running engines.
- www.fueleconomy.gov compares the miles-per-gallon ratings of different vehicle models manufactured since the mid-1980s.
- www.fueleconomy.gov/feg/savemoney.shtml calculates annual fuel estimates.
- www.epa.gov/carlabel allows you to compare the fuel economy of different types of vehicles (diesel, hybrid, electric, gasoline).

## BUYING A USED CAR

- To learn what rights you have when buying a used car, contact your state or local consumer protection office (p. 112).
- Find out in advance what paperwork you will need to register a vehicle. Contact your state's motor vehicle department. See www.usa.gov/Topics/Motor_Vehicles.shtml.
- Check prices of similar models using the *NADA Official Used Car Guide* (www.nadaguides.com) published by the National Automobile Dealers Association or the *Kelley Blue Book* (www.kbb.com). These guides are usually available at local libraries.

To contact an organization, use the directory beginning on page 63.

- Research the vehicle's history. Ask the seller for details concerning past owners, use, and maintenance. Next, find out whether the car has been damaged in a flood, involved in a crash, been labeled a "lemon," or had its odometer rolled back.
- Your state motor vehicle department can research the car's title history.
- The National Highway Traffic Safety Administration's (NHTSA) website (www.safercar.gov) lets you search an online database of manufacturer service bulletins and review crash test ratings.
- The website www.vehiclehistory.gov and the National Insurance Crime Bureau's free database (www.nicb.org) are centralized places for consumers to buy information on the history of vehicles gathered from state motor vehicle departments and other sources. These reports are helpful but do not guarantee that a vehicle is accident-free.
- The Center for Auto Safety (www.autosafety.org) provides information on safety defect recalls, complaints and service bulletins.
- Make sure any mileage disclosures match the odometer reading on the car.
- Check the warranty. If a manufacturer's warranty is still in effect, contact the manufacturer to make sure you can use the coverage.
- Ask about the dealer's return policy. Get it in writing and read it carefully.
- Have your mechanic inspect the car. Talk to the seller and agree in advance that you'll pay for the examination if the car passes inspection, but the seller will pay if significant problems are discovered. A qualified mechanic should check the vehicle's frame, tires, air bags, and undercarriage as well as the engine.
- Examine dealer documents carefully. Make sure you are buying—not leasing—the vehicle. Leases use terms such as "balloon payment" and "base mileage" disclosures.

## DEALER VERSUS PRIVATE-PARTY PURCHASES

In general, buying a used car from a dealer is a safer option because you are dealing with an institution, which means you are better protected by law. The FTC requires dealers to post a Buyer's Guide in the window of each used car or truck on their lot. This guide specifies whether the vehicle is being sold "as is" (in the vehicle's current condition, without a warranty) or with a warranty, and what percentage of repair costs a dealer will pay under the warranty. Keep in mind that private sellers generally have less responsibility than dealers do for defects or other problems. FTC rules do not apply to private-party sales.

Expect to pay higher prices at a dealer than if you buy from an individual. Many dealers inspect their cars and provide an inspection report with each one. However, this is no substitute for your own inspection. Some dealers provide limited warranties, and most sell extended warranties. Watch out for dealer warranties that are "power train" warranties only, and not "bumper-to-bumper," full-coverage warranties. It's best to compare warranties that are available from other sources.

Some dealers sell "certified" cars. This generally means that the cars have had a more thorough inspection and come with a limited warranty. Prices for certified cars are generally higher. Be sure to get a list of what was inspected and what is covered under the warranty.

Purchasing a car from a private seller may save you money, but there are risks. The car could be stolen, damaged, or still under a finance agreement. If a private

### CHOOSE A SAFE VEHICLE

Crash tests can help you determine how well a vehicle will protect you in a crash. These organizations perform crash tests and rate vehicles:

- **The National Highway Traffic Safety Administration.** Each year, NHTSA (www.nhtsa.gov) crashes vehicles head-on into a wall and bashes them broadside to test their ability to protect their occupants. NHTSA focuses on evaluating vehicle restraints such as air bags and safety belts.
- **The Insurance Institute for Highway Safety.** A different test by the IIHS (www.hwysafety.org) uses offset-frontal car crashes to assess the protection a vehicle's structure provides.
- **Consumer Reports.** The annual auto issue of Consumer Reports (www.consumerreports.org) rates vehicles in terms of overall safety. Its safety score combines crash test results with a vehicle's accident-avoidance factors—emergency handling, braking, acceleration, and even driver comfort.
- **The National Motor Vehicle Title Information System.** The NMVTIS (www.vehiclehistory.gov) provides information about a vehicle's history and condition, including information about its title, odometer reading, brand history, and, in some cases, theft.

To find out whether a manufacturer has recalled a car for safety defects, contact NHTSA (p. 104). If a vehicle has been recalled, ask the dealer for proof that the defect has been repaired. Used vehicles should also have a current safety inspection sticker if your state requires one.

seller lies to you about the condition of the vehicle, you may sue the individual if you have evidence and you can find him or her. An individual is very unlikely to provide a written warranty.

### FINANCING

Most car buyers today need some form of financing to purchase a new vehicle. Many use direct lending, that is, a loan from a finance company, bank, or credit union. In direct lending, a buyer agrees to pay the amount financed, plus an agreed-upon finance charge, over a specified period. Once a buyer and a vehicle dealership enter into a contract to purchase a vehicle, the buyer uses the loan proceeds from the direct lender to pay the dealership for the vehicle.

### LONG-TERM CAR LOANS

Some car dealers and banks offer loans that allow you to finance your car for longer periods than a traditional auto loan (more than six years). Before you decide on the length of your auto loan, weigh the pros and cons. Long-term loans can make your monthly payments smaller and allow you to refinance the loan after a few years, to reduce the length of the loan. Remember, however, that these loans can cost more over the life of the loan because you are paying interest for a longer period. Also, as the car depreciates, you may end up owing more on your loan than the value of the car. This is called negative equity.

For more information about auto loans, visit www.ftc.gov/bcp/edu/pubs/consumer/autos/aut04.shtm. For information about negative equity, visit www.ftc.gov/bcp/edu/pubs/consumer/alerts/alt083.shtm.

Another common form is dealership financing, which offers convenience, financing options, and sometimes special, manufacturer-sponsored, low-rate deals. Before you make a financing decision, it's important to do your research:

- Decide in advance how much you can afford to spend and stick to your limit.
- Get a copy of your credit report and correct any errors before applying for a loan.
- Check buying guides to identify price ranges and best available deals.

More information about vehicle financing, deciding what you can afford, and consumer protections is available at www.ftc.gov/bcp/menus/consumer/autos/finance.shtm. If you need to file a complaint about your auto loan, visit www.consumerfinance.gov.

### LEASING

When you lease, you pay to drive someone else's vehicle. Monthly payments for a lease may be lower than loan payments, but at the end of the lease, you do not own or have any equity in the car. To get the best deal, follow this advice in addition to the general suggestions for buying a car (p. 8):

- To help you compare leasing versus owning, the Consumer Leasing Act requires leasing companies to give you information on monthly payments and other charges. Check out www.leaseguide.com and www.leasecompare.com for more information.
- Consider using an independent agent rather than the dealer; you might find a better deal. Most financial institutions that offer auto financing also offer leasing options.
- Ask for details on wear and tear standards. Dings that you regard as normal wear and tear could be billed as significant damage at the end of your lease.
- Find out how many miles you can drive in a year. Most leases allow 12,000 to 15,000 miles a year. Expect a charge of 10 to 25 cents for each additional mile.
- Check the manufacturer's warranty; it should cover the entire lease term and the number of miles you are likely to drive.
- Ask the dealer what happens if you give up the car before the end of your lease. There may be extra fees for doing so.
- Ask what happens if the car is involved in an accident.
- Get all of the terms in writing. Everything included with the car should be listed on the lease to avoid your being charged for "missing" equipment later.

The Consumer Financial Protection Bureau offers a consumer guide to auto leasing at www.consumerfinance.gov.

### RECALLS, "LEMON" LAWS, AND SECRET WARRANTIES

Sometimes a manufacturer makes a design or production mistake on a motor vehicle. A service bulletin notifies the dealer of the problem and how to resolve it. Because these free repairs are not publicized, they are called "secret warranties." The National Highway Traffic Safety Administration maintains a database of service bulletins filed by manufacturers.

If you have a problem with a vehicle that is a safety hazard, check whether the manufacturer has recalled your vehicle. You can find information about service bulletins, recalls, and other safety defects at www-odi.nhtsa.dot.gov/recalls/recallsearch.cfm or call DOT's Vehicle Safety Hotline at 1-800-424-9393. You should report hazards that aren't listed to your dealer, the manufacturer of the vehicle (p. 64), and NHTSA at www-odi.nhtsa.dot.gov/ivoq. If a safety-related defect exists, the maker must fix it at no cost to you—even if your warranty has expired.

If you have a vehicle with a unique problem that just never seems to get fixed, you may have a "lemon." Some states have laws concerning "lemons" that require a refund or replacement if a problem is not fixed within a reasonable number of tries. These laws might also go into effect if you haven't been able to use your vehicle for a certain number of days. Contact your state or local consumer protection office (p. 112) to learn whether you have such protections and what steps you must take to get your problem solved. If you believe your car is a "lemon":

- Give the dealer a list of the problems every time you bring it in for repairs.
- Get and keep copies of the repair orders listing the problems, the work done, and the dates the car was in the shop.
- Contact the manufacturer, as well as the dealer, to report the problem. Check your owner's manual or the directory for the auto manufacturer (p. 64).

The Center for Auto Safety (p. 109) gathers information and complaints concerning safety defects, recalls, service bulletins, and state "lemon" laws.

## RENTING

Before renting a car:

- Ask what the total cost will be after all fees are included. There may be an airport surcharge or fees for drop-off, insurance, fuel, mileage, taxes, additional-drivers, underage-driver, and equipment rental (for items such as ski racks and car seats). See drip pricing on p. 2.
- Ask whether the rental company checks the driving records of customers when they arrive at the counter. If so, you could be rejected, even if you have a confirmed reservation.
- Check in advance to be sure you aren't duplicating insurance coverage. If you're traveling on business, your employer may have insurance that covers accidental damage to the vehicle. You might also have coverage through your personal auto insurance (p. 32), a motor club membership, or the credit card you use to reserve the rental.
- Carefully inspect the vehicle and its tires before renting and when you return it. Try to return the car during regular hours so you and the rental staff can look at the car together to verify that you didn't damage it.
- Check refueling policies and charges.
- Pay with a credit card rather than a debit card, to avoid holds on the funds in your checking account. See "Before You Swipe Your Debit Card" (p. 6).
- Ask the rental company whether a deposit is required. If so, ask for a clear explanation of the deposit refund policies and procedures.

For more information about renting a car and the insurance options, visit www.insureuonline.org/consumer_auto_car_rental_insurance.htm.

Some state laws cover short-term car and truck rentals. Contact your state or local consumer protection office (p. 112) for information or to file a complaint.

## REPAIRS

Whenever you take a car to the repair shop:

- Choose a reliable repair shop. Family, friends, or an independent consumer-rating organization should be able to help you. Look for shops that display various certifications that are current. You should also check out the shop's record with your state or local consumer protection office (p. 112) or the Better Business Bureau (p. 67).
- Describe the symptoms. Don't try to diagnose the problem.
- Make it clear that work cannot begin until you have an estimate (in writing, preferably) and you give your okay. Never sign a blank repair order. If the problem can't be diagnosed on the spot, insist that the shop contact you for authorization once it has found the trouble.
- Ask the shop to return the old parts to you.
- Follow the warranty instructions if a repair is covered under warranty.
- Get all repair warranties in writing.
- Keep copies of all paperwork.

Some states, cities, and counties have special laws that deal with auto repairs. For information on the laws in your state, contact your state or local consumer protection office (p. 112). A consumer guide to auto repair is available at www.ftc.gov/bcp/edu/pubs/consumer/autos/aut13.shtm.

## CAR REPOSSESSIONS

When you borrow money to buy a car or truck, the lender can take your vehicle back if you miss a payment or in some other way violate the contract. You should also be aware that the lender:

- Can repossess with cause without advance notice
- Can insist you pay off the entire loan balance to get the repossessed vehicle back
- Can sell the vehicle at auction
- Might be able to sue you for the difference between the vehicle's auction price and what you owe
- Cannot break into your home or physically threaten someone while taking the vehicle

If you know you're going to be late with a payment, talk to the lender. If you and the lender reach an agreement, be sure to get the agreement in writing. Contact your state or local consumer protection office (p. 112) to find out whether your state gives you any additional rights.

# CREDIT

Like everything else you buy, it pays to comparison shop for credit. For up-to-date interest rate reports on mortgages, auto loans, credit cards, home equity loans, and other banking products, visit www.bankrate.com. The Equal Credit Opportunity Act protects you when dealing with anyone who regularly offers credit, including banks, finance companies, stores, credit card companies, and credit unions. When you apply for credit, a creditor may not:

- Ask about or consider your sex, race, national origin, or religion
- Ask about your marital status or your spouse—unless you are applying for a joint account or relying on your spouse's income, or you live in a community property state (Arizona, California, Idaho, Louisiana, Nevada, New Mexico, Texas, Washington, or Wisconsin)
- Ask about your plans to have or raise children
- Refuse to consider public assistance income or regularly received alimony or child support
- Refuse to consider income because of your sex or marital status or because it is from part-time work or retirement benefits

**You have the right to:**

- Have credit in your birth name, your first name and your spouse/partner's last name, or your first name and a combined last name
- Have a co-signer other than your spouse if one is necessary
- Keep your own accounts after you change your name or marital status or if you retire, unless the creditor has evidence that you are unable or unwilling to pay
- Know why a credit application is rejected—the creditor must give you the specific reasons or tell you where and how you can get a copy of the credit report it used to determine its rejection, if you ask within 60 days
- Have accounts shared with your spouse reported in both of your names
- Know how much it will cost to borrow money

For additional information on credit, see Buying a Home (p. 27) and Cars (p. 8). Other sources of information include the HUD Housing Counseling Clearinghouse at 1-800-569-4287, the FTC (p. 107), and the National Consumer Law Center (p. 110). You have the right to a FREE annual Credit Report (see Free Credit Reports box below).

## CREDIT CARDS

There are many types of credit cards with various features, but there is no one best credit card. The card you use depends entirely on how you plan to use it. Are you going to use it for everyday purchases or larger purchases? Do you plan to pay your balance off each month?

When you apply for a credit card, consider:

- **Annual Percentage Rate (APR)**. If the interest rate is variable, how is it determined, and when can it change?
- **Periodic rate**. This is the interest rate used to determine the finance charge on your balance each billing period.
- **Annual fee**. While some cards have no annual fee, others expect you to pay an amount each year for being a cardholder.
- **Rewards programs.** Can you earn points for flights, hotel stays, and gift certificates to your favorite retailers? Use the tool on www.creditcardtuneup.com to find the card that offers the best rewards for you.
- **Grace period**. This is the number of days you have to pay your bill before finance charges start. Without this period, you may have to pay interest from the date you use your card or the date the purchase is posted to your account.
- **Finance charges**. Most lenders calculate finance charges using an average daily account balance, which is the average of what you owed each day in the billing cycle. Look for offers that use an adjusted balance, which subtracts your payment from your beginning balance. This method usually has the lowest finance charges. Check whether there is a minimum finance charge.

## FREE CREDIT REPORTS

You can request a free credit report once a year from each of the three major credit reporting agencies—Equifax, Experian, and TransUnion. You may want to request your credit reports one at a time, every four months, so you can monitor your credit throughout the year without having to pay for a report. (If you ask the credit bureaus directly, they will charge you a fee to obtain your report.) To order your free report, you must go through www.annualcreditreport.com or call 1-877-322-8228.

To contact an organization, use the directory beginning on page 63.

## CARD ACT PROTECTIONS FOR CONSUMERS

The Credit Card Accountability Responsibility and Disclosure (CARD) Act brought about sweeping protections for consumers. Among other things, your credit card company must comply with the rules below:

**Fees**

- Cannot change rates or fees without sending you a notice 45 days in advance in most cases
- Cannot charge you a late payment fee of more than $25, regardless of how much you owe—unless one of your last six payments was late or the credit card company can justify a higher fee based on the cost of late payments

**Payments**

- Has to tell you how long it will take to pay off your balance if you make only minimum payments
- Must mail or deliver your credit card bill at least 21 days before your payment is due

**Interest Rates**

- Cannot increase your rate for the first 12 months after you open an account unless you have a variable interest rate or an introductory rate; you are more than 60 days late paying your bill; or you are in a workout agreement and don't make payments as arranged
- Cannot charge higher rates for purchases made before you receive notice of a new rate

What's more, a credit card company can grant credit cards to consumers under age 21 only if they can show they are able to make payments or have a cosigner for the card. More information about CARD Act protections is available from www.federalreserve.gov/creditcard.

- **Other fees**. Ask about fees when you get a cash advance, make a late payment, or go over your credit limit. Some credit card companies also charge a monthly fee. Be careful: sometimes companies may also try to upsell by offering other services such as credit protection, insurance, or debt coverage. Visit www.federalreserve.gov/creditcard/fees.html for more information.

The Fair Credit and Charge Card Disclosure Act requires credit and charge card issuers to include this information on credit applications. The Federal Trade Commission (p. 107) offers a wide range of free publications on credit and consumer rights at www.ftc.gov.

There are many websites available to help you compare credit cards; www.bankrate.com provides free credit card tips and information and www.cardratings.com lists and reviews credit cards, and offers tips and credit card calculators.

To view an interactive version of a sample credit card bill, visit www.federalreserve.gov/creditcard.

The Consumer Financial Protection Bureau (CFPB) provides useful information for consumers on selecting a credit card appropriate for their needs. See "How do I Shop for a Credit Card," on the CFPB website, www.consumerfinance.gov/how-do-i-shop-for-a-credit-card.

### Complaints

To complain about a problem with your credit card company, call the number on the back of your card or try to resolve it with the CFPB (p. 96). If you fail to resolve the issue, ask for the name, address, and phone number of the card company's regulatory agency. See the chart on page 7 to find the best federal or state regulatory agency to contact.

To complain about a credit bureau, contact the CFPB; for complaints about a department store that offers credit, or other Federal Deposit Insurance Corporation (FDIC)-insured financial institution, write to the agency's Consumer Response Center (p. 106). You may also file a complaint with the FTC at www.ftc.gov.

### Credit Card Billing Disputes

Under the Fair Credit Billing Act, you have the right to dispute charges on your credit card that you didn't make, are incorrect, or are for goods or services you didn't receive.

- Send a letter to the creditor within 60 days of the statement date of the bill with the disputed charge.
- Include your name and account number, the date and amount of the disputed charge, and a complete explanation of why you are disputing the charge. To ensure it's received, send your letter by certified mail, with a return receipt requested.
- The creditor or card issuer must acknowledge your letter in writing within 30 days of receiving it and conduct an investigation within 90 days. You do not have to pay the amount in dispute during the investigation.
- If there was an error, the creditor must credit your account and remove any fees.
- If the bill is correct, you must be told in writing what you owe and why. You must then pay it, along with any related finance charges.

If you don't agree with the creditor's decision, file an appeal with the CFPB (p. 96).

## CREDIT REPORTS AND SCORES

A credit report contains information on where you work and live, how you pay your bills, and whether you've been sued or arrested or have filed for bankruptcy. Credit reporting agencies (CRAs) gather this information and sell it to creditors, employers, insurers, and others. The most common type of CRA is the credit bureau. There are three major credit bureaus:

## BEWARE: "CREDIT REPAIR" SCAMS

Before you sign up for fee-based credit repair services, beware. Many of the promised services are either illegal or are ones you can do for free by yourself. Before you sign up to work with these companies, here are some tidbits to keep in mind:

- A credit repair company must give you a copy of the "Consumer Credit File Rights under State and Federal Law" before you sign a contract.

- The company cannot perform any services until you have signed a written contract and completed a three-day waiting period, during which time you can cancel the contract without paying any fees.

- The company cannot charge you until it has completed the promised services, according to the Credit Repair Organizations Act.

- It is illegal to erase timely and accurate negative information contained in your credit history.

- Suggestions that you create a new credit history (also called file segregation) by requesting an Employer Identification Number from the IRS are also illegal.

- You can solve your own credit challenges by requesting a free copy of your credit report through www.annualcreditreport.com, and by working with creditors to dispute incorrect information.

---

- Equifax: 1-800-685-1111 or www.equifax.com. To place a fraud alert on your credit report, call 1-888-766-0008.
- Experian: 1-888-397-3742 or www.experian.com
- TransUnion: 1-877-322-8228 or www.transunion.com or fraud alert 1-800-680-7289

The CFPB is now responsible for overseeing the credit reporting agencies and receive complaints about them (p. 96).

### FICO

The information in your credit report is used to calculate your FICO score, a number generally between 300 and 850. The acronym stands for Fair, Isaac and Company. The higher your score, the less risk you pose to creditors. A high score, for example, makes it easier for you to obtain a loan, rent an apartment, or lower your insurance rate. Your FICO score is available from www.myfico.com for a fee. Free credit reports do not contain your credit score, although you can purchase it when you request your free annual credit report through www.annualcreditreport.com.

### Tips for Building a Better Credit Score

- Pay your bills on time. Delinquent payments and collections negatively affect your score.
- Keep balances low on credit cards and other "revolving credit." High outstanding debt lowers your score.
- Apply for and open new credit accounts only as needed. Don't open an account just to have a better credit mix; it probably won't raise your score.
- Pay off debt instead of moving it around. Owing the same amount, but having fewer open accounts, may lower your score.

You don't rebuild your credit score; you rebuild your credit history. Time is your ally in improving credit. There is no "quick fix" for a bad credit score, so be suspicious of any deals that offer you a fast, easy solution.

### Negative Information in Your Credit Report

Negative information concerning your use of credit can be kept in your credit report for seven years. A bankruptcy can be kept for 10 years, and unpaid tax liens for 15 years. Information about a lawsuit or an unpaid judgment against you can be reported for seven years or until the statute of limitations runs out, whichever is longer. Inquiries remain on your report for two years.

## DEBT COLLECTION E-MAILS

When communicating with consumers through email, debt collectors must observe the Fair Debt Collection Practices Act (FDCPA). It is important for you and creditors or collection agencies to save and store copies of all communication, which will be important if there is a disagreement later.

To take steps towards maintaining privacy, conduct all communications via email using either secure email platforms or industry-specific communication platforms. Never give a workplace email account as a contact address, as there is no legal expectation of privacy for a workplace email account.

---

Anyone who denies you credit, housing, insurance, or a job as a result of a credit report must give you the name, address, and telephone number of the CRA that provided the report. Under the Fair Credit Reporting Act (FCRA), you have the right to request a free report within 60 days if a company denies you credit based on the report.

If there is inaccurate or incomplete information in your credit report:

- Contact the CRA and the company that provided the information.
- Tell the CRA in writing what information you believe is inaccurate. Keep a copy of all correspondence.

Under the FCRA, the information provider is required to investigate and report the results to the CRA. If the information is found to be incorrect, FCRA must notify all nationwide CRAs to correct your file. If the investigation does not solve your dispute, ask that your statement

## LOST AND STOLEN CREDIT CARDS

Immediately call the card issuer when you suspect a credit or charge card has been lost or stolen. Once you report the loss or theft of a card, you have no further responsibility for unauthorized charges. In any event, your maximum liability under federal law is $50 per card.

concerning the dispute be included in your file. A notice of your dispute must be included whenever the CRA reports the negative item.

If the information is accurate, only time, hard work, and a personal debt repayment plan will improve your credit report. Credit repair companies advertise that they can erase bad credit for a hefty fee. Don't believe it. Under the Credit Repair Organizations Act, credit repair companies can't require you to pay until they have completed promised services. They must also give you:

- A copy of the "Consumer Credit File Rights Under State and Federal Law" before you sign a contract
- A written contract that spells out your rights and obligations
- Three days to cancel without paying any fees

Some credit repair companies promise to help you establish a whole new credit identity. You can be charged with fraud if you use the mail or telephone to apply for credit with false information. It is also a federal crime to make false statements on a loan or credit application, to give a false Social Security number, or to obtain an Employer Identification Number from the Internal Revenue Service under false pretenses. If you have lost money to a credit repair scam, contact your state or local consumer affairs office (p. 112).

## DEALING WITH DEBT

If you want to reduce your amount of debt, you can do some work on your own. First, develop a realistic budget so you can see your income and expenses in one place and look for ways to save money. For help in creating a budget, visit www.mymoney.gov or www.consumer.gov/articles/1002-making-budget#!what-it-is. Also, contact your creditors and inform them that you are having difficulty making payments; they may be able to modify your payment plan.

### Debt Collection

The Fair Debt Collection Practices Act applies to those who collect debts owed to creditors for personal, family, and household expenditures. These debts include car loans, mortgages, charge accounts, and money owed for medical bills. A debt collector is someone hired to collect money you owe.

Within five days after a debt collector first contacts you, the collector must send you a notice that tells you the name of the creditor, how much you owe, and what action to take if you believe you don't owe the money. If you owe the money or part of it, contact the creditor to arrange for payment. If you believe you don't owe the money, contact the creditor in writing and send a copy to the collection agency with a letter telling it not to contact you.

A debt collector may not:

- Contact you at unreasonable times, for example, before 8 am or after 9 pm, unless you agree
- Contact you at work if you tell the debt collector your employer disapproves
- Contact you after you write a letter telling the collector to stop, except to notify you if the collector or creditor plans to take a specific action
- Contact your friends, relatives, employer, or others, except to find out where you live and work
- Harass you with repeated telephone calls, profane language, or threats to harm you
- Make any false statement or claim you will be arrested
- Threaten to have money deducted from your paycheck or to sue you, unless the collection agency or creditor intends to do so and it is legal

To file a complaint about a debt collection company, contact your state or local consumer protection agency (p. 112) and the FTC (p. 107).

### Credit Counseling Services

Counseling services are available to help people budget money and pay bills. Credit unions, extension offices, military family service centers, and religious organizations are among those that may offer free or low-cost credit counseling.

Local, nonprofit agencies that provide educational programs on money management and help in developing debt payment plans operate under the name Consumer Credit Counseling Service (CCCS). Make certain that the agency is accredited by the Council on Accreditation (COA) or the International Organization for Standardization (ISO). The counselor should also be certified by the National Foundation for Credit Counseling (NFCC), an organization that supports a national network of credit counselors.

Typically, a counseling service will negotiate lower payments with your creditors, and then make the payments using money you send to it each month. The cost of setting up this debt-management plan is paid by

## PEER-TO-PEER LENDING

Peer to peer lending (P2P), or social lending, is a new process of connecting an individual borrower with lenders, without using traditional banks to obtain an unsecured loan. As a potential borrower, you can post a request for a loan, along with a brief description of how you will use it. The borrower and lenders are strangers; their only knowledge of each other is through the P2P website. Although the idea seems very informal, a peer-to-peer loan contract is a formal, legally binding agreement between two parties; checks and pay stubs are required. There can still be fees for late and missed payments. The lenders must report your loan payment history to the credit reporting agencies. For more information about peer-to-peer lending, visit www.consumer-action.org/news/articles/2012_p2p_lending_survey/#primer.

the creditor, not you. Ask these questions to find the best counselor for you:

- What services do you offer? Look for an organization that offers budget counseling and money management classes as well as debt-management planning.
- Do you offer free information? Avoid organizations that charge for information or make you provide a lot of details about your problem first.
- What are your fees? Are there set-up and/or monthly fees? A typical set-up fee is $10. Beware of agencies that charge large up-front fees.
- How will the debt-management plan work? What debts can be included in the plan, and will you get regular reports on your accounts?
- Ask whether the counselor can get creditors to lower or eliminate interest and fees. If the answer is yes, contact your creditors to verify this.
- Ask what happens if you can't afford to pay. If an organization won't help you because you can't afford to pay, go somewhere else for help.
- Will your counselor help you avoid future problems? Getting a plan for avoiding future debt is as important as solving the immediate debt problem.
- Ask for a contract. All verbal promises should be in writing before you pay any money.
- Are your counselors accredited or certified? Legitimate credit counseling firms are affiliated with the NFCC (p. 145) or the Association of Independent Consumer Credit Counseling Agencies (p. 143).

Check with your local consumer protection agency (p. 112) and the Better Business Bureau (p. 67) to see whether any complaints have been filed about the counseling service you're considering.

If you have concerns about approved credit counseling agencies or credit counseling providers, please contact the U.S. Trustee Program at www.justice.gov/ust or call 202-514-4100.

### Personal Bankruptcy

Bankruptcy generally is considered the debt management option of last resort because the results are long-lasting and far-reaching. The Bankruptcy Abuse and Prevention Act of 2005 established more stringent rules for consumers and attorneys.

The filing process may be difficult for debtors:

- Debtors must file documents, including itemized statements of monthly net income, proof of income (pay stubs) for the last 60 days, and tax returns for the preceding year (four years for Chapter 13 bankruptcies).
- Debtors must take a pre-filing credit counseling and post-filing education course to have debts discharged. To find an approved credit counseling provider, visit www.justice.gov/ust.
- Debtors face increased filing fees, plus fees for credit counseling/education.
- The bankruptcy petition and process are complicated, so it's very difficult to file without an attorney. However, attorneys are more apprehensive about filing bankruptcy because of sanctions.

The filing process for lawyers:

- An attorney's signature on a petition certifies that the attorney has performed reasonable investigation into circumstances giving rise to the petition.
- Attorneys must carefully review documents such as tax returns and pay stubs and ask clients for credit reports.

### LOANS

There are different types of loans. Some are secured loans. This mean that your property and things you own are used as collateral, and if you cannot pay back the loan, the lender will take your collateral to get their money back. Other types of loans, unsecured loans, don't use property as collateral. Lenders consider these as more risky than secured loans, so they charge a higher interest rate for them. Most credit cards are unsecured loans, although some consumers have secured credit cards. Two very common secured loans are home equity and installment loans.

### Home Equity Loans

A home equity loan is a form of credit where your home is used as collateral for the loan. This type of loan is often used to pay for major expenses, such as education, medical bills, and home repairs. Consider carefully before taking out a home equity loan. If you are unable to make payments on time, you could lose your home.

Home equity loans can be either a revolving line of credit or a lump sum. Revolving credit lets you withdraw funds when you need them. A lump sum is a one-time, closed-end loan for a particular purpose, such as remodeling or tuition. Apply for a home equity loan through a bank or credit union first. These loans are likely to cost less than those offered by finance companies.

Please see Housing (p. 27) for helpful information about buying, leasing, renting, or repairing a home.

### Installment Loans

Installment loans are loans that are repaid over time with a set number of scheduled payments; the most common installment loans are home or car loans. Before you sign an agreement for a loan to buy a house, a car, or other large purchase, make sure you fully understand all of the lender's terms and conditions, including:

- The dollar amount you are borrowing
- The payment amounts and when they are due
- The total finance charge, including all interest and fees you must pay to get the loan
- The APR, the rate of interest you will pay over the full term of the loan
- Penalties for late payments
- What the lender will do if you can't pay back the loan
- Penalties if you pay the loan back early

The Truth in Lending Act requires lenders to give you this information so you can compare different offers.

## PAYDAY AND TAX REFUND LOANS

Payday loans are designed to stretch your budget until your payday. Beware; these loans charge high annual interest rates and excessive fees that are due every few weeks. Because of these excessive fees, payday loans are illegal in some states and for all members of the military. With a typical payday loan, you might write a personal check for $115 to borrow $100 for two weeks, until payday. The Annual Percentage Rate (APR) in this example is 390%! If you can repay the loan quickly, it may not appear to be such a bad deal. But if you have to renew the loan, that relatively small loan can grow into a major debt.

Another high-cost way to borrow money is a tax refund loan. This type of credit lets you get an advance on a tax refund—for a fee. APRs as high as 774% have been reported. If you're short of cash, avoid both of these loans by asking for more time to pay a bill or seeking a traditional short-term bank loan.

## FINANCING YOUR EDUCATION

The U.S. Department of Education's website, www.studentaid.ed.gov, provides information on preparing for and funding education beyond high school with details on the federal aid programs. Another source of information on financial assistance is www.finaid.org. Both sites offer calculators to help you determine how much school will cost, how much you need to save, and how much aid you will need.

Before selecting a college, you must understand the earning potential of your chosen career. You need to make sure that your annual salary after you graduate will be high enough to cover any student loan payments you may need to make in addition to your other living expenses. The Department of Labor has a web-based career search tool that will give you information concerning the average annual salary for various career options at www.studentaid.ed.gov/prepare-for-college/careers/search.

### PAYING FOR COLLEGE 101

Many state governments have created 529 plans that make it easier for families to save for their child's education. These plans, which can be sponsored by states or institutions of higher learning, encourage saving for future college costs, and the earnings grow tax-free. There are two main types: "pre-paid tuition plans" and "college savings plans." Pre-paid plans allow you to pay for your child's college tuition based on today's costs, and then pay out at the future (higher) cost once your child is in college. College savings plans allow you to invest money in several investment funds, ranging in risk level, to pay for your child's college education. For more information about the different types of 529 plans and the plans available in each state, visit www.collegesavings.org.

## BEWARE: SCHOLARSHIP AND FINANCIAL AID SCAMS

Scholarships and financial aid do not require up-front fees. While there are legitimate companies that will help guide you through the financial aid and college application process for a fee, disreputable companies may ask you for money up front and provide nothing in return. Red flags to watch out for include the following:

- A "money-back guarantee" to secure a scholarship. Don't believe it. Unscrupulous companies attach conditions that make it impossible to get the refund.

- "Secret scholarships." If a company claims to have inside knowledge of scholarship money, it's lying. Information on scholarships is freely available to the public. Ask your librarian or school counselor.

- Telling students they've been selected as "finalists" for awards.

- Asking for a student's checking account to "confirm eligibility." If a company wants bank account information or your credit card number to confirm or reserve a scholarship, it's a scam.

- Quoting a relatively small "monthly" or "weekly" fee, then asking for authorization to debit your checking account for an unspecified length of time. Ongoing fees are a sure sign of a scam.

- Unsolicited offers. Whether it's an e-mail or phone call, or it arrives in your mailbox, if you didn't request the information, ignore the offer.

### Financial Aid

Student financial aid is available from a variety of sources, including the federal government, individual states, colleges and universities, and other public and private agencies and organizations. The four basic types of college aid are:

- **Grants.** Gift aid that does not have to be repaid and is generally awarded according to financial need.
- **Work-Study.** The Federal Work-Study Program (FWS) is a federally funded source of financial assistance used to offset financial education costs. Students who qualify earn money by working while attending school. This money does not have to be repaid.
- **Loans.** Funds are borrowed and must be repaid with interest. As a general rule, federal student loans have more favorable terms and lower interest rates than traditional consumer loans do.
- **Scholarships.** Funds are offered by the school, local/community organizations, private institutions, and trusts. Scholarships do not have to be repaid and are generally awarded based on specific criteria.

### Applying for Aid

You must complete and submit a Free Application for Federal Student Aid (FAFSA$^{SM}$) to apply for federal student aid. FAFSA on the Web$^{SM}$ is the quickest and easiest method of applying. Go to www.fafsa.gov to apply.

### Education Tax Benefits

The federal government allows you to receive tax credits, deductions, and savings plans that can help with your expenses for higher education. The tax credits can reduce the amount of income tax you have to pay, while deductions reduce the amount of your income that is taxable. Visit www.irs.gov/uac/Tax-Benefits-for-Education:-Information-Center for information on specific types of credits and deductions.

### Federal Student Aid Information Center

The Federal Student Aid Information Center (FSAIC) can answer your federal student financial aid questions and can give you all the help you need for free. You can also use the FSAIC automated response system to find out whether your FAFSA$^{SM}$ has been processed and to request a copy of your Student Aid Report (SAR). For FSAIC contact information, see page 97.

## FEDERAL STUDENT AID

- You can order many helpful publications at www.edpubs.gov, or by calling 1-877-433-7827.
- The U.S. Department of Education's federal student aid website, www.studentaid.ed.gov.
- The U.S. Department of Labor's Occupational Outlook Handbook, www.bls.gov/ooh, provides information on various careers and their earning potential.
- The National Association of Student Financial Aid Administrators provides Cash for College with advice, tips, and information on financing your education at www.nasfaa.org.

### Federal Loan Program Repayment Information

- **Public Service Loan Forgiveness Program**. Offers forgiveness for outstanding federal loans for individuals working full time in public service jobs.
- **Income-Based Repayment Plan.** Helps to make repaying education loans more affordable for low-income borrowers.

Both programs offer generous benefits, but the rules may seem complex, so it is important to get all of the details. For more information on these programs as well as other repayment options:

To contact an organization, use the directory beginning on page 63.

- U.S. Department of Education/Federal Student Aid: www.studentaid.ed.gov/repay-loans and www.myedaccount.com
- National Association of Student Financial Aid Administrators: www.nasfaa.org

### Comparing Student Loans

The Consumer Financial Protection Bureau (CFPB) has a Know Before You Owe Student Loan website, developed in partnership with the Department of Education. It provides financial aid shopping sheets that help schools communicate the financial aid options available to students. Visit www.consumerfinance.gov/students/knowbeforeyouowe.

---

## COLLEGE ACCREDITATION

Accreditation ensures that education provided by institutions of higher education meets acceptable levels of quality. The Secretary of Education is required by law to publish a list of nationally recognized accrediting agencies that it determines to be reliable authorities on the quality of education or training provided by the institutions of higher education and the higher education programs they accredit. You can access the list at www.ope.ed.gov/accreditation.

---

### Defaulting on Student Loans

You can take steps to avoid defaulting on your student loan. Before you get the loan, determine how much money you need to borrow and only borrow that amount. When you get the loan, make certain that you understand the details such as the payment terms and what type of loan you have. Once your student loan becomes due:

- Maintain accurate records of your loan, including the loan agreement, interest rates, and account numbers.
- Track your loans to stay updated on how much you owe.
- Make certain that the loan servicer has your current contact information and bank account (if payments are withdrawn automatically).

If you default, it means you failed to make payments on your student loan as scheduled. Your loan becomes delinquent the first day after you miss a payment. However, the loan isn't in default until 270 days have passed without a payment. The consequences of default can be severe, including:

- The entire unpaid balance of your loan and any interest is immediately due and payable.
- Your loan account is assigned to a collection agency.
- The loan will be reported as delinquent to credit bureaus, damaging your credit.
- Your federal and state taxes may be withheld through a tax offset. This means that the Internal Revenue

Service can take your federal and state tax refund to collect any of your defaulted student loan debt.
- Your employer can withhold money from your pay and send the money to the government. This process is called wage garnishment.

If you are having difficulty making your payments, contact your loan servicer immediately. The servicer may be able to help by changing your repayment plan, switching the due date, getting a deferment or forbearance, or consolidating your student loans.

For information about these consequences and how to avoid defaulting, visit studentaid.ed.gov/repay-loans/default.

Times have changed for job searching, and numerous websites are now available that post private industry jobs. Many companies also offer a way to apply online. However, these sites and new methods do not replace traditional and proven job-hunting approaches such as networking, personal contacts, business organizations, and interviewing.

## EMPLOYMENT AGENCIES AND RECRUITERS

If you're looking for a job, you may come across ads from employment agencies or receive calls from recruiters that promise wonderful opportunities. While some companies honestly want to help you, others are more interested in taking your money. Be wary of:

- Promises to get you a job and a guaranteed income
- Up-front fees, even when you are guaranteed a refund if you are dissatisfied
- Employment agencies whose ads read like job ads
- Promotions of "previously undisclosed" government jobs. All federal jobs are announced to the public at www.usajobs.gov.

Get a copy of the employment agency contract and review it carefully before you pay any money. Check with your local consumer protection agency (p. 112) and the Better Business Bureau (p. 67) to see whether any complaints have been filed about a company.

The FTC (p. 107) investigates businesses that fraudulently advertise employment openings and guarantee job placement. Contact the FTC if you have a complaint.

## WORK-AT-HOME COMPANIES

Not all work-at-home opportunities deliver on their promises. Some classic work-at-home schemes are medical billing, envelope stuffing, and assembly or craftwork. Ads for these businesses say, "Be part of one of America's Fastest-Growing Industries. Earn thousands of dollars a month from your home!" Legitimate work-at-home program sponsors should tell you, in writing, what's involved in the program they are selling. Here are some questions you might ask a promoter:

---

### CREDIT CHECKS: A NEW PART OF THE HIRING PROCESS

Are you in the market for a new job? If so, remember that potential employers aren't just reading your résumé; they are also reviewing your credit history. Before you apply for any job, get your free credit report (see p. 12) for information about your credit history, including:

- If you pay your bills on time or late
- How much money you owe
- If someone has sued you

Before a potential employer can request your credit report or use it, the company must notify you and ask your permission. And if a company decides not to hire you because of information in your credit report, it must tell you (orally or in writing), along with information about the credit reporting company and your rights to dispute the accuracy of the report. For more information about what to know when looking for a job, visit www.ftc.gov/bcp/edu/pubs/consumer/alerts/alt080.shtm.

---

- What tasks will I have to perform? (Ask the program sponsor to list every step of the job.)
- Will I be paid a salary, or will my pay be based on commission?
- Who will pay me?
- When will I get my first paycheck?
- What is the total cost of the work-at-home program, including supplies, equipment, and membership fees? What will I get for my money?

The answers to these questions may help you determine whether a work-at-home program is appropriate for your circumstances and whether it is legitimate.

### Multilevel Marketing

Some multilevel marketing plans are legitimate; however, others are illegal pyramid schemes. In pyramids, commissions are based on the number of distributors recruited. Most of the product sales are made to these distributors, not to consumers in general. The underlying goods and services, which vary from vitamins to car leases, only make the schemes look legitimate. Most people end up with nothing to show for their money except the expensive products or marketing materials they were pressured to buy for resale.

If you're thinking about joining what appears to be a legitimate multilevel marketing plan, take time to learn about the plan:

- What is the company's track record?
- What products does it sell?
- Does it sell products to the public at large?
- Does it have the evidence to back up the claims it makes about its product?
- Is the product competitively priced?
- Is it likely to appeal to a large customer base?
- How much does it cost to join the plan?
- Are monthly minimum sales required to earn a commission?
- Will you be required to recruit new distributors to earn your commission?

### Net-Based Business Opportunities

The FTC says that many Internet business opportunities are scams that promise more than they can possibly deliver. These companies lure would-be entrepreneurs with false promises of big earnings for little effort. Some tips for finding a legitimate opportunity:

- Consider the promotion carefully.
- Study the business opportunity's franchise disclosure document.
- Get earnings claims in writing and compare them with the experience of previous franchise and business opportunity owners.
- Visit previous franchise and business opportunity owners in person, preferably at their places of business.
- Check out the company with the local consumer protection agency (p. 112) and Better Business Bureau (p. 67) to see whether there have been any complaints.
- If the business opportunity involves selling products from well-known companies, verify the relationship with the legal department of the company whose merchandise you would promote.
- Consult an attorney, accountant, or other business advisor before you put any money down or sign any papers.
- Take your time. Promoters of fraudulent business opportunities are likely to use high-pressure sales tactics to get you to buy in. If the business opportunity is legitimate, it will still be around when you're ready to decide.

20  www.USA.gov

To contact an organization, use the directory beginning on page 63.

## UNEMPLOYMENT

The government's Unemployment Insurance Program provides benefits to eligible workers who become unemployed through no fault of their own and who meet other eligibility requirements. Each state administers its own program under federal guidelines. Eligibility requirements, benefit amounts, and length of benefits are determined by the states. For more information, go to www.dol.gov/dol/topic/unemployment-insurance/index.htm.

In addition, some states are extending unemployment benefits for eligible recipients for up to 13 additional weeks. Visit workforcesecurity.doleta.gov for the latest information regarding your state's benefit programs.

## FOOD AND NUTRITION

Consumers have a wide variety of food choices available. You want food that is safe, nutritious, and won't break your budget, but it's important to remember that making healthier choices can help you feel your best and stay strong. You can also reduce the risk for many diseases, including heart disease, cancer, stroke, and diabetes.

## HEALTHY FOOD CHOICES

To help you make healthy food choices, the federal government posts dietary guidelines at www.health.gov/dietaryguidelines. Federal regulations also require many foods to identify fat content, fiber, and nutrients on their labels. For more information about food labels, visit www.fda.gov/Food/ResourcesForYou/Consumers/NFLPM.

Check out these resources for advice, tips, and information on food shopping and nutrition:

- U.S. Department of Agriculture (p. 96)
- U.S. Food and Drug Administration (p. 100)
- Nutrition.gov (www.nutrition.gov)
- MedlinePlus.gov (www.nlm.nih.gov/medlineplus)
- Center for Nutrition Policy and Promotion (www.choosemyplate.gov)

## FOOD SAFETY

Food safety in the home revolves around three main functions: food storage, food handling, and cooking. By practicing a few simple rules for cleaning, separating, cooking, and chilling, you can prevent most food-borne illness in the home. The website www.foodsafety.gov is your gateway to government food safety information, including publications you can download or request. You can also visit www.recalls.gov for the latest food safety alerts and recalls.

For more information, here are some additional resources:

- Centers for Disease Control and Prevention (p. 99)
- FDA's Food Information Hotline, 1-888-SAFEFOOD (723-3366)
- Partnership for Food Safety Education, www.fightbac.org
- American Cleaning Institute, www.cleaninginstitute.org
- U.S. Department of Health and Human Services (p. 98)
- USDA Food Safety and Inspection Service, www.fsis.usda.gov
- USDA Meat and Poultry Hotline, 1-888-674-6854

## SAVING MONEY ON GROCERIES

It can be a challenge to make healthy food choices and stay within your food budget. Here are some tips to help you get the most from your grocery budget:

- Take an inventory of the food you already have in your home. Plan your meals for the week, keeping in mind what you already have.
- Make a shopping list and stick to it.
- Compare unit prices (cost per ounce or pound) to get the best deal.
- Buy the generic store brand versions of foods.
- Take advantage of store loyalty savings programs as well as clipping coupons and online discounts. Remember that stores retain your purchase habits and use them for marketing purposes. See Protecting Your Privacy (p. 38) for more information.
- Only take advantage of the deal if you know you will eat the discounted item. It's not a deal if the food goes to waste.
- Shop the perimeter of the store for nutrient-dense foods. Processed and packaged foods tend to be more expensive.
- Visit your local farmer's market to find fresh produce. Arrive early to get the best selection or late to get the best deals. Fresh food spoils quickly, so don't buy more than you can eat or freeze. Find your local farmers market at search.ams.usda.gov/farmersmarkets.
- Shop for foods that are in season. When the supply is plentiful, the prices tend to be lower.

## SNAP: SUPPLEMENTAL NUTRITION ASSISTANCE PROGRAM

The Supplemental Nutrition Assistance Program (SNAP) helps low-income people buy the food they need to maintain good health. To receive these benefits, you must apply and participate in an interview. If you are eligible, you will receive benefits in approximately 30 days. You may qualify if you are:

- Working for low wages or working part time
- Unemployed
- Receiving welfare or other public assistance payments
- Elderly or disabled and low-income
- Homeless

Benefits are distributed on a prepaid electronic benefit card (EBT) with a PIN. Use this card at approved food stores, like any other debit card. For more information about using a prepaid card, see page 7. For more information about SNAP and how to apply for benefits, visit www.fns.usda.gov/snap/applicant_recipients.

- Some stores offer discounts to customers for bringing their own bags.

For more grocery shopping tips visit www.extension.org and www.choosemyplate.gov.

### ORGANIC FOODS

Buying organic food is a way to eat in a healthy manner and protect the environment. These foods are grown and processed according to USDA regulations and follow specific rules concerning pest control, raising animals, and the use of additives. Keep in mind that organic and natural foods tend to be more expensive than conventionally grown foods, and that the USDA does not claim that organic food is safer or more nutritious than other foods.

To make sure a product is certified organic, look for the USDA organic seal. You can also tell whether produce was grown organically by checking the price look up code (PLU); if the first number starts with a 4, then the food was grown conventionally, if it starts with a 9, it was grown organically.

Other common labels that help you choose certain types of food products include:

**Free-Range or Cage-Free**. The flock was provided shelter in a building, room, or area with unlimited access to food, fresh water, and the outdoors during its production cycle.

**Natural**. As required by USDA, meat, poultry, and egg products labeled as "natural" must be minimally processed and contain no artificial ingredients.

**Grass-Fed**. Grass-fed animals receive a majority of their nutrients from grass throughout their life, while organic animals' pasture diet may be supplemented with grain.

For more information about organic foods, visit www.ams.usda.gov.

## GOING GREEN

"Going Green" means practicing an environmentally friendly and ecologically responsible lifestyle as well as making decisions to help protect the environment and sustain natural resources. There are lots of reasons to consider going green—too much trash, greenhouse gases, air and water pollution, damage to the ozone layer, and saving money. For example, switching all of the light bulbs in a home from conventional incandescent light bulbs to compact fluorescent light (CFL) bulbs could save about $40 over the life of the bulb. Other examples include:

- Turn your thermostat down two degrees in winter and up two degrees in summer.
- Make sure your walls and ceilings are well insulated.
- Replace bathroom and kitchen faucets with low-flow models.

## ENERGY STAR APPLIANCES

ENERGY STAR-qualified appliances use about 33% less energy than standard units. You can find the ENERGY STAR logo on TVs, clothes washers and dryers, water heaters, furnaces, and many other products.

Home electronics that have earned the ENERGY STAR rating deliver exceptional features while using less energy. Saving energy helps you save money on utility bills and helps to protect the environment by reducing greenhouse gas emissions to counter climate change. For more information, visit www.energystar.gov.

## BEWARE: VERIFY GREEN MARKETING CLAIMS

The number of products claiming they are "eco-friendly" or "all-natural" has increased due to a growing demand for "green" products. You may be unsure about which environmental standards and labels can be trusted. You can use the FTC's Green Guides (www.ftc.gov/bcp/grnrule/guides980427) as a resource to verify that the environmental attributes or products are truthful. Here are some tips to help you sort through eco-label marketing:

- Look for specific (for example, "contains 75% post-consumer recycled materials") rather than vague statements about environmental impact.
- Determine whether the green marketing claims apply to the packaging, the product, or both.
- Beware of fake third-party certification. Visit *Consumer Reports'* website (www.greenerchoices.org/eco-labels) to find reliable environmental labels.

For more information about environmental advertising and labeling, contact the FTC (p. 107) or EPA (p. 105).

For more ideas to help the environment and your wallet, check the EPA Pick 5 at www.epa.gov/pick5.

### BUYING GREEN

The U.S. Environmental Protection Agency (EPA) has a green products web portal (www.epa.gov/greenerproducts) to help you navigate the complex world of green products. The EPA also has a number of eco-labeling partnership programs to help you identify greener, safer, and more efficient products. Look for these EPA program labels when buying:

- **ENERGY STAR**—For energy-efficient electronics and appliances (www.energystar.gov)

## WATERSENSE MAKES SENSE

The EPA WaterSense program can help protect the future of our nation's water supply by promoting water efficiency and enhancing the market for water-efficient products, programs, and practices. To learn more and see what you can do to conserve water, visit www.epa.gov/watersense.

- **WaterSense**—For water-efficient products (www.epa.gov/watersense)
- **Design for the Environment (DfE)**—For household cleaners and other products that have been determined to be safer for both your health and the environment (www.epa.gov/dfe)
- **SmartWay Certified Vehicle**—For cleaner, more fuel efficient cars and trucks (www.epa.gov/smartway/vehicles)

You can also choose to buy organic or locally produced food and eco-friendly clothing. For more information about national standards covering organic food, go to the U.S. Department of Agriculture's Agricultural Marketing Service at www.ams.usda.gov/AMSv1.0. There are no national standards for organic clothing, but some fabrics to consider include organic cotton, bark cloth, bamboo, and organic wool.

By making greener product choices, you are saving money on utilities and fuel, and protecting public health and the environment.

### REUSING AND RECYCLING

You can make a big impact by using the products you buy in ways that respect the environment:

- Use fewer products and follow instructions for product use.
- Conserve energy, water, and materials.
- Recycle items made of materials such as glass, metal, plastic, or paper.
- Dispose of products properly.

Many utility companies now offer curbside recycling programs that provide U.S. households with a responsible and convenient way to recycle materials. To locate information on recycling services and efforts in your area, visit Earth 911's website (www.earth911.org) or call its toll-free hotline, 1-800-CLEANUP (253-2687).

It is easy to dispose of many products safely. Others, such as car batteries, cell phones, televisions, paints, oils, and solvents, require special handling. You can dispose of these products responsibly through your local household hazardous waste (HHW) collection facility or at your local government's annual HHW collection day. Some items may be given to charitable organizations or even dropped off at electronics retailers. Contact the EPA (p. 105) to help you make the right decisions about the best way to dispose of waste.

GOING GREEN

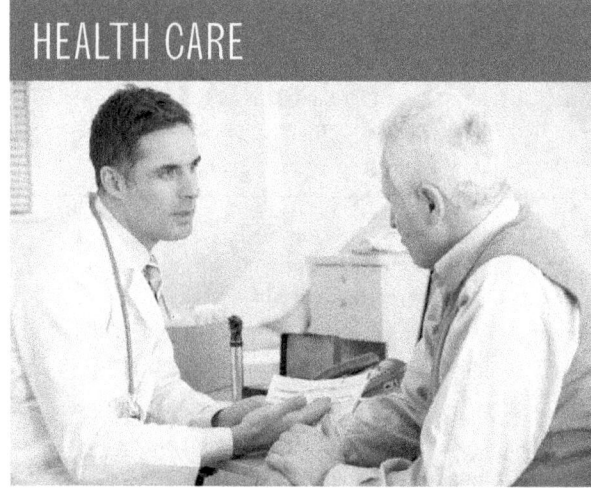

HEALTH CARE

There are plenty of resources available to help you make health care decisions. Be wary of websites sponsored by companies that are trying to sell you a particular treatment. It's better to contact reputable associations or visit sites run by government agencies and recognized organizations such as the Mayo Clinic or the American Medical Association (AMA). This information should complement, not replace, what you receive from a doctor. Here are some sites that are generally recognized as reliable information sources:

- **HealthFinder.gov and MedlinePlus** (www.medlineplus.gov) provide information on health issues, health care programs, and organizations.

- **Mayo Clinic** (www.mayoclinic.com) offers an index of diseases and much more.

- **Medical Library Association** (www.mlanet.org) links to websites suggested by librarians.

- **National Institute of Mental Health** (www.nimh.nih.gov) provides information on research about understanding and treating mental illness.

- **Substance Abuse and Mental Health Services Administration** (www.samhsa.gov) provides information on prevention, treatment, and recovery from substance abuse or mental health issues.

- **HealthCare.gov** (www.healthcare.gov/compare) provides tools that help compare doctors, hospitals, and nursing homes.

## CHOOSING A DOCTOR

When searching for a primary care doctor, dentist, specialist, or other health care professional:

- Find out whether the health care professional is licensed in your state. A state or local occupational and professional licensing board will be able to give you this information.

- Research whether the health care professional is board-certified in the appropriate specialty. Visit www.ama-assn.org and www.abms.org for more information.

- Ask how often the health care professional has done the procedure you need or has treated your condition. You may be able to find some of this information on the Internet. For example, the Centers for Disease Control and Prevention (CDC) reports the success rates and number of procedures performed by fertility clinics at www.cdc.gov. Some states also collect and post data on the success of heart-bypass surgery.

- Check whether there have been any complaints or disciplinary actions taken against the provider you are researching. Visit www.docboard.org for more information. There are also pay-for-use sites with similar information, including www.docinfo.org and www.mdnationwide.org. Visit www.healthfinder.gov and www.ahrq.gov/consumer for more advice on identifying providers.

- Find out what doctors participate in your health insurance plan. If you are having surgery, check that all providers (radiologists, anesthesiologists) are also covered by your plan, to avoid surprise bills.

Consider these questions regarding your health care provider and his or her practice:

- Does the doctor participate in your insurance plan?

- Is the office in an area that you can get to easily or does it have hours during times when you can make an appointment?

- Does the doctor have privileges at the hospital you prefer?

- Do you get along well with the doctor? Do you feel that you communicate well with each other and that he or she listens to your concerns and explains diagnoses and benefits of new treatments and prescriptions clearly?

- What is the doctor's cancelation policy?

- Will you have to pay for the visit if you cancel your appointment?

### Filing a Complaint

If you have a complaint about the medical services you received from a physician, you may file a complaint with your state medical board. For a complete directory from the Federation of State Medical Boards, visit www.fsmb.org/directory_smb.html. You can also call the Federation at 817-868-4000 to get the phone number of your state's medical board.

## CHOOSING A HEALTH CARE FACILITY

Report cards on the Internet can help you compare health care facilities. Compare doctors and health care facilities at www.healthcare.gov/compare. In addition, www.usnews.com and www.healthgrades.com rate hospitals based on information collected from Medicare records and other sources. As of October 2012, the Affordable Care Act requires all hospitals to report performance publically.

## MEDICAL IDENTITY THEFT

Medical identity theft can occur when someone steals your personal information number to obtain medical care, buy medication, or submit fake claims to your insurer or Medicare in your name. To prevent medical identity theft, you can:

- Guard your Social Security, Medicare, and health insurance identification numbers. Only give your number to your physician or other approved health care providers.

- Review your explanation of benefits or Medicare Summary Notice to make sure that the claims match the services you received. Report questionable charges to your health insurance provider or Medicare.

- Request and carefully review a copy of your medical records for inaccuracies and conditions that you don't have.

If you believe you have been a victim of medical identity theft, file a complaint with the FTC at 1-877- 438-4338 or ftccomplaintassistant.gov and your health insurance company's fraud department. If you suspect that you have been the victim of Medicare fraud, contact the U.S. Department of Health and Human Services' Inspector General at 1-800-447-8477 or by e-mail at HHSTips@oig.hhs.gov.

For more information about Medicare fraud, visit www.stopmedicarefraud.gov.

When determining the best health care facility for you, consider these factors:

- Does the facility accept payment from your insurance plan?

- Does your doctor have privileges to provide treatment to patients at the facility?

- What is the quality of the facility?

- Does the facility specialize in services and procedures that fit with your medical needs?

- Is the facility in an area you can travel to and from easily? Find health care facilities in your area at findahealthcenter.hrsa.gov.

### Elder Care

As people live longer, the need for services for seniors has become more important. The Eldercare Locator (www.eldercare.gov), a public service of the Administration on Aging, U.S. Department of Health and Human Services, is a nationwide service that connects older Americans and their caregivers with information on senior services. Visit www.aoa.gov/Elders_Families for a list of resources to connect older persons, caregivers, and professionals with important federal, national, and local programs.

The Joint Commission (p. 145) accredits hospitals as well as nursing homes and other health care organizations. Specially trained investigators assess whether these organizations meet set standards. At www.qualitycheck.org, you can check on a local facility, including how it compares with others. The Joint Commission also accepts consumer complaints. You can post a complaint on its website, www.jointcommission.org.

If you are looking for a nursing home or other assisted-living facility, these organizations can help:

- Nursing Home Compare, operated by the U.S. Department of Health and Human Services, will help you compare the facilities in many states. Go to www.medicare.gov/nhcompare/home.asp or call 1-800-MEDICARE (633-4227).

- Eldercare Locator (www.eldercare.gov) provides information and referral services for those seeking local and state support resources for the elderly (p. 99).

- LeadingAge (www.leadingage.org) is a trade group that represents many nonprofit facilities that serve and support the elderly (p. 145).

- The Assisted Living Federation of America (www.alfa.org) represents both for-profit and nonprofit assisted-living facilities; call 703-894-1805 (p. 143).

- The Commission on Accreditation of Rehabilitation Facilities (www.carf.org) gives its seal of approval to qualifying facilities; call 1-888-281-6531 (p. 143).

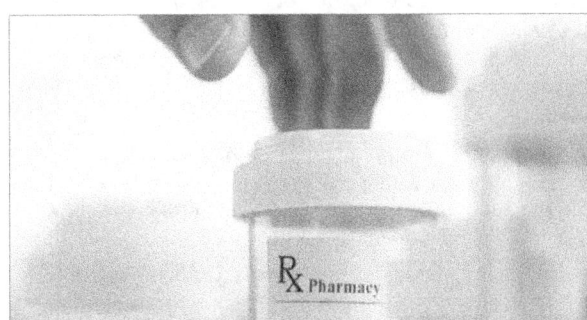

## PRESCRIPTION DRUGS

Your pharmacist oversees an important part of your health care by providing the medications prescribed by other health care professionals. It's important that you are proactive and communicate honestly with your pharmacist. Topics you should discuss with your pharmacist include:

- What other medications you take

- Whether you have allergic reactions to any medications

- Whether there is a generic version of the medication you can take instead

- Any questions about the medication you are receiving

- Whether there is a risk that your medications don't mix well with each other

- Whether there any side effects to the medications

## WHERE TO GO FOR MEDICAL CARE

When you are sick, you may not know the best place to go for medical care. In non-emergency situations, your first choice should be your primary care provider (PCP). Your PCP knows your medical history and treats common ailments. Urgent care is best when you need medical attention for a non-life threatening illness quickly or after regular hours. Go to the emergency room if your illness is serious or life-threatening, such as:

- Choking
- Stopped breathing
- Head injury with passing out, fainting, or confusion
- Injury to neck or spine, especially if there is loss of feeling or inability to move
- Electric shock or lightning strike
- Severe burn
- Seizure that lasts three to five minutes

To learn more about the differences among health care providers, visit www.medlineplus.gov or www.ucaoa.org.

Remember to finish your entire prescription, since some illnesses require treatment to continue past the time when symptoms go away. Make certain that your pharmacy has your current health and prescription insurance on record so you get the best price possible. If you have difficulty paying for your medications, contact the manufacturer; some pharmaceutical companies have patient assistance programs to help you afford your medication.

An increasing number of consumers are replacing a trip to the pharmacy with a visit to the Internet. While there are online pharmacies that provide legitimate prescription services, there are also some questionable sites that make buying medicines online risky. Do business only with a licensed U.S. pharmacy. Check with the National Association of Boards of Pharmacy to determine whether the site is licensed and in good standing. Visit www.nabp.net or call 847-391-4406.

If you suspect a site is not a licensed pharmacy, report it and any complaints to the Food and Drug Administration (p. 100) at www.fda.gov/Safety/ReportaProblem/ucm059315.htm.

Want to know the side effects of a particular medication? Curious whether a drug has been approved by the FDA? For answers to these questions and other information on approved prescription and over-the-counter and discontinued drugs, visit www.accessdata.fda.gov/scripts/cder/drugsatfda. For general drug information, you can also contact the FDA (p. 100).

## MEDICARE PRESCRIPTION DRUG COVERAGE

Medicare offers prescription drug coverage to help senior citizens and others who need medical assistance get the prescription drugs they need, under Part D of the program (or Part C if you are enrolled in the Medicare Advantage Plan). Everyone with Medicare can join a drug plan to get this coverage. Not all Medicare drug plans are the same, however. If you aren't sure whether a drug plan is approved by Medicare, call 1-800-MEDICARE (633-4227). Look for the "Medicare Approved" seal on drug discount cards to make sure you are getting the best deal.

Medicare prescription drug coverage pays expenses up to $2,800; once your prescription costs exceeds that amount, you will no longer have coverage and will be responsible for the full cost of your drugs. However, once your out-of-pocket spending reaches $4,550, your prescription coverage will kick back in. Any amount of prescription drug spending between $2,800 and $4,550 is called the coverage gap or "Medicare donut hole." Beginning in 2013, if you reach the coverage gap, you will automatically get a 52.5% discount on covered brand-name drugs and a 14% discount on generic drugs. If you have limited income and resources, you may get extra help to cover prescription drugs for little or no cost. For more information, contact the Centers for Medicare & Medicaid Services (p. 100).

For more information about Medicare, go to www.medicare.gov.

## ADVANCE MEDICAL DIRECTIVES

We all face the possibility that we may become incapacitated sometime during our lifetime. This often happens when nearing death, but it can also be the result of a temporary condition. Many people assume their spouses or children will automatically be allowed to make financial and/or medical decisions for them, but this is not necessarily true.

Advance directives are written documents that tell your doctors what kind of treatment you want if you become unable to make medical decisions (for example, if you're in a coma). Forms and laws vary from state to state, so it's a good idea to understand the laws of the state where you live when you write advance directives. It's also a good idea to make them before you are very ill. Federal law requires hospitals, nursing homes, and other institutions that receive Medicare or Medicaid funds to provide written information regarding advance medical directives to all patients upon admission.

A living will is one type of advance directive that goes into effect when a person is terminally ill. A living will does not give you the opportunity to select someone to make decisions for you, but it does allow you to specify the kind of treatment you want in specific situations. For example, you might choose to specify that you do not want to be treated with antibiotics if death is imminent. You can, if you choose, include an advance directive that you do not wish to be resuscitated if your heart stops or if you stop breathing. In this case, a Do Not Resuscitate (DNR) order would be entered on your medical chart.

### Naming a Durable Power of Attorney for Health Care

A durable power of attorney for health care (sometimes called a durable medical power of attorney) specifies the person you've chosen to make medical decisions for you. It is activated when you're unconscious or unable to make medical decisions, or when you have specified. You need to choose someone who meets the legal requirements in your state for acting as your agent. State laws vary, but most states disqualify anyone under the age of 18, your health care provider, or employees of your health care provider.

The person you choose as your agent must:

- Be willing to speak and advocate on your behalf
- Be willing to deal with conflict among friends and family members, if it arises
- Know you well and understand your wishes
- Be willing to talk with you about these issues
- Be someone you trust with your life

When choosing among housing options, there are many decisions you must make. Should you rent or buy? If you buy, what sort of financing should you choose, and what type of mortgages is best for you? The U.S. Department of Housing and Urban Development (HUD) funds housing counseling agencies throughout the country to help you make these decisions. These organizations can give you advice on buying a home, renting, defaults, foreclosures, credit issues, and reverse mortgages. To contact the agency nearest you, call 1-800-569-4287 or visit www.hud.gov. Homeowners with problems that could result in default on their mortgage or foreclosure on their property are encouraged to contact a HUD-approved housing counseling agency immediately.

If you believe you are being discriminated against during your housing search because of your race, color, nationality, religion, sex, familial status, or disability, contact HUD's Office of Fair Housing and Equal Opportunity (p. 102).

## BUYING A HOME

Buying a home is one of the most complex financial decisions you'll ever make. In addition to the financial and legal issues involved, real estate agents and lenders may not be acting in your best interest.

- Real estate agents represent the seller, not the buyer. Consider hiring a buyer's agent who works for you, not for the seller.
- Get prices on other homes. Knowing the price of other homes in a neighborhood will help you avoid paying too much.
- Have the property inspected. Use a licensed home inspector to inspect the property carefully before you agree to buy it.
- Check to see if a particular home requires you to pay any ongoing homeowners association or condo fees. For more information, visit www.bankrate.com/finance/real-estate/check-out-hoa-finances-before-buying-condo-1.aspx.

### Mortgages

When shopping for a home mortgage, make sure you obtain all of the relevant information:

- Research current interest rates. Check the real estate section of your local newspaper, use the Internet, or call at least six lenders for information.
- Check the rates for 15-year, 20-year, and 30-year mortgages. You may be able to save thousands of dollars in interest charges by getting the shortest-term mortgage you can afford.
- Ask for details on the same loan amount, loan term, and type of loan from multiple lenders so you can compare the information. Be sure to get the APR, which takes into account not only the interest rate, but also points, broker fees, and other credit charges expressed as a yearly rate.
- Ask whether the rate is fixed or adjustable. The interest rate on adjustable-rate mortgages (ARMs) can vary a great deal over the lifetime of the mortgage. An

### UNDERWATER/UPSIDE-DOWN MORTGAGES

When describing a mortgage in trouble, the terms "underwater" or "upside-down" mean the same thing—when the amount of money you still have to pay on the loan is more than the actual value of the loan. For more information about underwater or upside-down mortgages, visit www.makinghomeaffordable.gov/programs/fallen-value-help.

increase of several percentage points might raise payments by hundreds of dollars per month.

- If a loan has an adjustable rate, ask when and how the rate and loan payment can change.
- Find out how much of a down payment is required. Some lenders require 20% of the home's purchase price as a down payment. But many lenders now offer loans that require less. In these cases, you may be required to purchase private mortgage insurance (PMI) to protect the lender if you fall behind on payments.
- If PMI is required, ask what the total cost of the insurance will be. How much will the monthly mortgage payment be when the PMI premium is added, and how long you will be required to carry PMI?
- Ask whether you can pay off the loan early, and whether there is a penalty for doing so.

There is a long list of sources for mortgage loans: mortgage banks, mortgage brokers, banks, thrifts and credit unions, home builders, real estate agencies, and Internet lenders.

For more information on home buying and mortgages, visit www.hud.gov. Other good sources include the Mortgage Bankers Association at www.homeloanlearningcenter.com and Neighborworks America's home ownership website at www.keystomyhome.org.

## Mortgage Transfers

CFPB rules help mortgage borrowers by requiring that mortgage companies notify them when their loans are transferred to another company. The rules ensure that you know who owns your loan, which is important information if you have questions or payment disputes or want to discuss loan modifications.

Under these rules, the company that takes over your loan must send you a notice within 30 days of acquiring it. Even with a new loan owner, the company that "services" or handles your loan might not change, and you might continue to send your mortgage payments to the same address. If that loan servicer changes, you will receive a separate notice.

For more information about servicing companies, read the FTC's publication, Mortgage Servicing: Making Sure Your Payments Count at www.ftc.gov/bcp/edu/pubs/consumer/homes/rea10.shtm.

## AVOIDING FORECLOSURE

If you miss your mortgage payments, foreclosure may occur. This is the legal means your lender can use to repossess your home. If you owe more than your property is worth, a deficiency judgment is pursued. Both foreclosures and deficiency judgments have a negative impact on your future credit. You should avoid foreclosure if at all possible.

---

**Fixed-rate and adjustable-rate mortgages are the two main types of mortgages, but there is a wide variety of other mortgage products available. Below are pros and cons of some of the mortgage products you want to consider:**

| TYPE OF MORTGAGE | PROS | CONS |
| --- | --- | --- |
| Fixed-rate mortgage | No surprises. Interest rate stays the same over the entire term, usually 15, 20, or 30 years. | If interest rates fall, you could be stuck paying a higher rate. |
| Adjustable-rate (ARM) or variable-rate mortgage | Usually offers a lower initial rate of interest than fixed-rate loans. | After an initial period, rates fluctuate over the life of the loan. When interest rates rise, generally so do your loan payments. |
| FHA (Federal Housing Administration) loans | Allows buyers who may not qualify for a home loan to obtain one with a low down payment. | The size of your loan may be limited. |
| VA loan | Guaranteed loans for eligible veterans, active duty personnel, and surviving spouses. Offers competitive rates, low or no down payments. | The size of your loan may be limited. |
| Balloon mortgage | Usually a fixed-rate loan with relatively low payments for a fixed period. | After an initial period, the entire balance of the loan is due immediately. This type of loan may be risky for some borrowers. |
| Interest-only | Borrower pays only the interest on the loan in monthly payments for a fixed term. | After an initial period, the balance of the loan is due. This could mean higher payments, paying a lump sum, or refinancing. |
| Reverse mortgage | Allows seniors to convert equity in their homes to cash; you don't have to pay back the loan and interest as long as you live in the house. | Subject to aggressive lending practices and false advertising promises, particularly by lenders that prey on seniors. Check to make sure the loan is Federally insured. |

## MORTGAGE REFINANCING

Consider refinancing your mortgage if you can get a rate that is at least one percentage point lower than your existing mortgage rate and if you plan to keep the new mortgage for several years. When comparing mortgages, don't forget to include the extra fees you must pay for the new mortgage. You may be able to get some fees waived if you are able to refinance with your current mortgage holder.

In addition, the Making Home Affordable Program offers opportunities to modify or refinance your mortgage to make your monthly payments more affordable. It also includes the Home Affordable Foreclosure Alternatives Program for homeowners who are interested in a short sale or deed-in-lieu of foreclosure. Visit www.makinghomeaffordable.gov or call 1-888-995-HOPE (4673).

**These steps can help:**

- Do not ignore letters from your lender. If you're having problems making your payments, call or write to your lender's Loss Mitigation Department immediately. Explain your situation. Be prepared to provide financial information, such as your monthly income and expenses. Without this information, the lender may not be able to help you.

- Stay in your home for now; you may not qualify for assistance if you abandon your property.

- Contact a HUD-approved housing counselor. Call 1-800-569-4287 or TDD 1-800-877-8339 for the housing counseling agency nearest you. These agencies are valuable resources.

- Contact Making Home Affordable for help. Call 1-888-995-4673, or 1-877-304-9709 for hearing-impaired homeowners, to talk to a HUD-approved credit counselor who will guide you through your options for free.

HUD counselors frequently have information on services and programs offered by government agencies as well as private and community organizations that could help you. The housing counseling agency may also offer credit counseling. These services are usually free of charge.

For more information, contact The U.S. Department of Housing and Urban Development (p. 102).

Additional advice, resources, and tips for homeowners can be found under Home Equity Loans (p. 16), Insurance (p. 33), and Home Improvement and Repairs (p. 29).

## MOVING COMPANIES

Not all moving companies are the same. Although many are legitimate, some attempt to take advantage of their clients. Follow these guidelines to help you choose the right mover:

**Get a written estimate from several movers.** Be wary of very low estimates. Some companies quote a low price to get a contract and later ask for more money before they will remove your belongings from their truck.

**Make sure the mover has an operating license.** For moves from one state to another, visit www.protectyourmove.gov to verify a mover's license. For moves within a state, check your state, county, or local consumer affairs agency (p. 112).

**Make sure the mover has insurance.** If furniture is damaged during the move, the mover's insurance should cover it. Ask how to file a complaint if there are limits to the coverage. For more information about the levels of mover's insurance coverage, visit www.protectyourmove.gov/consumer/awareness/valuation/valuation-insurance.htm.

**Check the mover's record.** Contact your state or local consumer protection agency (p. 112) or the Better Business Bureau (p. 67) to see whether there is a history of complaints.

If you have a dispute with a moving company, you can file a complaint with the Federal Motor Carrier Safety Administration by calling 1-888-368-7238 or by visiting www.fmcsa.dot.gov.

## HOME IMPROVEMENT AND REPAIRS

Home improvements and repairs can cost thousands of dollars and are the subject of frequent complaints.

When selecting a contractor:

- Get recommendations and references. Talk to friends, family, and others who have used the contractor for similar work.

- Get at least three written estimates. Insist the contractors come to your home to evaluate what needs to be done. Be sure the estimates are based on the same work so you can make meaningful comparisons.

- Check contractor complaint records with your state or local consumer protection agency (p. 112) or the Better Business Bureau (p. 67).

- Make sure the contractor meets licensing and registration requirements. Your state or local consumer protection agency (p. 112) can help you determine the necessary requirements.

- Get the names of suppliers and ask them whether the contractor makes timely payments.

- Contact your local building inspection department to check for permit and inspection requirements. Be wary if the contractor asks you to get the permit; it could mean the firm is not licensed.

- Be sure your contractor is insured. The contractor should have personal liability, property damage, and workers' compensation insurance for workers and subcontractors. Also check with your insurance company to find out whether you are covered for any injury or damage that might occur.

## BEWARE: FORECLOSURE RESCUE SCAMS

Scam artists often target homeowners who are struggling to meet their mortgage commitment or are anxious to sell their homes. Recognize and avoid common scams:

- **Lease-back or rent-to-buy scams:** You are asked to transfer the title to your home "temporarily" to the scam artist who promises to obtain better financing for your mortgage and allow you to stay in your home as a renter with the option to purchase the home back. However, if you do not comply with the terms of the rent-to-buy agreement, you will lose your money and be evicted like any other tenant.

- **Fake "government" modification programs:** These scams claim to be affiliated with the government or require that you pay high fees to benefit from government modification programs. Remember that you do not have to pay any fees to participate in government-approved programs. Some frauds may even use words like "Federal" or "government-approved" or acquire website names that make consumers think they are associated with the government.

- **Refinance fraud:** The scam artist offers to be an intermediary between you and your mortgage lender to negotiate a loan modification. The scam artist may even instruct you to make payments directly to him or her, which the scammer will send to the lender. However, the scam artist will not forward the payments to your lender and you could still lose your home.

- **"Eliminate your debt" claims:** Some companies may make false legal claims that you are not required to repay your mortgage or that they know of "secret laws" that can eliminate your debt. Do not believe these claims.

- **Refinance scams:** You are encouraged to sign "foreclosure rescue" loan documents to refinance your loan. In reality, you have surrendered ownership of your home because the loan documents are actually deed transfer documents. You may falsely believe that your home has been saved from foreclosure until you receive an eviction notice months or even years later.

Remember: Foreclosure assistance from a HUD-approved housing counselor is free. Visit www.makinghomeaffordable.gov or call 1-800-569-4287.

- Insist on a written contract that states exactly what work will be done, the quality of materials that will be used, warranties, timetables, the names of any subcontractors, the total price of the job, and the schedule of payments.

- Try to limit your down payment. Some states have laws limiting the amount of down payment required.

- Understand your payment options. Compare the cost of getting your own loan versus contractor financing.

- Don't make a final payment or sign a final release until you are satisfied with the work and know that subcontractors and suppliers have been paid. Some state laws allow unpaid subcontractors and suppliers to put a lien on your home for bills the contractor failed to pay.

- Pay by credit card when you can. You may have the right to withhold payment to the credit card company until problems are corrected (see p. 13).

**Be especially cautious if the contractor:**

- Comes door-to-door or seeks you out
- Just happens to have material left over from a recent job
- Offers you discounts for finding other customers
- Quotes a price that's out of line with other estimates
- Pressures you for an immediate decision
- Can only be reached by leaving messages with an answering service
- Drives an unmarked van
- Has out-of-state license plates

- Asks you to pay for the entire job up front

With most home improvements, federal law gives you three business days to cancel without penalty. See the 3-Day Cooling-Off Rule (p. 4). Of course, you would be liable for any benefit already received. State laws may also provide some protection. And remember, if you finance home improvements with a home equity loan (p. 16) and don't make your payments, you could lose your home.

## RENTING/LEASING

A lease is an agreement that outlines the obligations of the owner and the tenants of a house or apartment. It is a legally binding document that courts will generally uphold in legal proceedings, so it is important for you to know the exact terms of the lease agreement before you sign it. Before agreeing to lease an apartment to you, a landlord may review your credit report, so you may want to get a copy before you start your apartment search. Some things to look for in a lease:

- Clauses that allow the landlord to change the terms of the lease after it is signed
- Requirements/responsibilities of the tenants to do routine repairs such as lawn maintenance, cleaning, or notification about needed repairs
- Restrictions that would prevent you from living normally or comfortably in the home
- Terms of the lease and any important dates such as when the rent is due or garbage pickup days
- Extra fees for parking spaces or storage, garbage collection, and pets

- Information regarding utility providers, how to arrange for service and whether the landlord or tenant is responsible for paying the bills (see Utilities, p. 52)

Read the lease carefully and discuss anything you don't understand or any issues you might have. All landlord responsibilities should be stated clearly. Always get a copy of the signed lease to keep in your records. Any clause or terms in the agreement affects ALL parties who sign.

Check with the Better Business Bureau (p. 67) or your local consumer protection office (p. 112) to determine if your prospective landlord has any existing complaints from previous tenants.

The Fair Housing Act protects tenants who lease or rent property. If you think your rights have been violated, you may write a letter to or call the HUD office nearest you (p. 102). You have one year after the alleged violation to file a complaint with HUD, but you should file as soon as possible.

Each state has its own set of tenant rights, laws, and protections. For a state-by-state directory, visit www.hud.gov/local. You can also find available public housing at www.hud.gov. HUD (p. 102) offers several housing assistance programs for tenants and landlords as well as information on rights of residents and displaced tenants.

## Ten Tips for Renters

1. The best way to win over a prospective landlord is to be prepared by bringing a completed rental application with you; written references from previous landlords, employers, friends, and colleagues; and a current copy of your credit report.
2. Carefully review all of the important conditions of the tenancy before you sign.
3. To avoid disputes or misunderstandings with your landlord, get everything in writing.
4. Ask about your privacy rights before you sign the lease.
5. Know your rights to live in a habitable rental unit—and don't give them up.
6. Keep communication open with your landlord.
7. Purchase renters insurance to cover your valuables. See more information under Homeowners/Renters Insurance (p. 33).
8. Make sure the security deposit refund procedures are spelled out in your lease or rental agreement.
9. Learn whether your building and neighborhood are safe, and what you can expect your landlord to do if they aren't.
10. Know when to fight an eviction notice and when to move. Unless you have the law and provable facts on your side, fighting an eviction notice is usually shortsighted.

INSURANCE

General sources of insurance information include the American Council of Life Insurers (p. 142), the Insurance Information Institute (p. 144), the National Association of Insurance Commissioners (p. 145), and your state insurance department (p. 130). You can also visit www.insure.com.

When buying any type of insurance (home, life, auto, rental, or other), you should:

- Find out whether your state insurance department (p. 130) offers any information concerning insurance companies and rates. This is a good way to get a feeling for the range of prices and the lowest-cost providers in your area.
- Check several sources for the best deal. Try getting quotes online, but be aware that many online services may provide prices for just a few companies. An independent insurance agent who works with several insurers in your area may be able to get you a better deal.
- Make sure the insurance company is licensed and covered by the state's guaranty fund. The fund pays claims in case the company defaults. Your state insurance department (p. 130) can provide this information.
- Check the financial stability and soundness of the insurance company. Ratings from A.M. Best (www.ambest.com), Standard & Poor's (www.standardandpoors.com), and Moody's Investors Services (www.moodys.com) are available online and at most public libraries.
- Research the complaint record of the company. Contact your state insurance department (p. 130), or visit the website of the National Association of Insurance Commissioners (www.naic.org), which has a database of complaints filed with state regulators.
- Find out what others think about the company's customer service. Consumers can rate homeowner insurance companies at www.jdpower.com/insurance.

- Once you pay your first insurance premium, make sure you receive a written policy. This tells you that the agent forwarded your premium to the insurance company. If you don't receive a policy within 60 days, contact your agent and the insurance company.

If you suspect fraud, call the National Insurance Crime Bureau's hotline, 1-800-835-6422. For more information, check out www.insurancefraud.org.

## AUTO INSURANCE

The requirements for auto insurance vary from state to state. Check with your state insurance regulator (p. 130) to learn more about individual requirements as well as insurers you may be considering for your policy.

To get the best coverage at the best price, get several quotes from insurance companies; it may save you hundreds of dollars a year. Other ways to reduce your insurance premium include:

- Raise your deductible on collision and comprehensive coverage. If you have an older car, you might want to drop this coverage altogether.

- Take advantage of discounts. You may be eligible for a discount based on the number of miles you drive; your age (turning 25 or 50); your good grades if you are a student; your driving record (no moving vehicle violations or accidents in three years); or if you've taken a safe-driving course. You might also be able to get discounts if you insure more than one vehicle, insure your vehicle and your home with the same company, have anti-theft devices, or have safety features such as air bags or anti-lock brake system.

You can also find valuable information about car ownership in Cars (p. 11), as well as information about insurance for rental cars.

## DISABILITY INSURANCE

Disability can be more disastrous financially than death. If you are disabled, you lose your earning power, but you still have living expenses and often huge fees for medical care. Disability insurance helps you replace lost income. Many employers offer some type of disability insurance coverage for employees, or you can get an individual disability insurance policy. There are two types of disability policies: short-term disability (STD) and long-term disability (LTD). Short-term disability policies have a maximum benefit of two years, while long-term disability policies have benefits that can last the rest of your life. When purchasing disability insurance, ask:

- **How is disability defined?** Some policies consider you disabled if you are unable to perform the duties of any job. Better plans pay benefits if you are unable to do the usual duties of your own occupation.

- **When do benefits begin?** Most plans have a waiting period after an illness before payments begin.

---

## INSURANCE VOCABULARY

**Claim**—a request for your insurance provider to pay for services provided by a medical professional

**Co-payment (co-pay)**—the amount, set by your insurer, that you pay when you receive medical service or for a prescription

**Deductible**—amount you must pay before your insurance company will pay a claim. There are multiple types of deductibles, but in general, a lower deducible will have a higher-cost policy.

**Explanation of benefits (EOB)**—a statement from your health insurance company that shows what claims it has paid on your behalf

Visit www.HealthCare.gov for more important definitions related to health insurance.

---

- **How long do benefits last?** After the waiting period, payments are usually available until you reach age 65, though shorter or longer terms are also available.

- **What dollar amount is promised?** Can benefits be reduced by Social Security disability and workers' compensation payments? Are the benefits adjusted for inflation? Will the policy provider continue making contributions to your pension plan so you have retirement benefits when the disability coverage ends?

For more information on disability insurance, visit www.iii.org.

## HEALTH INSURANCE

### Affordable Care Act

The 2010 Affordable Care Act (ACA) puts in place comprehensive health insurance reforms that will roll out over several years. Most provisions will take effect by 2014; a timeline is available at healthcare.gov/law/timeline. The law is intended to lower health care costs, provide more health care choices, and enhance the quality of health care for all Americans. Major provisions affecting consumers include:

- Coverage for seniors who hit the Medicare Prescription Drug "donut hole," including a rebate for those who reach the gap in drug coverage.

- Expanded coverage for young adults, allowing them to stay on their parents' plan until they are 26 years old.

- Providing access to insurance for uninsured Americans with pre-existing conditions.

- Expanded preventive care (for example, wellness visits and mammograms) to Medicare and Medicaid participants.

- Medical coverage to children not eligible for care under Medicaid.

- In 2013, you can set aside up to $2,500 in a flexible spending account (FSA) for medical expenses that aren't covered by insurance.

For more information about the law as well as basic information about health insurance, go to www.healthcare.gov.

### Group Policies

Many consumers have health care coverage from their employers. Others have medical care paid through a government program such as Medicare (p. 100), Medicaid (p. 100), or the Veterans Health Administration (p. 105).

If you have lost your group coverage from an employer as the result of unemployment, death, divorce, or loss of "dependent child" status, you may be able to continue your coverage temporarily under the Consolidated Omnibus Budget Reconciliation Act (COBRA). You, not the employer, pay for this coverage. When one of these events occurs, you must be given at least 60 days to decide whether you wish to purchase the coverage.

Some states offer an insurance pool to residents who are unable to obtain coverage because of a health condition. To find out whether a pool is available in your state, check with your state department of insurance (p. 130).

### Medicare and Medicaid

There are also health insurance programs for people who are seniors, disabled, or have low incomes.

- **Medicaid** provides health insurance for people with low incomes, children, and pregnant women. Eligibility is determined by your state.
- **Medicare** provides health insurance for people who are 65 years or older, some younger people with disabilities, and those with kidney failure.

Contact the Centers for Medicare & Medicaid Services (p. 100) for more information on benefits.

Most states also offer free or low-cost coverage for children who do not have health insurance. Visit www.insurekidsnow.gov or call 1-877-KIDS-NOW (543-7669) for more information.

## HEALTH CARE PLANS

When purchasing health insurance, your choices typically will fall into one of three categories:

- **Traditional** fee-for-service health insurance plans are usually the most expensive choice, but they offer you the most flexibility in choosing health care providers.
- **Health maintenance organizations (HMOs)** offer lower co-payments and cover the costs of more preventive care, but your choice of health care providers is limited. The National Committee for Quality Assurance evaluates and accredits HMOs. You can find out whether one is accredited in your state by calling 1-888-275-7585. You can also get this information, as well as report cards on HMOs, by visiting www.ncqa.org.
- **Preferred provider organizations (PPOs)** offer lower co-payments like HMOs, but give you more flexibility in selecting a provider. A PPO gives you a list of providers you can choose from.

**WARNING: If you go outside the HMO or PPO network of providers, you may have to pay a portion or all of the cost.**

When choosing among different health care plans, you'll need to read the fine print and ask lots of questions, such as:

- Do I have the right to go to any doctor, hospital, clinic, or pharmacy I choose?
- Are specialists such as eye doctors and dentists covered?
- Does the plan cover special conditions or treatments such as pregnancy, psychiatric care, and physical therapy?
- Does the plan cover home care or nursing home care?
- Will the plan cover all medications my physician may prescribe?
- What are the deductibles? Are there any co-payments?
- What is the most I will have to pay out of my own pocket to cover expenses?
- If there is a dispute about a bill or service, how is it handled? In some plans, you may be required to have a third party decide how to settle the problem.

## HOMEOWNERS/RENTERS INSURANCE

You may be able to save hundreds of dollars a year on homeowners insurance by shopping around. You can also save money by following these tips:

- Consider a higher deductible. Increasing your deductible by just a few hundred dollars can make a big difference in your premiums.
- Ask your insurance agent about discounts. You may be able to get a lower premium if your home has safety features such as dead-bolt locks, smoke detectors, an alarm system, storm shutters, or fire-retardant roofing

material. Persons over 55 years of age or long-term customers may also be offered discounts.

- Insure your house, NOT the land under it. After a disaster, the land is still there. If you don't subtract the value of the land when deciding how much homeowners insurance to buy, you will pay more than you should.

- Don't wait until you have a loss to find out whether you have the right type and amount of insurance.

- Make certain you purchase enough coverage to replace what is insured. "Replacement" coverage gives you the money to rebuild your home and replace its contents. An "Actual Cash Value" policy is cheaper but pays the difference between your property's worth at the time of loss minus depreciation for age and wear.

- Ask about any special coverage you might need. You may have to pay extra for computers, cameras, jewelry, art, antiques, musical instruments, stamp collections, etc.

- Remember that flood and earthquake damage are not covered by a standard homeowners policy. The cost of a separate earthquake policy will depend on the likelihood of earthquakes in your area. Homeowners who live in areas prone to flooding should take advantage of the National Flood Insurance Program (p. 102).

- If you are a renter, do not assume your landlord carries insurance on your personal belongings. Purchase a separate policy for renters.

## LIFE INSURANCE

Your need for life insurance will change with changes in your life. For example, the arrival of children usually triggers a sharp increase in the amount you will need. As children grow older and leave the nest, you will probably need less protection. You should also consider your life insurance policies as you are planning for retirement (p. 37).

Term life insurance policies are the least costly. They pay death benefits but have no cash value if you decide to stop making payments. As the word "term" suggests, these policies are in effect for a specific period—one year or until you reach a certain age are common. Visit www.accuquote.com for online comparisons of term life insurance.

Whole life, universal life, and other cash value policies combine a long-term savings and investment product with life insurance. Canceling these policies after only a few years can more than double your life insurance costs.

If you have misplaced a life insurance policy, your state's insurance commission may be able to help you locate it. Or you can search for it at www.policylocator.org. If the insurance company knows that an insured person has died, but cannot locate the beneficiaries, the company must turn the benefits over to the state's unclaimed property office. Check with that office if you believe that you are due a benefit.

You can avoid losing your life insurance policy by alerting the policy beneficiaries and filing a copy with your will.

## LONG-TERM CARE INSURANCE

Medical advances have resulted in greater need for nursing home care and assisted living. Most health insurance plans and Medicare severely limit or exclude long-term care. You should consider these costs as you plan for your retirement (p. 37).

Here are some questions to ask when considering a separate long-term care insurance policy:

- **What qualifies you for benefits?** Some insurers say you must be unable to perform a specific number of the following activities of daily living: eating, walking, getting from bed to a chair, dressing, bathing, using the restroom, and remaining continent.

- **What type of care is covered?** Does the policy cover nursing home care? What about coverage for assisted-living facilities that provide less client care than a nursing home? If you want to stay in your home, will it pay for care provided by visiting nurses and therapists? What about help with food preparation and housecleaning?

- **What will the benefit amount be?** Most plans are written to provide a specific dollar benefit per day. The benefit for home care is usually about half the nursing home benefit, but some policies pay the same for both forms of care. Other plans pay only for your actual expenses.

- **What is the benefit period?** It is possible to get a policy with lifetime benefits, but this can be very expensive. Other options for coverage are from one to six years. The average nursing home stay is about 2.5 years.

- **Is the benefit adjusted for inflation?** If you buy a policy before age 60, you face the risk that a fixed daily benefit will not be enough by the time you need it.

- **Is there a waiting period before benefits begin?** A 20- to 100-day period is not unusual. See page 26 for more information about advance medical directives.

## OTHER INSURANCE

- **Travel Insurance.** There are four kinds of travel insurance: Travel Cancellation Insurance, Baggage or Personal Effects Coverage, Emergency Medical Coverage, and Accidental Death. To learn more, a helpful website is www.insuremytrip.com. See page 49 for additional insight on travel concerns and problems.

- **Dental and Vision Insurance.** Some companies that offer health insurance plans may also allow employees to purchase separate dental and vision plans, which are not part of most standard health plans. Contact your state insurance commission (p. 130) or individual insurance companies to find out more about purchasing dental and vision insurance.

- **Identity Theft Insurance**. This type of insurance provides reimbursement to crime victims for the cost of restoring their identity and repairing credit reports. Some companies now include this as part of their homeowners insurance policy; others sell it as a stand-alone policy. Ask your homeowner policy company for information.

- **International Health Care Insurance**. A policy that provides health coverage no matter where you are in the world. The policy term is flexible, so you can purchase it only for the time you will be out of the country. Contact your current health care provider for coverage information.

- **Catastrophic Health Care Insurance**. A health plan that only covers certain types of expensive care, like hospitalizations.

- **Liability Insurance**. Insurance for what the policyholder is legally obligated to pay because of bodily injury or property damage caused to another person. Search online or ask your personal insurance agent for more information.

- **Umbrella Insurance**. A policy that supplements the insurance you already have for home, auto, and other personal property. Umbrella insurance can help cover costs that exceed the limits of other policies.

INVESTING

If you have a financial goal in mind, such as saving for retirement, paying for college, or buying a new house, then you may decide to invest your money to earn enough to fund your goals. Before you invest, do some homework. What is your tolerance for risk? What do you want to invest in? Stocks? Bonds? Mutual funds? Do you want to open an IRA or buy an annuity? Does your employer offer a 401(k)? Remember, every investment involves some degree of risk. Most securities are not insured by the federal government if they lose money or fail, even if you purchase them through a bank or credit union that offers federally insured savings accounts. Make sure you have answers to all of these questions before you invest:

- **How quickly can you get your money back?** Stocks, bonds, and shares in mutual funds usually can be sold at any time, but there is no guarantee you will get back all the money you paid for them. Other investments, such as limited partnerships, certificates of deposit (CDs), or IRAs, often restrict your ability to cash out your holdings.

- **What can you expect to earn on your money?** While bonds generally promise a fixed return, earnings on most other securities go up and down with market changes. Keep in mind that just because an investment has done well in the past, there is no guarantee it will do well in the future.

- **What type of earnings can you expect?** Will you get income in the form of interest, dividends, or rent? Some investments, such as stocks and real estate, have the potential for earnings and growth in value. What is the potential for earnings over time?

- **How much risk is involved?** With any investment, there is always the risk that you won't get your money back or the earnings promised. There is usually a trade-off between risk and reward—the higher the potential return, the greater the risk. The federal government insures bank savings accounts and backs up U.S. Treasury securities (including savings bonds). See FDIC on page 106 and the chart on page 7 for regulatory information. Other investment options are not protected.

- **Are your investments diversified?** Some investments perform better than others in certain situations. For example, when interest rates go up, bond prices tend to go down. One industry may struggle while another prospers. Putting your money in a variety of investment options can help to reduce your risk.

- **Are there any tax advantages to a particular investment?** U.S. Savings Bonds are exempt from state and local taxes. Municipal bonds are exempt from federal income tax and, sometimes, state income tax as well. Tax-deferred investments for special goals, such as paying for college and retirement, are available that let you postpone or even avoid paying income taxes.

For more information about investing, check out the Securities and Exchange Commission's (SEC's) website: www.investor.gov. Be sure to note specific tips at investor.gov/Saving-and-Investing. The SEC requires public companies to disclose financial and other information to help you make sound decisions. View the text of these files at www.sec.gov/edgar.shtml, or call the SEC toll-free Investor Information Service at 1-800-732-0330 to obtain free publications and investor alerts, or to learn how to file a complaint.

The Financial Industry Regulatory Authority (FINRA) also provides up-to-date market data and information for a wide range of stocks, bonds, mutual funds, and other

## BEWARE: INVESTMENT FRAUD

Deceptive pitches for investments often misrepresent or leave out facts to promote fantastic profits with little risk. No investment is risk-free, and a high rate of return means greater risk. Before investing, get written information such as a prospectus or annual report. Beware if a salesperson:

- Encourages you to borrow money or cash in retirement funds to invest
- Pressures you to invest immediately
- Promises quick profits
- Says the disclosure documents required by federal law are just a formality

- Tells you to write false information on your account form
- Sends material with typos or misspellings or not printed on letterhead
- Does not send your money promptly
- Offers to share inside information
- Uses words such as "guarantee," "high return," "limited offer," or "as safe as a CD"
- Claims that "off-shore investments are tax-free and confidential"

If you need more information or have an investment advisor problem you are unable to resolve directly, you can contact the SEC (p. 108) or FINRA (p. 144).

securities through its Market Data Center at www.finra.org/marketdata.

The following companies rate the financial condition of corporations and municipalities issuing bonds. Their ratings are available online and at many public libraries:

- Standard & Poor's (www.standardandpoors.com)
- Moody's Investors Services (www.moodys.com)

For ratings of mutual funds, consult personal finance magazines such as *Kiplinger's Personal Finance*, *Money*, *Consumer Reports*, *Smart Money*, and *Worth*. To compare expenses, use the FINRA Mutual Fund Expense Analyzer at apps.finra.org/fundanalyzer/1/fa.aspx.

## ONLINE TRADING

Stocks can be bought and sold with a mouse click from a wide range of online brokers, often with low transaction fees. However, the price of some stocks can instantly go from high to low. Online trading is quick and easy, but online investing requires research and takes time. Before you trade, ask questions and learn how to limit losses in this fast-moving marketplace by:

- Knowing what you're buying
- Understanding why you're buying or selling
- Being aware of how quickly trading changes during fast markets

Like other purchases, you should set a price limit, to avoid buying or selling at prices above or lower than you wanted. For more detailed information about online investing, visit www.investor.gov.

## FINANCIAL BROKERS AND ADVISORS

When selecting a broker or investment advisor, research the person's education and professional history as well as the firm the person works for. Ask:

- Has the person worked with others who have circumstances similar to yours?

- Is the person licensed in your state? Your state securities regulator (p. 134) lists individuals and firms that are registered in your state. Ask whether the regulatory office has any other background information. You can find out how to reach your state securities regulator by visiting www.nasaa.org.
- Has the person had any run-ins with regulators or received serious complaints from investors? Call your local state securities regulator or the SEC (p. 108). You can also check out www.finra.org/brokercheck to find licensing, employment, and disciplinary information.
- How is the person paid? Is it an hourly rate, a flat fee, or a commission that depends on the investments you make? Does the person get a bonus from his or her firm for selling you a particular product?
- What are the fees for setting up and servicing your account?

### Additional organizations that could be helpful are:

- The Commodity Futures Trading Commission (CFTC) provides consumer alerts and advisories. Visit www.cftc.gov/ConsumerProtection. The CFTC oversees the Reparations Program that resolves disputes between commodity customers and commodity professionals. You can institute "reparations" proceedings against commodity professionals registered with the CFTC if they violate the anti-fraud or other provisions of the Commodity Exchange Act. To ask a question, report information, or submit a complaint, contact the CFTC (p. 108).
- Both the North American Securities Administrators Association and the National Futures Association (p. 146) can offer helpful information.
- FINRA (p. 144) provides a dispute resolution program among investors, brokers, and brokerage firms.

## INVESTING IN GOLD AND COMMODITIES

Many financial experts recommend buying gold as part of a balanced portfolio. Some suggest buying only a small amount because values can fluctuate; others recommend larger investments.

There are a number of ways to invest in precious metals; common ones include bullion, certificates, and coins. Most people depend on an investment advisor or company to help them choose. Make sure the person or company you choose is licensed with your state securities administrator (p. 134). If you're considering investing in gold, check the U.S. Mint website at www.usmint.gov. Before you purchase coins or coin-related products, research the seller with your state consumer protection office (p. 112) or Better Business Bureau (p. 67).

Commodity futures are an agreement to buy or sell a specific quantity of metals, grains, or other foods. Anyone who trades or gives advice to the public about futures must be registered with the National Futures Association (NFA). The CFTC also provides additional information about investing in gold and other commodities at www.cftc.gov/ConsumerProtection/FraudAwarenessPrevention/CFTCFraudAdvisories.

## RETIREMENT PLANNING

Part of smart investing is planning for retirement. The average American spends 20 years in retirement, but fewer than half of Americans calculate how much they need to save for their retirement years. Regardless of your age, it's never too early or too late to start.

The three major components of a retirement portfolio are generally benefits from pensions, savings and investments, and Social Security.

If you are still working and your employer offers a plan, find out how it works. If your employer has a 401(k) plan and offers to put some money in if you do (called a match), this should be the first place where you save. Make sure you understand how a job change might

| TYPE OF INVESTMENT | WHAT IS IT? | RISK LEVEL |
|---|---|---|
| Traditional IRA | Traditional IRA is a personal savings plan that gives tax advantages for savings for retirement. Investments may include a variety of securities. Contributions may be tax-deductible; earnings are not taxed until distributed. | Risk levels vary according to the holdings in the IRA. |
| Roth IRA | A personal savings plan where earnings that remain in the account are not taxed. Investments may include a variety of securities. Contributions are not tax-deductible. | Risk levels vary according to the holdings in the IRA. |
| Money Market Funds | Mutual funds that invest in short-term bonds. Usually pay better interest rates than a savings account but not as much as a certificate of deposit (CD). | Low risk. |
| Bonds and Bond Funds | Also known as fixed-income securities because the income they pay is fixed when the bond is sold. Bonds and bond funds invest in corporate or government debt obligations. | Low risk. |
| Index Funds | Invest in a particular market index such as the S&P 500 or the Russell 2000. An index fund is managed passively and mirrors the performance of the designated stock or bond index. | Risk level depends on which index the fund uses. A bond index fund involves a lower risk level than an index fund of emerging markets overseas. |
| Stocks | Stocks represent a share of a company. As the company's value rises or falls, so does the value of the stock. | Medium to high risk. |
| Mutual Funds | Invest in a variety of securities, which may include stocks, bonds, and/or money market securities. Costs and objectives vary. | Risk levels vary according to the holdings in the mutual fund. |
| Market-linked CDs (or structured cds) | Returns are linked to the future performance of a market index and may include stocks, bonds, foreign currency, or other assets. These are designed for long-term commitment (up to 20 years). | Medium to high risk. |
| Commodities | Physical commodities, such as an agricultural product or a natural resource (like gold). A futures contract is an agreement to purchase or sell a commodity for delivery in the future. | High risk. |

affect your employer-based retirement plan and what your options are for saving that money. If you switch jobs before you are fully vested, you may lose a significant amount of money.

As you approach retirement, there are many factors to consider. Experts advise that you will need about 80% of your pre-retirement income in your retirement years. The exact amount, of course, depends on your individual needs (see Elder Care, p. 25). For example:

- At what age do you plan to retire?
- Will your spouse or partner retire when you do?
- Where do you plan to live? Will you downsize, own, or rent?
- Do you expect to work part time?
- Will you have the same medical insurance you had while working? Will coverage change?
- Do you want to travel or pursue a new hobby that might be costly?
- If you have a financial advisor, talk to him or her about your plans.

In addition to planning to maintain your lifestyle during retirement, you may need to purchase long-term health insurance (p. 34) or to pay for assisted-living services (p. 25).

**For more information go to:**

- AARP: www.aarp.org
- American Savings Education Council: www.asec.org
- Certified Financial Planner Board of Standards: www.cfp.net
- Investopedia: www.investopedia.com/university/retirement
- U.S. Department of Labor: www.dol.gov/ebsa
- The Investor's Clearinghouse: www.investoreducation.org
- MyMoney.gov: www.mymoney.gov
- Securities and Exchange Commission: www.investor.gov
- Social Security Administration: www.socialsecurity.gov

# PROTECTING YOUR PRIVACY

Identity thieves steal your personal information to commit fraud. They can damage your credit status and cost you time and money to restore your good name. To reduce your risk of becoming a victim, follow these tips:

- **Don't carry your Social Security card** in your wallet or write your number on your checks. Only give out your SSN when absolutely necessary.
- **Protect your PIN.** Never write a PIN on a credit/debit card or on a slip of paper kept in your wallet.
- **Watch out for "shoulder surfers."** Use your free hand to shield the keypad when typing your passwords on computers and at ATMs.
- **Collect mail promptly.** Ask the post office to put your mail on hold when you are away from home for more than a day or two.
- **Pay attention to your billing cycles.** If bills or financial statements are late, contact the sender.
- **Keep your receipts.** Ask for carbons and incorrect charge slips as well. Promptly compare receipts with account statements. Watch for unauthorized transactions.
- **Tear up or shred** unwanted receipts, credit offers, account statements, expired cards, etc., to prevent "dumpster divers" (see p. 7) from getting your personal information.
- **Store personal information in a safe place** at home and at work. Don't leave it lying around.
- **Don't respond to unsolicited requests** for personal information in the mail, over the phone, or online.
- **Install firewalls** and virus-detection software on your home computer.
- **Create complex passwords** that identity thieves cannot guess easily. For tips on creating secure passwords, see p. 40.
- **Check your credit report once a year.** Check it more frequently if you suspect someone has gained access to your account information. See Free Credit Reports (p. 12).

38  www.USA.gov

To contact an organization, use the directory beginning on page 63.

## REPORTING IDENTITY THEFT

If you suspect or become a victim of identity theft, follow these steps:

- **Report it to your financial institution.** Call the phone number on your account statement or on the back of your credit or debit card.
- **Report the fraud to your local police.** Keep a copy of the police report, which will make it easier to prove your case to creditors and retailers.
- **Contact the credit reporting bureaus** (p. 13) and ask them to flag your account with a fraud alert, which asks merchants not to grant new credit without your approval.

If your identity has been stolen, you can use an ID Theft affidavit to report the theft to most of the parties involved. All three credit bureaus and many major creditors accept the affidavit. Request a copy of the document by calling toll-free 1-877-ID-THEFT (438-4338) or visit www.ftc.gov/idtheft. You can also use this website to file a complaint with the FTC.

The FTC also publishes a series of publications about the importance of personal information privacy. To download copies, go to www.ftc.gov or request free copies of brochures by calling 1-877-FTC-HELP (382-4357).

### IF YOUR WALLET IS STOLEN

Your wallet contains some of your most important personal items, from hard-earned money to credit cards and driver's license. For an identity thief, your wallet offers a treasure trove of personal information. If your wallet is lost or stolen:

- File a report with the police immediately.
- Cancel your credit and debit cards and request new cards and account numbers.
- Report the missing cards to the major credit reporting agencies.
- Report your missing license to the department of motor vehicles.

Visit www.ftc.gov/opa/1996/08/purse.shtm for a complete list of steps you should take.

## PROTECTING YOUR PRIVACY

Today, it's quick and easy to get a credit card approved, transfer money from one account to another, renew your driver's license, fill a prescription from your doctor at your local pharmacy, use store loyalty cards, and purchase products online. But you pay for this convenience by providing more opportunities for your personal information to be changed, stolen, or reported inaccurately. Companies can also use the information you have shared to direct their future marketing efforts or can sell the information to other companies.

### CHILD ID THEFT

Children are especially vulnerable to identity theft. The danger is that child ID theft goes unnoticed for years, until the child becomes an adult and tries to apply for credit or to college. Scam artists use the stolen ID to get credit, jobs, medical care, and more. To protect your child's future, shred all documents with their personal information. Also check your child's credit report (if there is a credit report, this is a clue that theft has occurred). For more information contact the FTC (p. 107).

To help protect your privacy, follow these tips:

- Look for privacy statements on websites, sales materials, and forms you fill out. If a website claims to follow a set of established voluntary standards, read the standards. Don't assume it provides the level of privacy you want.
- Ask how your personal information will be stored and used.
- Only provide the purchase date, model/serial numbers, and your contact information on warranty registration forms.
- Discuss privacy with others in your home. Everyone, even children, should understand what information is not appropriate to share on the phone, while using a computer, and in other situations.

Check with your state or local consumer agency (p. 112) to find out whether any state laws help protect your privacy. Some companies and industry groups have also adopted voluntary policies that address privacy concerns.

## FINANCIAL PRIVACY

The FDIC (p. 106) and other federal regulators require banks, insurance companies, brokerage firms, and certain businesses that share financial information to inform you of their privacy policies. They must give you this information when you open an account and at least once every year. This includes:

- The kinds of information being collected
- How the confidentiality and security of this information will be protected
- What types of businesses may be provided this information

If a business is going to share the information with anyone outside its corporate family, it must also give you the chance to "opt out" or say no to information sharing. Even if you don't opt out, your account numbers may not be shared with third parties for marketing purposes.

You cannot prevent certain types of information from being shared, including information needed to conduct

## TAX ID THEFT

Identity theft occurs when someone uses your personal information such as your name, Social Security number (SSN), or other identifying information, without your permission, to commit fraud or other crimes. Usually, an identity thief uses a legitimate taxpayer's identity to file a tax return fraudulently and claim a refund early in the filing season.

If you believe someone has used your SSN fraudulently, contact the IRS immediately at 1-800-908-4490. You will need to fill out the IRS Identity Theft Affidavit, Form 14039. For more information, visit www.irs.gov/uac/Taxpayer-Guide-to-Identity-Theft.

normal business or protect against fraud, or information that is already publicly available. Also, a bank can share your information with a partner company to market products.

Your credit information has additional privacy protections under the FCRA. Only people with a legitimate business need can get a copy of your report. An employer can only get your report with your written consent. For more information on your rights under this federal law, and to find out how you can get a copy of your credit reports, see Credit Reports and Scores on page 13.

### MEDICAL PRIVACY

Personal information you give to your doctor is shared with insurance companies, pharmacies, researchers, and employers based on specific regulations. The privacy of your health records is protected by federal law, specifically under the Health Insurance Portability and Accountability Act, also known as HIPAA. HIPAA:

* Defines your rights over your health information
* Sets rules and limits on who is allowed to receive and/or see your health information

## CREATE SECURE PASSWORDS

The number of passwords you need daily can be overwhelming. It is tempting to use the same password across several sites; however to get the most protection available, you should use different passwords on each site and change your passwords periodically. The goal for creating passwords is to strike a balance between being something that is easy to remember and unique.

Some general tips for creating a secure password include:

* Use a mix of uppercase and lowercase letters, numbers, and special characters.
* The longer the password, the better it is.
* Don't use your name, birthday, license plate, favorite sports teams, or other facts that are easily guessed.
* Create a password based on a phrase. For example, "A stitch in time saves nine," can be translated into the password "Ast!Ts9", where each character represents a word in the phrase.
* If you must use the same password on several websites, add a prefix or suffix. For example, use "Ast!Ts9:4bnk" for your bank account and "Eml: Ast!Ts9" for your email account.

The U.S. Department of Health and Human Services, Office for Civil Rights (www.dhhs.gov/ocr or 1-800-368-1019) is an excellent resource for complete details and advice about the HIPAA ruling. The Office for Civil Rights provides a listing of resources for consumers, providers, and advocates, along with fact sheets and other educational materials.

You can request a copy of your medical records from the provider or from the hospital where medical services were provided. You will probably be charged a fee to cover retrieving and mailing copies to you.

If you believe that a person, agency, or organization covered under the HIPAA Privacy Rule violated your health information privacy rights or committed another violation of the Privacy Rule, you may be able to file a written complaint with the Department of Health and Human Services, Office for Civil Rights (p. 98).

For more information on how the federal government protects your personal health information, visit the U.S. Department of Health and Human Services, Office for Civil Rights website at www.hhs.gov/ocr/privacy.

### ONLINE PRIVACY

In addition to following the general advice on protecting your privacy, make sure you only use websites with acceptable privacy policies.

* Look for a privacy policy statement or seal that indicates the site abides by privacy standards. Take the time to read how your privacy is protected.
* Look for signals that you are using a secure web page. A secure site encrypts or scrambles personal information so it cannot be intercepted easily. Signals include a screen notice that says you are on a secure site, a closed padlock or unbroken key in the bottom corner of your screen, or the first letters of the Internet address you are viewing change from "http" to "https."

Another threat to your privacy is spyware, software that is secretly installed when you download screensavers, games, music, and other applications. Spyware sends information about your online activities to a third party, usually to target you with pop-up ads. Browsers like Internet Explorer and Firefox, and search engines like Google and Bing, enable you to block pop-ups. You can also install anti-spyware software to stop this threat to your privacy. For more information, see Internet on page 41.

40    www.USA.gov

To contact an organization, use the directory beginning on page 63.

# TELECOMMUNICATIONS

Choices for phone service, Internet, and television have never been greater. As devices have multiple functions, such as the ability to watch television shows on your computer or surf the Internet using your phone, your decisions about each of these services may overlap. Most consumers are now able to bundle phone, TV, and Internet service for a discount; however, buying a bundle of services could make it more difficult to change providers for any one service if you're tied into a long-term contract. Before you buy, compare services and prices and think about what you really need.

## INTERNET

### Choosing Service Providers

To connect your computer to the Internet, you'll need an Internet Service Provider (ISP). Some ISPs are large and well known, while others are literally one-person operations. Some companies limit their service to providing Internet access only. Others, such as a telephone or cable company, may offer Internet access as part of a larger package of services. It is important to compare service providers and options to make sure you are getting what you want as well as the best deal possible to meet your needs.

If you have limited Internet expertise, you may want to start with one of the well-known ISPs. They usually offer user-friendly startup software that often includes features such as a browser, instant messaging, parental controls, and pop-up blockers. Many also offer 24-hour tech support. However, this convenience results in higher monthly user fees. Once you are comfortable with how the Internet works, you may decide you don't need the "extras" and can switch to a lower-cost ISP.

Consider these factors when selecting a provider:

- **Speed**. If you only want to check e-mail and read web pages, a dial-up connection may be enough. But if you want to download music or television shows or watch videos, you will need a faster connection with broadband access, such as a digital subscriber line (DSL), cable modem, or satellite.

- **Availability**. Which companies offer service in your area?
- **Wireless access**. Can you get a wireless connection for other computers in your home?
- **E-mail**. Do e-mail accounts come with the service? What will be the storage limit on your mailbox?
- **Software**. Is any software required to activate the service?
- **Support**. What kinds of support are available—phone, e-mail, chat, etc.? Is the support free?
- **Special features**. What services are provided for spam blocking, virus protection, instant messaging, and chat rooms?
- **Terms of service**. Is there a limit to the amount of data you can use per month?
- **Cost**. What is the monthly fee for the service? Are there fees for renting a modem or set up?

### WiFi (Wireless)

Going wireless provides you with the freedom to use your computer in multiple locations, without dragging cables and cords with you. However, with the privilege of increased freedom comes the danger of increased vulnerability. Wireless Internet requires that you have access to a wireless network via a wireless router. It is important that you secure your network so strangers (or neighbors) can't use your network without your knowledge (also known as "piggybacking"). Also, computer hackers could use your network to access personal information you save or send from your computer. This is particularly important if you conduct financial transactions online. If you use the wireless (Wi-Fi) network at bookstores, airports, or other public places, there are other precautions you should take to protect your privacy.

At home:

- **Turn on encryption.** When you buy a wireless router, it is important to turn on the encryption feature. This scrambles information that you send over the Internet so other people cannot access it.
- **Rename your router.** Change the name from the default to something only you would know.
- **Change the password.** Routers come with a standard password. Create a new one with a mix of letters, numbers, and special characters. For help creating passwords, see page 40.

## PROTECTING CHILDREN ONLINE

The Children's Online Privacy Protection Act requires commercial websites to obtain parental consent before collecting, using, or disclosing personal information from children under age 13. For more information, contact the FTC (p. 107) or visit www.ftc.gov.

## BEWARE: SCAREWARE

If you've ever received a "security alert" stating that malicious software was found on your computer, it may have been scareware. These messages will persuade you that your computer is infected with a virus that you can eliminate only by purchasing and installing specific software. Don't follow that advice; shut down your browser without clicking on the message. If you believe your computer is infected, you should run a scan using a known anti-virus software. For more information about scareware and protecting your computer, visit www.onguardonline.gov.

- **Turn off your router** when you are not using it.
- **Be aware of cookies.** Cookies are small text files that some websites place on your computer to collect information about the pages you view and your activities on the site. They also allow the site to recognize you when you return. For more information, visit www.ftc.gov/ftc/cookies.shtm.

On public wireless networks:

- **Don't assume the network is secure.** Most public wireless networks don't encrypt information you send. Avoid sending private information from public locations.
- **Use encrypted websites.** If you must send sensitive information from a public network, make certain that URL starts with "https" ("s" means secure). Look for that on every page you visit.
- **Log off** sites after you finish using them rather than using "remember me" features. It is better to log in again than give away your login credentials to someone else on the network.

For more information about wireless computing, visit www.onguardonline.gov.

### Online File Sharing

Every day, millions of computer users share files online. Whether music, games, video, or software, peer-to-peer (P2P) file sharing allows users to share all kinds of content. To share files, you download special software that connects your computer to an informal network of other computers running the same software. The software is often free and easy to access.

However, file sharing can have a number of risks. For example, when you are connected to file-sharing programs, you unknowingly could allow others to copy private files you never intended to share. You could download material that is protected by copyright laws and find yourself mired in legal issues; you could download a virus or facilitate a security breach; or you could unwittingly download pornography labeled as something else.

To secure the personal information stored on your computer, the FTC suggests that you:

- Set up the file-sharing software very carefully.
- Be aware of spyware and use a good anti-spyware program.
- Close your connection when you're not using it.
- Use an effective anti-virus program and update it regularly.
- Talk with your family about file sharing.

For more information on P2P, visit www.onguardonline.gov.

### Online Copyright Issues

Quite simply, it's illegal to make or download unauthorized copies of software or online media, such as books, music, and videos. Whether you are casually making a few copies for friends, lending disks, distributing and/or downloading pirated software via the Internet, or buying a single software program and then installing it on 100 computers, you are committing a copyright infringement. It doesn't matter whether or not you make money doing it. If you or your company is caught copying software, you may be held liable under both civil and criminal law. If the copyright owner brings a civil action against you, the owner can seek to stop you from using its software immediately and can request monetary damages. The copyright owner can sue for as much as $150,000 for each program copied. In addition, the government can prosecute you criminally for copyright infringement. If convicted, you can be fined up to $250,000, sentenced to jail for up to five years, or both.

For more information, visit the Business Software Alliance's online piracy site, www.bsa.org.

### DO YOU REALLY OWN THOSE SONGS?

Today many consumers purchase music and e-books as digital downloads to play on digital music players or mobile devices. However, just because you buy the file, doesn't mean you actually own the song. A media service provider sells you a license to listen to your downloaded music, but that license may restrict your ability to lend, share, transfer, or burn the contents of your music library. You may be able to use the songs on several devices; the rules vary from provider to provider. Before you download or click "I Agree," know your rights under the terms of service agreement. For more information about digital copyright, contact the United States Patent and Trademark Office (p. 97).

42   www.USA.gov

To contact an organization, use the directory beginning on page 63.

## BUYING TICKETS ONLINE

When buying tickets online, be mindful of convenience or venue fees that can raise the price. Also, be mindful of the fine print. Some tickets are tied to your credit card, restricting your ability to donate, give them as gifts or resell them if you cannot attend because the same credit card must be shown at the event venue to enter. For more information about restricted ticketing, visit fanfreedom.org.

### Preventing Online Fraud

The Internet gives you easy access to information, entertainment, financial offers, and countless other services. The flip side, however, is that it can leave you vulnerable to online scammers, identity thieves, and criminals.

Online frauds are not limited to fake companies. Thieves will often try to disguise a fraudulent website by giving the site a URL close to the URL of a legitimate, well-known site. Internet criminals try to trick customers of these legitimate sites into sharing their personal information on fake sites, so they can use that information for identity theft or credit card fraud schemes. Some scam artists have even used the IRS name and logo to collect taxpayers' personal information so they can steal taxpayers' identity. Visit www.irs.gov/uac/Suspicious-e-Mails-and-Identity-Theft to learn more about tax-related online fraud and how to identify a fraudulent e-mail or website.

To guard against Internet fraud, follow these tips:

- **Know your seller.** If you don't, do some research.
- **Company websites** often provide information in a section called "About Us." Some online sellers participate in programs, such as BBBOnLine, that help resolve problems. Look for a logo or endorsement seal on the company website; this indication, however, is not a guarantee of the seller's reliability.
- **Check with state** and/or local consumer offices.
- **Reading comments from other consumers** is another way to check the integrity of online sellers. Some Internet auction sites post ratings of sellers based on buyers' comments. Beware of too many glowing stories the sellers themselves might have placed.
- **Protect your personal information**. Don't provide it in response to an e-mail, a pop-up, or a website you've linked to from an e-mail or web page.
- **Take your time** and resist any urge to "act now" to keep your account open or take advantage of a special offer.
- **Use anti-virus and anti-spyware software**, as well as a firewall, and update them all regularly. Make sure your operating system and web browser are set up properly and update them regularly as well.

- **Protect your passwords**. Don't share your passwords with anyone. Memorize them.
- **Don't take the bait.** Don't reply to e-mail messages that claim your credit card information or other personal information needs to be updated.
- **Back up important files**. Copy them onto another computer or a removable hard drive such as a flash memory stick.

Learn whom to contact if something goes wrong online. Report suspected fraud to your bank, credit card company, or relevant authority.

## SOCIAL NETWORKING

Social networking sites such as Facebook, Twitter, LinkedIn, Pinterest, and others continue to gain popularity. These sites make it easy to reconnect, stay in touch, and even do business. But recent reports involving privacy concerns and crimes should make users more careful about the information they share. Some tips to consider to protect your privacy and safety include:

- Make your contact information private.
- Limit who can search your profile from Internet search engines.
- Manage who can view your images; untag photos if necessary.
- Create separate lists to manage who can see the information you've posted.
- Be careful about who can see your status updates.
- Refrain from telling people where you are at any specific time.
- Be cautious about arranging meetings in person with online acquaintances.
- Keep in mind that current or prospective employers may be able to see your social network pages and photos.

### For more information go to:

- Federal Communications Commission: www.reboot.fcc.gov/consumers
- Federal Trade Commission: www.onguardonline.gov
- GetNetWise: www.getnetwise.org
- Internet Keep Safe Coalition: www.ikeepsafe.org
- i-SAFE: www.i-safe.org
- National Center for Missing & Exploited Children: www.missingkids.com
- National Crime Prevention Council: www.ncpc.org; www.mcgruff.org
- National Cyber Security Alliance: www.staysafeonline.org
- Wired Safety: www.wiredsafety.org

For additional information, visit www.ftc.gov or call 1-877-382-4357; TTY: 1-866-653-4261.

The FTC (p. 107) provides tips to help secure your computer, guard against Internet fraud, and protect your personal information. If you have been the victim of an online fraud, report it to the Internet Crime Complaint Center at www.ic3.gov. Visit www.onguardonline.gov for more information.

To keep up to date with the latest computer threats, sign up for alerts from the U.S. Department of Homeland Security at www.uscert.gov.

### Spam

E-mail spam is not just unwanted; it can be offensive. Decrease the number of spam e-mails you receive by making it difficult for spammers to get and use your e-mail address:

- Don't use an obvious e-mail address, such as JaneDoe@isp.com. Instead use numbers or other digits, such as Jane4oe6@isp.com.

- Use one e-mail address for close friends and family and another for everyone else. Free addresses are available from Yahoo!, Gmail, and Hotmail. You can also get a disposable forwarding address from www.spammotel.com. If an address attracts too much spam, get rid of it and establish a new one.

- Don't post your e-mail address on a public web page. Spammers use software that harvests text addresses. Substitute "jane4oe6 at isp.com" for "jane4oe6@isp.com," or display your address as a graphic image, not text.

- Don't enter your address on a website before you check its privacy policy.

- Uncheck any checked boxes. These often grant the site or its partners permission to contact you.

- Don't click on an e-mail's "unsubscribe" link unless you trust the sender. This action tells the sender you are there.

- Never forward chain letters, petitions, or virus warnings. All could be a spammer's trick to collect addresses.

- Disable your e-mail "preview pane." This stops spam from reporting to its sender that you've received it.

- Choose an ISP that filters e-mail. If you get lots of spam, your ISP may not be filtering effectively.

- Use spam-blocking software. Web browser software often includes free filtering options. You can also purchase special software that will accomplish this task.

- Report spam. Alert your ISP that spam is slipping through its filters. The FTC also wants to know about "unsolicited commercial e-mail." Forward spam to spam@uce.gov. For more information, visit www.ftc.gov/spam.

### PHONES

The choices for phone service have never been greater. Most consumers are now able to buy local and long-distance phone service from their telephone company, cable or satellite TV provider, or ISP. Services such as voice mail, call waiting, caller ID, and wireless may be offered as a package deal or sold separately. Before you buy, compare services and prices and think about what you really need:

- Whom do you call most often?
- What time of day or day of the week do you call?
- Do you want to get messages? If so, do you need voice mail, or will an answering machine do?
- Do you want call waiting and/or caller ID?
- How important is it for you to have your phone with you when you are away from home?

Find out how each company prices its services. Are there minimum use, time-of-day, or distance requirements; flat monthly fees; or special plans? For example, wireless service may be cheaper than regular local service if you don't make many calls. Make sure you're comparing prices on similar plans and features. Understand that many service providers offer contracts for specific periods. Read the fine print and ask questions if there is anything you're not clear about.

## BUNDLING, PROMOTIONS, AND DEALS

Do you want to get Internet, telephone, and TV service from the same provider? Buying a bundle of services from one provider can be a good deal, but it can also make it more difficult to change providers for any one service if you're tied into a long-term contract.

Special promotions such as introductory pricing may be enticing, but read the fine print. The promotion price probably does not include taxes or the cost of extra equipment or fees. Ask the provider to explain all the one-time, recurring, and special charges, including taxes and fees. Get all promises in writing. Ask when the special promotions end and what the post-promotion cost will be. Also find out whether you have to install any special equipment and whether the provider will help troubleshoot on the phone if you have any problems.

Some deals are available only online or by phone. Even if you have to order online, call the provider first to ask questions. When you are online, review any frequently asked questions, minimum system requirements, and fine-print terms and conditions. Read the entire customer service agreement and print a copy for your records. For more information, visit www.ftc.gov/bcp/consumer.shtm. For help deciding on the best values from Internet, telephone, and TV service providers; filing a complaint; or learning more about consumer protections, go to www.reboot.fcc.gov/consumers.

44   www.USA.gov

To contact an organization, use the directory beginning on page 63.

## BEWARE: CALLER ID SPOOFING

Scammers have adopted the practice of Caller ID spoofing to obtain personal information from consumers. In this fraud, someone calls you using a false name and phone number for the Caller ID screen. During the call, the scammer describes an urgent scenario, such as the cancellation of an account. The caller may say you can avoid the cancellation if you provide your bank account or credit card number to pay the company. If you give the sensitive information, the caller can use it to steal your identity or use your bank accounts.

You can prevent being a victim of caller ID spoofing. Don't give out personal information on an incoming call. Hang up and call the customer service phone number printed on your statement, on the company's website, or in the phonebook.

Report caller ID spoofers to the Federal Communications Commission at fcc.gov/complaints or 1-888-225-5322.

The FCC (p. 106) offers consumer information about choosing a long-distance carrier, understanding new phone fees and taxes, and more at www.fcc.gov/consumers. The National Consumers League also maintains a web page (www.nclnet.org/technology/88-telecommunications/228-understanding-your-phone-bill) to help you understand phone charges and recognize fraud.

### Slamming and Cramming

"Slamming" occurs when a phone company illegally switches your phone service without your permission. If you notice a different company name on your bill or see phone charges that are higher than normal, contact the company that slammed you and ask to be switched back to your original company. Tell the company you are exercising your right to refuse to pay charges, then report the problem to your original company and ask to be re-enrolled in your previous calling plan.

"Cramming" occurs when companies add charges to your phone bill without your permission. These charges may be for services such as voice mail, ringtones, or subscriptions. You may not notice these monthly charges because they are relatively small, $5 to $30, and look like your regular phone charges.

### Take These Steps to Avoid Slammers and Crammers:

- **Block changes to your phone service.** Ask your telephone service provider if it offers a blocking or account protection service, which usually requires the company to notify you before making any changes to your service.
- **Read the fine print** on contest entry forms and coupons. You could be agreeing to switch your phone service or to buy optional services.
- **Watch out for impostors.** Companies could falsely claim to be your regular phone company and offer some type of discount plan or change in billing. They may also say they are taking a survey or they may pretend to be a government agency.

- **Beware of "negative option notices."** You can be switched or signed up for optional services unless you say "NO" to telemarketers.
- **Examine your telephone bill** carefully, including pages that show the details, and look for suspicious charges.

Your phone service cannot be shut off for refusal to pay for unauthorized services. For help, contact your local or state consumer protection agency (p. 112), state public utilities commission (p. 138), or the FCC (p. 106).

### Cell Phones

Before you sign a contract and choose a plan and a company that meets your needs, you should ask these types of questions:

**Where can you make and receive calls?** Most providers now offer a choice of local, regional, or national plans. A local plan offers low-cost options if most of your calls are near your home. Regional plans cover a larger geographic area—sometimes several states. If you call outside the area covered by these plans, you will pay long-distance and roaming charges in addition to the airtime used. National plans are the most expensive, but they let you use your phone anywhere in the country for a single per-minute price.

**How frequently will you use the phone?** If you just want a phone for emergencies, an economy plan with a few minutes a month may be all you need. On the other hand, if your cell phone is your primary phone, a plan with the lowest airtime rate is a wiser choice. If you plan to use texting, pick a plan that will meet your needs and avoid surprises on your bills. Most services allow you to upgrade a plan without an added one-time charge.

**Is a family plan option available?** You can share one cellular service plan and a pool of monthly usage minutes among several phone lines. The cost of the additional numbers per month is usually less than if you purchased individual accounts.

**Is there a trial period?** There are "dead spots" where a cell phone doesn't work. A trial period lets you test your service and try the features of the phone without incurring a termination fee.

**Know your options.** Make sure you are only buying the options or features you really need. It is always easier to upgrade a plan later if you feel you need another feature.

**What if you want to cancel your service?** Most providers have a penalty. This is a concern if you have to move out of the area covered by your plan.

Be sure to keep track of your usage and understand your cell phone bill to avoid "bill shock." Visit www.fcc.gov/encyclopedia/bill-shock to learn more about reading your cell phone bill and how to better monitor your usage.

## GPS ON YOUR SMARTPHONE

Retailers can use your phone's GPS for geofencing—sending you coupons and promotions when you are near their stores so you'll buy the items there instead of buying the same item online for a possibly cheaper price. If you have signed up to receive text messages from stores, they may send you an alert with a coupon when you are nearby, based on your phone's GPS.

### Smart Phones

Smart phones are like miniature computers; they provide basic phone functions, along with advanced features, including browsing the Internet, accessing e-mail, interacting on online social networks, listening to music, watching videos, uploading pictures, and using apps. They also allow use of a QWERTY keyboard to make texting and e-mailing easy. (The keys are arranged the same way they are on a computer keyboard.)

When shopping for a smart phone, consider these tips:

- Consider the shape and size of the phone.
- Make sure you can use the keypad easily to make calls and send messages.

- Do you need to access the Internet with your phone? If so, a data plan is required. Find out how much it costs; compare options carefully. Data plans govern use and costs associated with mobile access for e-mail, text messaging, web browsing, social networking, and other applications.
- Take advantage of special pricing and promotions.
- Is there a limit on the amount of data you can use each month?
- Be wary of buying phone insurance, which may sound tempting; consumer groups generally advise against it.

## MOBILE PAYMENTS USING A DIGITAL WALLET

Paying for your purchases using a smart phone app has become more common and convenient. In a sense you have a digital wallet that contains your credit card numbers, store loyalty cards, and even digital coupons. When you get to the checkout counter, you pay by swiping your phone at the checkout. You can also use it online. Before you decide to use a digital wallet provider, make certain that your phone has the required chip that allows you use the mobile payment app. Also find out how the company ensures the security of your cards and each transaction. Some questions to ask:

- Is it possible to freeze your wallet if your phone is lost or stolen?
- Are the details of your purchases shared or sold for marketing purposes?
- Is there a PIN to secure access to your digital wallet?
- Are there other security measures in place (encryption of your cards, security codes)?
- Who is responsible for fraudulent or unauthorized purchases, and what is your liability if this happens?
- How do you dispute a purchase dispute?

For more information about e-payments, visit www.ftc.gov/bcp/edu/pubs/consumer/tech/tec01.shtm.

## APPS FOR YOUR SMARTPHONE

"Apps," short for applications, are tools that help you accomplish tasks or find information when you are on the go. Apps are designed to work on smart phones and may be downloaded or accessed using your phone's web browser. Some apps are designed for specific platforms (Android, Blackberry, or iPhone), so be sure to purchase apps that are compatible with your phone's software requirements.

While some apps are free, many of them do charge a small fee. Before you click "download," keep in mind that the cost of your purchases is deducted automatically from your bank account or charged to your credit card or phone bill. Keep track of the amount of money you spent on apps to avoid shock when you receive your bill.

Visit Apps.usa.gov to download free apps from the government. Look for some of the consumer apps for product recalls, fuel economy, food safety, nutrition, and health information.

Since smart phones are like miniature computers, many of the same privacy and safety concerns apply; however, unlike computers, these devices do not have anti-virus software to protect them from malware attacks. For more information on how to protect yourself from these concerns, see Online Privacy (p. 40) and Internet (p. 41).

### Pay-As-You-Go Plans

If you want cell phone service only for emergencies, or you aren't sure how much you will actually use a cell phone once you get it, you may want to consider a prepaid cell phone before you commit to a long-term wireless contract. With a prepaid cell phone, there is no contract to sign and no monthly bill. You will know exactly how much you spend. The downside of prepaid plans is that you pay more per minute, and, if you don't use the phone for an extended period, you may lose the money in your account.

### TV

There are many choices for consumers looking to buy new televisions today. Before buying a new TV, do your homework. It is important to see the monitors in person before buying to make sure the one you select will meet your needs. For independent ratings and reviews, check out *Consumer Reports* at www.consumerreports.org. Additional information is also available at www.energystar.gov.

### Cable

You can start with a basic lineup of channels and go from there. The more channels you want, the more it will cost. You may want to consider video on demand so you can order movies and sports events and watch them when you like (usually within a 24-hour window). You can also buy a bundle of services that includes digital TV, digital phone, and broadband Internet access at discounted rates. Bear in mind, however, that you may be asked to sign a contract for bundled services.

### Satellite

This requires a dish that's mounted outside (service requires an unobstructed view of the satellite) and a receiver that's placed by your television. Satellite TV offers comparable channels to cable TV, and you can add a digital video recorder to record shows for viewing later. One downside to satellite TV is occasional interference during periods of rain or snow. Check with your satellite TV provider for channel options and prices. As with cable TV, you may be asked to sign a contract for a package of services.

### Internet TV

If you have a high-speed Internet connection, you're already able to watch thousands of videos on your computer. Movies and TV shows are also available and becoming more prevalent as large online companies start distributing TV programming. You may even be able to connect your computer to your television so that shows you would normally watch online can project on a larger screen. Several services allow Internet streaming for a fee, along with free access to shows on network websites.

## TELEMARKETING AND UNWANTED MAIL

What can you do about the growing pile of unwanted mail in your mailbox and unwelcome telemarketers on your phone? Actually, there's a lot you can do:

- Tell companies you do business with to remove your name from customer lists they rent or sell to others. Look for information on how to opt out of marketing lists on sales materials, order forms, and websites.
- Use the services provided by the Direct Marketing Association (p. 144) to remove your name from most national telemarketing, mail, and e-mail lists.
- Call the credit reporting agencies' notification system at 1-888-567-8688. This will reduce the number of unsolicited credit and insurance offers you get. All three major credit bureaus participate in this program.
- Under U.S. Postal Service (USPS) rules, it is illegal to send mail that looks like it is from a government agency when it isn't. It is also illegal to send mail that looks like a bill when nothing was ordered, unless it clearly states that it is not a bill. Report violations of this rule to the USPS (p. 108).

### NATIONAL DO NOT CALL REGISTRY

The federal government's Do Not Call Registry allows you to restrict telemarketing calls permanently by registering your phone number at www.donotcall.gov or by calling 1-888-382-1222. If you receive telemarketing calls after your number has been in the national registry for three months, you can file a complaint using the same web page and toll-free number.

Placing your number on this national registry will stop most telemarketing calls, but not all of them. Calls that are still permitted include those from political organizations, charities, telephone surveyors, and some organizations with which you have a relationship.

In addition, the standard has always been that telemarketers are not allowed to call cell phones. Cell phone numbers can also be added to the Do Not Call Registry (www.donotcall.gov), but it is not necessary, since telemarketers are already forbidden to call them.

### PRE-RECORDED MESSAGES

Pre-recorded sales calls or robocalls are illegal. Companies cannot transmit these messages to consumers who have not agreed, in writing, to accept such messages. Pre-recorded calls may only be made to residential telephone numbers in the following cases:

- Emergency calls needed to ensure your health and safety
- Non-commercial calls
- Calls that don't include any unsolicited advertisements
- Calls by, or on behalf of, tax-exempt nonprofit organizations
- Calls for which you have given prior consent
- Calls from entities with which you have an established business relationship

If you receive pre-recorded telemarketing calls but have not agreed to get them, file a complaint with the FTC at www.donotcall.gov or by calling 1-888-382-1222.

### TELEMARKETING SALES CALLS

An FTC rule defines what telemarketers can and cannot do when making a sales call. Callers must:

- Provide the seller's name
- Disclose that the call is a sales call
- Tell you exactly what they're trying to sell
- Disclose the total cost and other terms of sale before you make any payment for goods or services
- Tell you if they don't allow refunds, exchanges, or cancellations

### OPTING OUT

Tired of unwanted e-mail filling up your inbox? You can opt out of most unsolicited e-mail lists by going to the "unsubscribe" button, usually found at the bottom of the message. Some senders make the button difficult to find, so you may have to do some searching.

In addition, the Direct Marketing Association lets you opt out of receiving unsolicited commercial mail from many national companies for three years. You can register with this service for a small fee, but your registration only applies to organizations that use the association's Mail Preference Service. To register, go to www.dmachoice.org. If you would like to opt out of credit and insurance offers, you can call 1-888-567-8688 or go online at www.optoutprescreen.com, which is managed by the major credit reporting companies.

To contact an organization, use the directory beginning on page 63.

If a prize is involved, the caller must give you the odds of winning, inform you that no purchase is necessary, and tell you how to get instructions for entering without buying anything. It's illegal for telemarketers to:

- Misrepresent what they're offering
- Call before 8 am or after 9 pm
- Threaten, intimidate, or harass you, or call again if you ask them not to

This FTC rule applies even when you receive a call from a telemarketer in another state or country. It also applies when you make a call to a company in another state or country in response to a mail solicitation.

The rule generally does not apply when you call to order from a catalog or in response to an ad on television or radio, or in a magazine or newspaper. It also does not apply to solicitations you receive by fax or e-mail. Beware that certain types of businesses, including nonprofit organizations, investment brokers and advisors, and banks and financial institutions, are exempt from the rule.

If you get a phone call from someone who says he or she is with your bank and/or credit company and the person asks you to provide or confirm any personal information:

- Do NOT answer any questions.
- Hang up immediately.
- Call your bank or credit company directly and describe what happened.

Whether reserving a hotel room, buying plane tickets, or making other travel arrangements, these tips will help you get the deal you've been promised:

- **Plan as far ahead as you can.** Special deals on hotel rooms and airline seats often sell out very quickly.
- **Be flexible in your travel plans.** Hotels usually offer better rates on days when they expect fewer guests. Once you get a fare quote from an airline, ask if you can save money by leaving a day earlier or later, by taking a different flight on the same day, or by using a different

airport. Changing planes during your trip is sometimes cheaper than a nonstop flight.

- **Check out the seller.** Ask tour operators and travel agents whether they belong to a professional association, then check to see if they are members in good standing. Contact your state or local consumer protection agency (p. 112) and the Better Business Bureau (p. 67) to find their complaint history.
- **Comparison shop.** Determine the complete cost of the trip in dollars, including all service charges, taxes, processing fees, etc.
- **Beware of unusually cheap prices and freebies.** These could be a scam, and you could end up paying more than the cost of a regular package tour. See information on Drip Pricing on p. 2.
- **Make sure you understand the terms of the deal.** If you hear you've won a free vacation, ask whether you have to buy something in order to get it. If the destination is a beach resort, ask the seller how far the hotel is from the beach. Then ask the hotel.
- **Ask about cancellation policies.** You may want to look into travel insurance for added protection (see p. 34). The website www.insuremytrip.com offers pricing and policy information on plans from different companies and describes the different forms of policies available.
- **Insist on written confirmations.** Ask for written proof of reservations, rates, and dates.
- **Pay by credit card.** It's not unusual to make a deposit or even pay in full for travel services before the trip. Paying by credit card gives you the right to dispute charges for services that were misrepresented or never delivered. If a travel agent or service provider says you can't leave for at least two months, be very cautious— the deadline for disputing a credit card charge is 60 days, and most scam artists know this. (See Credit Card Billing Disputes, p. 13).

In some states, travel sellers must be registered and insured. Advance payments for travel must be placed in an escrow account until services are provided. Prizes or "free" gifts may also be regulated. Contact your state or local consumer protection agency (p. 112) to find out about your rights and how to file complaints. The American Society of Travel Agents (p. 143) also helps to resolve disputes with member agents.

## RESOLVING AIR TRAVEL PROBLEMS

No matter how well you plan, you might encounter these common air travel hassles.

### Delayed and Canceled Flights

Airline delays caused by bad weather, traffic control problems, and mechanical repairs are hard to predict. If your flight is canceled, most airlines will rebook you on the earliest flight possible to your destination, at no additional charge. If you're able to find a flight on another

## AIRLINE FEES

Many airlines charge extra fees for checked baggage and some charge for carry-ons. Others charge for advance seat assignments, meals, unaccompanied minors, and other services. The Department of Transportation has ruled that an airline must prominently disclose all mandatory taxes and fees on their websites. The airline must also refund baggage fees if it loses your baggage. In addition, airlines are required to include all government taxes and fees in the advertised price. However, air carriers may still charge optional fees not included in the standard price. Each airline's fee schedule is different, so check with the airline before you head to the airport. For more information, go to airconsumer.dot.gov/subjects.htm.

Keep in mind—using frequent flyer points doesn't necessarily mean you are exempt from additional fees. When booking a flight using frequent flyer points, airlines may still charge you a booking fee or pet fee.

airline, ask the first airline to endorse your ticket to the new carrier. This could save you from a fare increase, but there is no rule requiring the airline to do this.

Each airline has its own policies about what it will do for delayed passengers; there are no federal requirements. If your flight is delayed or canceled, ask the airline whether it will pay for meals or a phone call. Contrary to what many people believe, airlines are not required to do so.

### Delayed or Damaged Bags

If your bags aren't on the conveyor belt when you arrive, file a report with the airline before you leave the airport:

- Insist the airline fill out a form and give you a copy, even if personnel say the bag will be on the next flight.
- Get the name of the person who filled out the form and a phone number.
- Confirm that the airline will deliver the bag to you without charge when it's found.

Some airlines will give you money to purchase a few necessities. If they don't provide you with cash, ask what types of articles are reimbursable and keep all receipts.

If a suitcase arrives damaged, the airline may pay for repairs if you file a claim immediately (before you leave the airport). If an item can't be fixed, the airline will negotiate to pay you its depreciated value. The same is true for belongings packed inside a suitcase. However, airlines may refuse to pay for damage if it was caused by your failure to pack something properly rather than by the airline's handling.

### Lost Bags

If your bag is declared officially lost, you will have to submit a second, more detailed form within a time period set by the airline. The information on the form is used to estimate the value of your lost belongings. Airlines

can limit their liability for delay, loss, and damage to baggage; however, they must prominently display a sign that explains the limit. According to the Office of Aviation Consumer Protection and Enforcement (airconsumer.ost.dot.gov/SA_Baggage_Limits.htm), the maximum an airline pays on lost bags and their contents is limited to $3,300 per passenger on domestic flights, and approximately $1,500 per passenger for unchecked baggage on international flights. See www.thetravelinsider.info/travelaccessories/lostbaggagerights.htm for more information on maximum liability, including special rates that change daily.

If the airline's offer doesn't cover your loss fully, check your homeowners or renters insurance to see whether it covers losses away from home. Some credit card companies and travel agencies also offer optional or even automatic supplemental baggage coverage.

On those trips when you know you're carrying more than the liability limits, you may want to ask about purchasing "excess valuation" from the airline when you check in. Of course, there is no guarantee the airline will sell you this protection. The airline may refuse, especially if the item is valuable or breakable.

### Overbooked Flights

Selling more tickets than there are seats is not illegal. Most airlines overbook their flights to compensate for "no-shows." If there are more passengers than seats just before a plane is scheduled to depart, you can be "bumped" or left behind against your will. Whether you are bumped may depend on when you officially checked in for your flight, so check-in early. The U.S. Department of Transportation requires airlines to ask people to give up their seats voluntarily, in exchange for compensation. Airlines decide what to offer volunteers, such as money, a free trip, food, or lodging.

Federal rules protect you if you are "bumped" on most flights within the United States and on outbound international flights. Passengers who are bumped involuntarily are protected under Federal Aviation Administration guidelines (www.faa.gov). If you volunteer to be bumped, your agreement with the airline is not regulated and will depend on negotiating at the gate.

The airline must give you a written statement describing your rights as well as the airline's boarding priority rules and criteria. If the airline is not able to get you to your final destination within two hours of your original arrival time, you may be entitled to a maximum of $800 compensation if you are delayed (that is, more than two hours for domestic and four hours for international) from your original arrival time. The amount depends on the price of the ticket and the length of the delay. To receive this payment, you must have a confirmed reservation. You must also meet the airline's deadlines for ticketing and check-in. An airline may offer you a free ticket on a future flight in place of a check, but you have the right to insist on a check.

**Tarmac Delays**

Under new federal rules, U.S. airlines operating domestic flights must allow passengers to deplane after a tarmac delay of three hours. The only exceptions allowed are for safety or security, or if air traffic control advises the pilot otherwise. Carriers are also required to provide adequate food and drinking water within two hours of being delayed on the tarmac; they must also maintain operable lavatories and, if necessary, provide medical attention.

There are other protections as well, such as prohibiting airlines from scheduling chronically delayed flights. For more information, go to www.airconsumer.ost.dot.gov, and search for Airline Passenger Protections.

## PASSPORTS

A valid U.S. passport is required to enter and leave most foreign countries. The Passport Services Office provides information and services to American citizens about how to obtain, replace, or change a passport. All American citizens must now have a valid U.S. passport to re-enter the country, regardless of what nations they have been visiting while traveling. For more information on how to get a new passport, visit www.travel.state.gov/passport.

Acceptance facilities include many federal, state, and probate courts; post offices; some public libraries; and a number of county and municipal offices. There are also 25 regional passport agencies, and one Gateway City Agency, that serve customers who are traveling within two weeks (14 days), or who need foreign visas for travel. Appointments are required in such cases.

To obtain a passport for the first time, you need to appear in person at one of 7,000 passport acceptance facilities located throughout the United States with:

- Two photographs of you taken within the last six months
- Proof of U.S. citizenship
- A valid form of photo identification (such as a driver's license)

Passports can be renewed by mail if the applicant is an adult; however, passports for minors must be renewed in person. Guidelines for renewing passports as well as the appropriate forms can be found at www.travel.state.gov/passport/renew/renew_833.html.

## TRAVEL SAFETY

Several federal agencies offer advice and information on the Internet or mobile apps available at apps.usa.gov that can help you have a safe trip. For advice on:

- **Airline, highway, and rail safety information**: Check out the U.S. Department of Transportation (p. 104) at www.dot.gov. Look up crash-safety reports on cars or find out how weather is affecting air travel and road conditions at www.fly.faa.gov or www.faa.gov/passengers.

- **Safe travel by air, land, and sea**: Contact the Transportation Security Administration (p. 101) at www.tsa.gov/travelers. This site posts tips on dealing with airline security checks, traveling with kids, and warnings on prohibited items.

- **What to do before, during, and when returning from a trip overseas**: Visit the U.S. Department of State (p. 104) at www.state.gov/travel. You can also get warnings on locations to avoid and what to do in an overseas emergency.

- **Health-related travel information**: Consult the Centers for Disease Control and Prevention (p. 99) at www.cdc.gov/travel. Research vaccination requirements, find information on how to avoid illnesses caused by food and water, and review inspection scores on specific cruise ships.

## CHECK BUS SAFETY RECORDS

Some travelers have turned to commercial buses as an inexpensive option for traveling long distances. Before planning a trip on a commercial bus or hired motorcoach, you should research the company's record. The Federal Motor Carrier Safety Administration (FMCSA) recommends that you contact the company and ask these questions:

- Do the drivers hold valid Commercial Driver's Licenses with a "passenger" endorsement?

- Does the company comply with the Department of Transportation's drug and alcohol testing requirements for drivers?

- Does the company conduct safety inspections of its buses?

You can find more information about the FMCSA's (p. 104) bus safety database and interstate travel safety at www.fmcsa.dot.gov/safety-security/pcs/Index.aspx. If you want to file a safety complaint, call 1-888-368-7238.

## UTILITIES

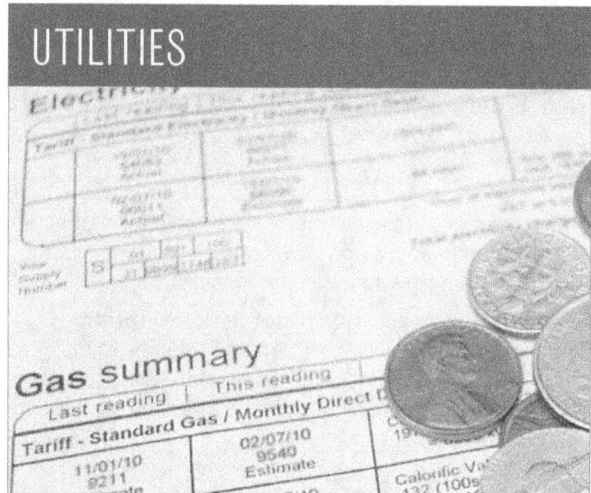

In many states, consumers can choose their telephone and energy service provider. Contact your state utility commission (p. 138) to find out whether you have a choice. Some commissions will provide a list of service providers and advice on making a choice, and most state utility commissions will take any complaints you have concerning utility sales and service.

### STARTING UTILITY SERVICE

When you move into a new home or apartment, you may also be required to have the utilities (electricity, gas, water, waste removal, and cable) turned on in your name. Your city or county government may handle some services, such as water, sewer, and garbage collection. If you live in an apartment or are leasing a house from a homeowner, the landlord may handle this for you, but that is not required. If you request service, provide as much advance notice to the utility company as you can, at least one week in advance of the date you need service to start. Also, if you are relocating, don't forget to have service turned off at your old address. Each company may require you to pay a fee to start service. You may also be required to pay a deposit or allow the company to check your credit to establish service at your home. If any of these companies fails to meet its service requirements, file a complaint with the company; you may be able to get a refund of your installation fee. If that doesn't work, contact your state's utility commission (p. 138).

### BILLING

Once you have established service, you should start receiving your bills at regular intervals, normally monthly or quarterly. Utility bills are based on the amount of energy or water you actually use. However, if you live in an apartment complex, the amount you pay for some utilities may be prorated or split, based on a mathematical formula, among all of the residents in your community, no matter how energy conscious you are; see Renting (p. 30). If the amount of energy varies by season, you may decide to sign up for a budget billing program. These programs

allow you to smooth out your monthly payments by paying more in lighter-use months, so your bills are still manageable in months with heavier use. Contact your utility companies to sign up for these programs. To learn ways to save on your energy bill, see Going Green (p. 22).

In addition to your actual service, you may have other fees on your bill, such as administrative fees, public surcharges, or local taxes. Contact the service provider if you see charges you don't understand or didn't authorize, or if you have difficulty making timely payments.

If you have difficulty paying your bills, especially for electricity or gas, help is available. Contact the company to find out if it has a program in place to help consumers. Also, your state's utility commission (p. 138) may sponsor a program to either reduce your bill or make your payments based on a set amount of your income each month. Programs like these from utility companies and local government are usually based on your income.

## WILLS AND FUNERALS

It's unfortunate how many people believe that estate planning is only for the wealthy. People at all economic levels benefit from an estate plan. Upon death, an estate plan legally protects and distributes property based on your wishes and the needs of your family and/or survivors with the fewest tax consequences.

### WILLS

A will is the most practical first step in estate planning. It makes clear how you want your property to be distributed after you die. Writing a will can be as simple as typing out how you want your assets to be transferred to loved ones or charitable organizations after your death. If you don't have a will when you die, your estate will be handled in probate, and your property could be distributed differently from what you would like.

It may help to get legal advice when writing a will, particularly when it comes to understanding all of the rules of the estate disposition process in your state. For information about legal issues, see page 58. Some

52    www.USA.gov

To contact an organization, use the directory beginning on page 63.

states, for instance, have community-property laws that entitle your surviving spouse to keep half of your wealth after you die, no matter what percentage you leave him or her. Fees for the execution of a will vary according to its complexity.

## CHOOSE AN EXECUTOR

An executor is the person who is responsible for settling the estate after death. Duties of an executor include:

- Taking inventory of property and belongings
- Appraising and distributing assets
- Paying taxes
- Settling debts owed by the deceased

Most important, the executor is legally obligated to act in the interests of the deceased, following the wishes provided by the will. Here again, it can be helpful to consult an attorney to help with the probate process or offer legal guidance. In most states, any person over the age of 18 who hasn't been convicted of a felony can be named executor of a will. Some people choose a lawyer, accountant, or financial consultant based on his or her professional experience. Others choose a spouse, adult child, relative, or friend. Since the role of executor can be demanding, it's often a good idea to ask the person if he or she is willing to serve.

If you've been named executor in someone's will but are not able or do not want to serve, you need to file a "declination," which is a legal document that declines your designation as an executor. The contingent executor named in the will then assumes responsibility. If no contingent executor is named, the court will appoint one.

## RULES TO REMEMBER WHEN WRITING A WILL

- In most states, you must be 18 years of age or older.
- To be valid, a will must be written when you are of sound judgment and have adequate mental capacity.
- The document must clearly state that it is your will.
- An executor of your will, who ensures your estate is distributed according to your wishes, must be named.
- It is not necessary to notarize or record your will, but doing so can safeguard any claims that it is invalid. To be valid, you must sign a will in the presence of at least two witnesses.
- A financial will and testament will always supersede a last will and testament when bestowing financial assets.

## WRITE A SOCIAL MEDIA WILL

Social media are a part of daily life, so what happens to the online content you created once you die? If you are active online, you should consider creating a social media will, or statement of how you would like your online identity to be handled. You should appoint someone you trust as an online executor. This person will be responsible for closing your email addresses, social media profiles, and blogs after you are deceased. Take these steps to help you write a social media will:

- Review the privacy policies and the terms and conditions of each website where you have a presence.
- State how you would like your profiles to be handled. You may want to cancel your profile completely or keep it up for friends and family to visit. Some sites allow users to create a memorial profile where other users can still see your profile but can't post anything new.
- Give the responsible person a document that lists all of the websites where you have a profile, along with your usernames and passwords.
- Stipulate in your will that the online executor should have a copy of your death certificate. The online executor may need this as proof for websites to take any actions on your behalf.

## FUNERALS

One of the most expensive purchases many consumers will ever make is arranging for a funeral. A traditional burial, including a casket and vault, costs about $7,000. Extras such as flowers, obituary notices, cards, and limousines can add thousands of dollars more. At such a highly emotional time, many people are easily swayed to believe that their decisions reflect how they feel about the deceased and wind up spending more than may be necessary.

Most funeral providers are professionals who work to serve their clients' needs and best interests. Unfortunately, some do not. They may take advantage of clients by insisting on unnecessary services and overcharging consumers. That's why there is a federal law, called the Funeral Rule that regulates the actions of funeral directors, homes, and services.

Many funeral providers offer a variety of package plans that include products and services that are most commonly sold. Keep in mind, you are not obligated to buy a package plan; you have the right to buy the individual products and services you prefer. As outlined by the Funeral Rule:

## THE FUNERAL RULE

A federal law makes it easier for you to choose only the goods and services you want or need when planning a funeral, and to pay only for those you select. The Funeral Rule, enforced by the FTC, requires funeral directors to give you itemized prices in person and, if you ask, over the phone.

- You have the right to choose the funeral goods and services you want (with some exceptions).
- The funeral provider must state this "Rule" in writing on the general price list.
- If state or local law requires you to buy any particular item, the funeral provider must disclose it on the price list, with a reference to the specific law.
- The funeral provider may not refuse, or charge a fee, to handle a casket that you bought elsewhere.
- A funeral provider who offers cremations must make alternative containers available.
- When prepaying for funeral services, do not agree to give the check from the life insurance company directly to the funeral home. You are paying for specific goods and services, and signing over the life insurance check might result in a significant overpayment for services rendered.

For more information about the Funeral Rule, visit www.ftc.gov/bcp/edu/microsites/funerals.

Planning ahead is the best way to make informed decisions about funeral arrangements. An advance plan also spares your family from having to make choices in the middle of grief and under time constraints. Every family is different, and funeral arrangements are influenced by religious and cultural traditions, budgets, and personal preferences.

You are not legally required to use a funeral home to plan and conduct a funeral, but most people find that the services of a professional funeral home make the process easier.

Comparison shopping, either in person or by phone, can save you money and is much easier when done in advance. Visit www.funerals.org to learn more about how to select a funeral home and research its history. Many funeral homes will also send you a price list by mail, but this is not required by law. If you have a problem concerning funeral matters, it's best to try to resolve it first with the funeral director. If you are dissatisfied, the Funeral Consumers Alliance (p. 110) may be able to advise you on how best to resolve your issue. You can also contact your state or local consumer protection agencies (p. 112) or the Funeral Service Consumer Assistance Program at 1-800-662-7666. Most states have a licensing board that regulates the funeral industry. You can contact the board in your state for information or help.

### Prepaying

Millions of Americans have entered into contracts to prearrange their funerals and prepay some or all of the expenses involved. Various states have laws to help ensure that these advance payments are available to pay for the funeral products and services when they're needed; however, protections vary widely from state to state. Some state laws require the funeral home or cemetery to place a percentage of the prepayment in a state-regulated trust or to purchase a life insurance policy with the death benefits assigned to the funeral home or cemetery. For a list of questions to consider before prepaying for a funeral, visit www.ftc.gov/bcp/edu/pubs/consumer/products/pro19.shtm.

### VETERANS CEMETERIES

All veterans are entitled to a free burial in a national cemetery and a grave marker. This eligibility also applies to some civilians who have provided military-related service and some Public Health Service personnel. Spouses and dependent children also are entitled to a lot and marker when buried in a national cemetery. There are no charges for opening or closing the grave, for a vault or liner, or for setting the marker in a national cemetery. For more information, visit the Department of Veterans Affairs (p. 105) at www.cem.va.gov.

54  www.USA.gov

To contact an organization, use the directory beginning on page 63.

## FILING A COMPLAINT

Even the savviest consumer has problems with a good or service at one time or another. It is your right to complain if you have a genuine consumer problem. It is also your responsibility. A problem can't be fixed if no one knows it exists.

### CONTACT THE SELLER

The first step in resolving a consumer problem is contacting the seller. You can solve most consumer problems by talking to a salesperson or customer service representative. Do this as soon as possible because some retailers have time limits on returns and refunds. If this doesn't work, ask for a supervisor or manager. If this fails, try going higher up to the national headquarters of the seller or the manufacturer of the item. Many companies have a special customer relations or consumer affairs division whose primary function is solving consumer problems. Many companies provide a toll-free number or address for this office on the product label, warranty, or other papers you received at the time of purchase. If this is not the case:

- Check the Corporate Consumer Directory portion of this Handbook for the contact information of several hundred corporations (p. 72).
- Visit the company's website and look for a "Contact Us" link.
- Dial the directory of toll-free numbers at 1-800-555-1212 to see whether the company has a toll-free number listed.
- Ask your local librarian to assist you. Most public libraries have reference books with contact information.
- As you do your search, keep in mind that the name of the manufacturer or parent company is often different from the brand name. The Thomas Register of American Manufacturers, a book available at many public libraries, lists the manufacturers of thousands of products.

- With each person you contact, calmly and accurately explain the problem and what action you would like to be taken. A written letter is a good strategy because you will have a record of your communication with the company. The sample letter (p. 57) will help you prepare a written complaint.
- Be brief and to the point. Note all important facts about your purchase, including what you bought, serial or model numbers, the name and location of the seller, and when you made the purchase.
- State exactly what you want done about the problem and how long you are willing to wait for a response. Be reasonable.
- Don't write an angry, sarcastic, or threatening letter. The person reading your letter probably was not responsible for your problem but could be very helpful in resolving it.
- Send your letter as certified mail or request delivery confirmation.
- Include copies of all documents regarding your problem. Keep the originals.
- Provide your name, address, and phone numbers. If an account is involved, be sure to include the account number.
- Keep a record of your efforts to contact the seller; include the name of the person with whom you spoke and what was done, if anything.

### CONTACT THIRD PARTIES

Don't give up if you are not satisfied with the seller's response to your complaint. Once you have given the seller a reasonable amount of time to respond, consider filing a complaint with one or more of these outside organizations:

**State or local consumer protection offices** (p. 112). These government agencies mediate complaints, conduct investigations, and prosecute those who break consumer laws.

**State regulatory agencies** that have jurisdiction over the business. For example, banking (p. 126), insurance (p. 130), securities (p. 134), and utilities (p. 138) are regulated at the state level.

### STEPS TO FOLLOW TO RESOLVE A COMPLAINT

- Before starting, start a file or log to record all contacts and documents.
- Contact the seller.
- Contact the manufacturer.
- Contact industry trade associations.
- Contact local and state consumer protection/regulatory/licensing officers.
- Contact the local Better Business Bureau.

## FILE A COMPLAINT USING SOCIAL MEDIA

Social media offer an alternative to filing a formal consumer complaint. The customer relations staff at many major corporations monitor posts and complaints about their company's service. Someone may respond to your problem quickly, to avoid negative perceptions of their company's performance by other potential customers. While there is no guarantee that you'll get your problem resolved, it can be a worthwhile effort.

**Local politicians.** Your local and state politicians may be able to help you get your complaint addressed.

**State and local licensing agencies.** Doctors, lawyers, home improvement contractors, auto repair shops, debt collectors, and child care providers are required to register or be licensed. The board or agency that oversees this process may handle complaints and have the authority to take disciplinary action. Your state or local consumer protection office (p. 112) can help you identify the appropriate agency.

**Better Business Bureaus** (p. 67). This network of nonprofit organizations supported by local businesses tries to resolve buyer complaints against sellers. Records are kept on unresolved complaints as a source of information for the seller's future customers. The umbrella organization for the BBBs assists with complaints concerning the truthfulness of national advertising and helps to settle disputes with automobile manufacturers through the BBB AUTO LINE program (p. 66).

**Trade associations.** Companies selling similar products or services often belong to an industry association that will help resolve problems between its members and consumers (p. 142).

**National consumer organizations.** Some of these organizations assist consumers with complaints. Others may be unable to help individuals but are interested in hearing about problems that could influence their education and advocacy efforts (p. 109).

**Media programs.** Local newspapers, radio stations, and television stations often have action lines or hotline services that try to resolve consumer complaints they receive. Call for Action, Inc. is a nonprofit network of consumer hotlines that educate and assist consumers with consumer problems. For more information, visit www.callforaction.org to find your local action office, or call 240-747-0225.

## DISPUTE RESOLUTION PROGRAMS

Some companies and industries offer programs to address disagreements between buyers and sellers. The auto industry (p. 66) has several of these programs. The Financial Industry Regulatory Authority (FINRA) offers a program to resolve investment-related disputes (p. 66). Some small claims courts also offer a dispute resolution program as an alternative to a trial. The American Bar Association (p. 142) also publishes a directory of state and local dispute resolution programs.

Mediation, arbitration, and conciliation are three common types of dispute resolution. During mediation, both sides involved in the dispute meet with a neutral third party and create their own agreement jointly. In arbitration, the third party decides how to settle the problem. Conciliation is similar; however, you and the other party meet with the conciliator separately (not a group meeting). Request a copy of the rules of any program before deciding to participate. You will want to know beforehand whether the decision is binding; some programs do not require both parties to accept the decision. Also ask whether participation in the program places any restrictions on your ability to take other legal action.

Some contracts include a clause that prohibits you from taking legal action and require you to engage in mandatory arbitration with a company in the case of a dispute. The clause may limit your ability to take a case to court. Be sure to read contracts carefully to see whether they include a mandatory arbitration clause. If you do not wish to be prohibited from taking legal action if needed, you can choose not to purchase an item from the company. If you have no other option, write on the contract that you don't agree with the clause and initial next to the statement.

## SMALL CLAIMS COURT

Small claims courts resolve disputes over small amounts of money. While the maximum amount that can be claimed differs from state to state, court procedures are generally simple, inexpensive, quick, and informal. Court fees are minimal, and you often get your filing fee back if you win your case. Typically, you will not need a lawyer—some states do not permit them. If you live in a state that allows lawyers, and the party you are suing brings one, don't be intimidated. Most judges make allowances for consumers who appear without lawyers. Even though the court is informal, the judge's decision must be followed.

If you file a case and win, the losing party should give you what the court says you are owed without further action on your part. But some losers refuse to follow the court's decision. When this happens, you can go back to court and ask for the order to be enforced. Depending on local laws, law enforcement officials might sell a person's property or take money from a bank account or business cash register. If the person who owes the money receives a salary, the court might order an employer to garnish (deduct money from) each paycheck to pay you.

Keep copies of all of your letters, faxes, e-mails, receipts and related documents.

**Your Address**
**Your City, State, ZIP Code**
**Date**

**Name of Contact Person, if available**
**Title, if available**
**Company Name**
**Consumer Complaint Division (if you have no specific contact)**
**Street Address**
**City, State, Zip Code**

Dear (**Contact Person**):

Re: (**account number, if applicable**)

- describe purchase
- name of product, serial number
- include date and place of purchase

On (**date**), I (**bought, leased, rented, or had repaired**) a (**name of the product, with serial or model number or service performed**) at (**location, date and other important details of the transaction**).

- state problem
- give history

Unfortunately, your product (**or service**) has not performed well (**or the service was inadequate**) because (**state the problem**). I am disappointed because (**explain the problem: for example, the product does not work properly, the service was not performed correctly, I was billed the wrong amount, something was not disclosed clearly or was misrepresented, etc.**).

- ask for specific action
- enclose copies of documents

To resolve the problem, I would appreciate your (**state the specific action you want—money back, charge card credit, repair, exchange, etc.**). Enclosed are copies (**do not send originals**) of my records (**include receipts, guarantees, warranties, canceled checks, contracts, model and serial numbers, and any other documents**).

- allow time for action
- state how you can be reached

I look forward to your reply and a resolution to my problem and will wait until (**set a time limit**) before seeking help from a consumer protection agency or Better Business Bureau. Please contact me at the above address or by phone at (**home and/or office numbers with area code**).

Sincerely,

**Your name**

**Enclosure(s)**

Download a copy of the sample complaint letter at:
www.usa.gov/topics/consumer/complaint/complaint-letter.shtml

SAMPLE COMPLAINT LETTER

Check your local telephone book under the municipal, county, or state government headings for small claims court offices. Ask the clerk how to use the small claims court. Before taking your own case to court, observe a small claims court session and ask the court whether it has information that will help you prepare your presentation to the judge.

## LEGAL HELP AND INFORMATION

If you need an attorney to advise or represent you, ask friends and family for recommendations. You can also contact the Lawyer Referral Service of your state, county, or city bar association listed in your local phone directory. Websites such as www.americanbar.org (American Bar Association) and www.nolo.com can help you with answers to general legal questions.

### Tips for Choosing an Attorney

Many lawyers who primarily serve individuals and families are general practitioners with experience in frequently needed legal services, such as divorce and family matters, wills and probate, bankruptcy and debt problems, real estate, and criminal and/or personal injury. Some have a narrower focus. Be sure the lawyer you are considering has experience in the area for which you are seeking help.

### Once you've identified some candidates:

- Call each attorney on the telephone, describe your legal issue, and find out whether he or she handles your situation.
- Ask if you will be charged for an initial consultation.
- Ask for an estimate of what the lawyer usually charges to handle your kind of case.
- Ask whether there are hourly charges or your attorney accepts a percentage of the settlement as a fee contingency.

The initial consultation is an opportunity for you and the lawyer to get to know each other. After listening to the description of your case, the lawyer should be able to outline your rights and liabilities as well as alternative courses of action. The initial consultation is the lawyer's opportunity to explain what he or she can do for you and how much it will cost. You should not hesitate to ask about the attorney's experience in handling matters such as yours. Also, do not hesitate to ask about the lawyer's fees and the likely results. If you are considering going beyond the initial consultation and hiring the lawyer, request a written fee agreement before proceeding.

### What If You Can't Afford a Lawyer?

If you cannot afford a lawyer, you may qualify for free legal help from a Legal Aid or Legal Services Corporation (LSC) office. These offices generally offer legal assistance for such things as landlord-tenant relations, credit, utilities, family matters (for example, divorce and adoption), foreclosure, home equity fraud, Social Security, welfare, unemployment, and workers' compensation.

If the Legal Aid office in your area does not handle your type of case, it may refer you to other local, state, or national organizations that can provide help. Additional resources may be found at www.lawhelp.org or www.freeadvice.com.

- To find the Legal Aid office nearest to you, check a local telephone directory or contact:

  National Legal Aid and Defender Association
  1140 Connecticut Ave., NW, Suite 900
  Washington, DC 20036
  Phone: 202-452-0620
  www.nlada.org

- To find the LSC office nearest you, check a local telephone directory or contact:

  LSC Public Affairs
  3333 K St., NW, 3rd Floor
  Washington, DC 20007
  Phone: 202-295-1500
  www.lsc.gov

Free assistance may also be available from a law school program where students, supervised by attorneys, handle a variety of legal matters. Some of these programs are open to all; others limit their service to specific groups, such as senior citizens or low-income persons. Contact a law school in your area to find out whether such a program is available.

## REPORT FRAUD AND SAFETY HAZARD

If you suspect a law has been violated, contact your local or state consumer protection agency (p. 112). This agency may take action or refer you to another state organization that has authority where you live. A local law enforcement officer may also be able to provide advice and assistance.

Violations of federal laws should be reported to the federal agency responsible for enforcement. While federal agencies are rarely able to act on behalf of individual consumers, complaints are used to document patterns of abuse, allowing the agency to take action against a company.

Throughout Part I of this *Handbook*, you will find references to federal agencies you can contact for more information, which is usually the same agency to contact with your complaint. You can also find the appropriate federal agency by using the Federal Agency Directory (p. 96).

People who have no intention of delivering what is sold, misrepresent items, sell counterfeit goods, or otherwise try to trick you out of your money are committing fraud. If you suspect fraud, there are some additional steps to take:

- Contact the Federal Trade Commission (p. 107). Please note—the FTC does not handle individual consumer complaints.
- Report scams that use the mail or interstate delivery service to the U.S. Postal Inspection Service (p. 108). It is illegal to use the mail to misrepresent or steal money.
- Report scams that are Internet-based to the Internet Crime Complaint Center at www.ic3.gov.

Reporting fraud promptly improves your chances of recovering what you have lost and helps law enforcement authorities stop scams before others are victimized.

If you suspect you have a product that poses a safety hazard, report the problem to the appropriate federal agency:

- **Animal Products.** Food and Drug Administration (p. 100)
- **Automobiles.** National Highway Traffic Safety Administration (p. 104)
- **Consumer Household Products.** U.S. Consumer Product Safety Commission (p. 96)
- **Drugs, Cosmetics, and Medical Devices.** Food and Drug Administration (p. 100)
- **Food.** Food and Drug Administration (p. 100), U.S. Department of Agriculture (p. 96)
- **Household Chemicals.** Environmental Protection Agency (p. 105)
- **Seafood.** Food and Drug Administration (p. 100), U.S. Department of Commerce (p. 97)
- **Toys, Baby, and Play Equipment.** U.S. Consumer Product Safety Commission (p. 96)

# KEY INFORMATION RESOURCES

### Federal Citizen Information Center (FCIC)

FCIC is a one-stop source that provides government information and services directly to the public. FCIC offers information across various channels, including websites USA.gov and GobiernoUSA.gov (in Spanish), telephone at 1-888-333-4636, print publications available through the *Consumer Information Catalog* and at Publications.USA.gov, and via social media on Facebook at www.facebook.com/USAgov, and Twitter @USAgov.

### Center for the Study of Services

www.checkbook.org Evaluates quality and price for local services in major metropolitan areas; see page 109.

### Consumer Reports

www.consumerreports.org Researches and tests goods and services such as automobiles, appliances, food, clothing, luggage, and insurance; see page 110.

### Consumer World

www.consumerworld.org A public service website with links to hundreds of consumer resources, corporations and government agencies.

### National Institute of Food and Agriculture (NIFA)

Programs cover food and nutrition, housing, gardening, budgeting, using credit, saving for retirement, and more; visit www.nifa.usda.gov or www.extension.org. See page 96.

### Libraries

Publications from many of the organizations mentioned on this page are available at your local public library or by visiting www.publiclibraries.com.

## EMERGENCY PREPAREDNESS

Disasters can strike in many forms—fires, floods, hurricanes, tornadoes, and even national emergencies. Protecting yourself, your family, your pets, and your home or your business requires advance planning. It is equally important to know where to turn for help and information. You may even be eligible for government assistance.

## SERVICES AND RESOURCES FOR CONSUMERS WITH DISABILITIES

**Relay Services:**
Telecommunications relay services link telephone conversations between individuals who use standard voice telephones and those who use text telephones (TTYs). Calls may be made from either type of telephone to the other type through the relay service.

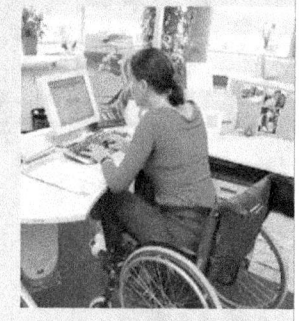

**Local Relay Services:** States provide relay services for local and long-distance calls. Consult your local telephone directory for information on use, fees (if any), services, and dialing instructions for that area.

**Federal Relay Service:** The FRS, a program of the U.S. General Services Administration (GSA), provides access to TTY users who wish to conduct official business nationwide with and within the federal government. The toll-free number is 1-866-377-8642. For more information on relay communications or to obtain a brochure on using the FRS, call 1-800-877-0996.

**Other Services:** Consumers who are deaf or hard of hearing, or who have speech impairment and use a TTY, may receive operator and directory assistance for calls by calling 1-800-855-1155. Check the introductory pages of your local telephone directory for additional TTY services.

There are numerous sources of information to help you prepare. To get started, check out these sites:

- www.disasterassistance.gov
- www.fema.gov
- www.ready.gov
- www.redcross.org

In case of a disaster, make certain that you have your ID, cash, debit and credit cards, and a list of your account numbers and insurance policy numbers. It is also helpful to have a home inventory; you can create one online that you can access anywhere at www.knowyourstuff.org. For more detailed information about financial preparation in disasters see the FDIC publication, www.fdic.gov/consumers/consumer/news/cnsum11/protectingyourfinances.html.

### FOR TEACHERS

Teachers often use the *Consumer Action Handbook* to teach essential information about credit, insurance, major purchases, complaint letters, saving and investing, and other consumer topics. For classroom copies of the *Handbook*, e-mail action.handbook@gsa.gov; include the name and address of your school and the number of copies you would like to receive.

### FOR PERSONS WITH DISABILITIES

**National Council on Disability**
www.ncd.gov A federal agency whose mission is to improve the quality of life for Americans with disabilities and their families; see page 107.

**National Disability Rights Network**
www.ndrn.org Provides legally based advocacy services for people with disabilities.

**Department of Education**
www.ed.gov Provides training and information to parents of disabled children and to people who work with them; see page 97.

**Department of Housing and Urban Development**
www.hud.gov/offices/fheo/disabilities Learn more about the housing rights of people with disabilities, and the responsibilities of housing providers and building and design professionals; see page 102.

**National Library Service for the Blind and Physically Handicapped**
www.loc.gov/nls Administers a free loan service of recorded and Braille books and magazines, music scores in Braille and large print, plus specially designed playback equipment.

### FOR MILITARY PERSONNEL

Today's military families face many common consumer challenges as well as the additional stress associated with frequent separation. To ease such difficulties, Family Centers, along with the other programs described below, provide help and support for military families.

**U.S. Military Family Centers**
Located on most military installations, Family Centers provide information, life skills education, and support services to military members and their families. One key function of the Family Center is to link customers with appropriate services available in the local community and/or through state and federal assistance programs such as those related to health and human services, school systems, employment assistance, law enforcement, and recreation.

If you cannot locate a Family Center, contact your respective military branch's headquarters office listed below. The designation "DSN," preceding some of the phone numbers, refers to the military phone system and does not apply to the civilian sector.

**Air Force Community Readiness and Family Support**
AF/A1SF 4E235, Force Sustainment Division
1040 Air Force Pentagon
Washington, DC 20330-1040
Phone: 703-697-0067
www.afcrossroads.com

Air Force Crossroads is a comprehensive resource for Air Force members and their families relating to nearly every aspect of personal and professional life. With topics that cover, among others, health and wellness, finances, family matters, and recreation, the network includes access to the Air Force Spouse Forum, chat rooms, an employment forum, a flea market, and links to news sources.

### Marine Corps Community Services (MCCS)

3280 Russell Rd.
Quantico, VA 22134-5103
703-784-0275
DSN: 278-0275
Toll-free: 1-800-627-4637
www.usmc-mccs.org

The Personal and Family Readiness Division (MR) provides a number of Marine Corps personnel service programs, such as Casualty Assistance, DEERS Dependency Determination, Voting Assistance, Postal Services, and Personal Claims.

### FedsHireVets

Veterans Employment Program Office
U.S. Office of Personnel Management
1900 E St., NW
Washington, DC 20415-0001
Phone: 202-606-5090
www.fedshirevets.gov

FedsHireVets is a one-stop resource for federal veteran employment information.

### Fleet and Family Support Programs

Commander, Navy Installations Command
716 Sicard St., SE Suite 1000
Washington Navy Yard, DC 20374-5140
ffsp.navy.mil

Visit ffsp.navy.mil and submit questions to "Sailor and Family Information & Referral". Response will be provided within one business day. The Fleet and Family Support Program delivered by Commander, Navy Installations Command, provides support, references, information and a wide range of assistance for members of the Navy and their families to meet the unique challenges of the military lifestyle. Up-to-date news, messages, links and resources are provided, including assistance with relocation, employment, career and benefits, healthy lifestyles, casualties, domestic violence, and retirement.

### Family and Morale, Welfare and Recreation Command Family Programs

Directorate, Army Community Service
4700 King St.
Alexandria, VA 22302
Phone: 703-681-5375
DSN: 761-5375

## PREDATORY LENDING RESTRICTIONS

As of October 1, 2007, the Talent-Nelson Amendment to the John Warner National Defense Authorization Act allows the Department of Defense to regulate the terms of payday loans, vehicle title loans, and tax refund loans to active-duty service members and their dependents. These three products have high interest rates, coupled with short payback terms.

The rule for service members and their dependents limits the Military Annual Percentage Rate (MAPR) on these loans to 36%. All fees and charges should be included in calculating the rate. The rule also prohibits contracts requiring the use of a check or access to a bank account, mandatory arbitration, or unreasonable legal notice. Any credit agreement subject to this regulation that fails to comply with the regulation is void and cannot be enforced. The rule further provides that a creditor or assignee that knowingly violates the regulation shall be subject to certain criminal penalties.

The Department of Defense strongly encourages service members and their families to choose alternatives that specifically help resolve financial crises, rebuild credit ratings, and establish savings for emergencies. Payday loans, vehicle title loans, and tax refund loans can propel an already overextended borrower into a deeper spiral of debt.

### MyArmyLifeToo

www.myarmylifetoo.com

This portal is the single gateway to comprehensive information on the support available to Army personnel and families, including resources to strengthen home and family life, Army basic training, lifelong learning, finances, employment, and relevant news, along with links to other key resources.

### U.S. Coast Guard

2100 Second St., SW, Room 6320
Washington, DC 20593
Phone: 202-267-6160
Toll-free: 1-800-368-5647 (Safety)
Toll-free: 1-877-669-8724 (Recruiting)
www.uscg.mil

The U.S. Coast Guard can provide key resources, including core publications, career information, and related news, as well as comprehensive background about its mission, community services, history, photos, and reports.

### Military HOMEFRONT

www.militaryhomefront.dod.mil

Military HOMEFRONT is the official Department of Defense website for information to help improve the quality of life for troops and their families. Members of all branches of the military service and their families will find reliable, up-to-date details and advice on such topics as education, housing, legal matters, parenting, personal

## BETTER BUSINESS BUREAU MILITARY LINE

The BBB Military Line, www.military.bbb.org, offers consumer education and advocacy to service members and their families. Five service-specific sites contain current military-related consumer news as well as links to local BBBs and other sites with useful consumer information:

www.bbb.org/us/army

www.bbb.org/us/navy

www.bbb.org/us/airforce

www.bbb.org/us/usmc

www.bbb.org/us/uscg

Users may request reports, file complaints, and sign up for a custom consumer newsletter. At the local level, area BBBs provide educational briefings for military personnel and their families and work with local businesses to promote ethical treatment of military consumers.

finances, pay and benefits, relocation, and health care. Military HOMEFRONT also makes it easier for leaders to locate official quality-of-life program information and resources for its troops and families. In addition, service providers can access desk guides, policies, forms, and other resources.

### Military Sentinel

www.ftc.gov/sentinel/military

Military Sentinel is a gateway to consumer education materials covering a wide range of consumer protection issues, from auto leasing to identity theft and work-at-home scams. It allows members of the U.S. Armed Forces to enter consumer complaints directly into a database that is immediately accessible by over 500 law enforcement organizations throughout the United States, Canada, and Australia. These law enforcement agencies use these complaint data to target cases for prosecution and other enforcement measures. Members of the Judge Advocate General's staff and others in the Department of Defense can also use this information to help protect armed services members and their families from consumer protection–related problems.

### Military OneSource

www.militaryonesource.com
Toll-free: 1-800-342-9647
Military OneSource is an excellent hub of information and assistance for military personnel and their families. This 24/7 resource offers a variety of services and tools to meet the special needs and improve the lives of service men and women, both personally and professionally. In addition to in-person counseling and direct links to all armed services home sites, Military OneSource offers advice and contact information on matters such as health, education, training, moving, shopping, legal

issues, and finances. Podcasts, webinars, discussion boards, and news feeds cover special topics and provide answers to help resolve problems.

### Commissaries and Exchanges

Consumers who shop at military commissaries and exchanges and who have a question or problem should contact the local manager before contacting the regional office. If your problem is not resolved at the local level, write or call the regional office nearest you. Be sure to discuss the problem with the local and regional offices of a commissary or exchange before contacting the national headquarters.

### Wounded Warrior Resource Center

www.woundedwarriorresourcecenter.com
The Wounded Warrior Resource Center (WWRC) website provides wounded service members, their families, and caregivers with information they need concerning military facilities, health care services, and benefits. It supports access to the Wounded Warrior Resource Call Center and trained specialists who are available 24 hours a day, seven days a week by phone at 1-800-342-9647 or by e-mail at wwrc@militaryonesource.com. Information is also available on how to connect to other families for support and recreation.

### National Resource Directory

www.nationalresourcedirectory.gov
The National Resource Directory provides wounded, ill, and injured service members; veterans; their families; and those who support them, with a web-based "yellow book." It has information on, and access to, the full range of medical and non-medical services and resources needed to achieve their personal and professional goals across the transitions from recovery to rehabilitation to community reintegration. The National Resource Directory, an online partnership of the departments of Defense, Labor, and Veterans Affairs, provides links to the services and resources of federal, state, and local government agencies; veterans' service, nonprofit, community-based, and philanthropic organizations; professional associations; and academic institutions.

## HELP FROM THE CONSUMER FINANCIAL PROTECTION BUREAU

The Consumer Financial Protection Bureau (CFPB) offers resources specifically for service members and their families. The Office of Service Member Affairs is dedicated to helping military personnel to plan for their financial futures and protect themselves from frauds that are targeted at military communities.
For more information visit,
www.consumerfinance.gov/servicemembers.

To contact an organization, use the directory beginning on page 63.

## SOCAP INTERNATIONAL

Many of the companies listed in this Handbook
are members of the Society of Consumer Affairs
Professionals International (SOCAP). Formed in 1973,
SOCAP is composed of over 2,000 best-in-class customer
care executives and professionals from over 100 brand
name companies throughout the U.S. and Canada.
SOCAP is committed to promoting customer care
and engagement as competitive advantages. SOCAP
members are identified in the automotive and corporate
directories by the SOCAP logo (see Key at right).
For more information, contact SOCAP (p.146).

**KEY:**

| | |
|---|---|
| ⊠ | Email |
| ς | SOCAP International Member |
| ◆ | Provided financial support for the publication of the *2013 Consumer Action Handbook*. |
| **TTY** | Numbers for people with hearing disabilities. For more information see the box on p. 59. |

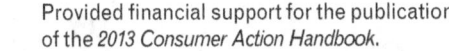

## Contacting Your Automotive Manufacturer

If you have a problem with a car purchased from a local dealer, first try to work it out with the dealer. If the problem is not resolved, contact the manufacturer's regional or national office. Ask for the Consumer Affairs Office.

If you are still unsuccessful, consider contacting the automotive dispute resolution resources listed at the end of this section. The method used to resolve your dispute may be mediation, arbitration, or conciliation. Decisions of arbitrators are usually binding and must be accepted by both the customer and the business. Ask for a copy of the rules of the program before you file your case. See page 55 for an overview of dispute resolution programs.

A local or state consumer agency (p. 112) could also be a useful resource in resolving problems with your vehicle. If you have a new vehicle, be sure to ask whether you have any protection under a state "lemon" law (p. 10).

**Acura**
1919 Torrance Blvd.
Mail Stop 500-2N7E
Torrance, CA 90501-2746
Toll free: 1-800-382-2238
**www.acura.com**

**American Honda Motor Company, Inc.** ↺
1919 Torrance Blvd.
Mail Stop 500-2N-7A
Torrance, CA 90501-2746
Toll free: 1-800-999-1009
**www.honda.com**

**American Suzuki Motor Corporation**
PO Box 1100
Brea, CA 92822-1100
714-572-1490 (Motorcycle/ATV/Marine)
Toll free: 1-800-934-0934 (Automotive)
**www.suzuki.com**

**Audi of America, Inc.**
3800 W. Hamlin Rd.
Auburns Hills, MI 48326
Toll free: 1-800-822-2834
✉: **auditalk@audi.com**
**www.audiusa.com**

**BMW of North America, LLC** ↺
300 Chestnut Ridge Rd.
Woodcliff Lake, NJ 07677-7731
201-307-4000
Toll free: 1-800-831-1117
✉: **customerrelations@bmwusa. com**
**www.bmwusa.com**

**Buick**
PO Box 33136
Detroit, MI 48232-5136
Toll free: 1-800-521-7300
TTY: 1-800-735-2900
**www.buick.com**

**Cadillac**
PO Box 33169
Detroit, MI 48232-5169
Toll free: 1-800-458-8006
TTY: 1-800-255-2683
**www.cadillac.com**

**Chevrolet**
PO Box 33170
Detroit, MI 48232-5170
Toll free: 1-800-222-1020
TTY: 1-800-735-2988
**www.chevrolet.com**

**Chrysler Group, LLC** ↺
PO Box 21-8004
Auburn Hills, MI 48321-8004
Toll free: 1-800-247-9753
**www.chrysler.com**

**Dodge**
PO Box 21-8007
Auburn Hills, MI 48321-8007
Toll free: 1-800-423-6343
**www.dodge.com**

**Ferrari North America, Inc.**
250 Sylvan Ave.
Englewood Cliffs, NJ 07632
201-816-2600
Toll free: 1-866-551-2828
✉: **support@ferrarisupport.com**
**www.ferrari.com**

**Ford Motor Company** ↺
PO Box 6248
Dearborn, MI 48126
Toll free: 1-800-392-3673
TTY: 1-800-232-5952
**www.ford.com**

**GMC** ↺
PO Box 33172
Detroit, MI 48232-5172
Toll free: 1-800-462-8782
TTY: 1-800-735-2988
**www.gmc.com**

**Harley-Davidson**
3700 W. Juneau Ave.
Milwaukee, WI 53208
Toll free: 1-800-258-2464
**www.harley-davidson.com**

**Hyundai Motor America** ↺
PO Box 20850
Fountain Valley, CA 92728-0850
714-965-3000
Toll free: 1-800-633-5151
✉: **consumeraffairs@hmausa. com**
**www.hyundaiusa.com**

**Infiniti**
See: Nissan North America, Inc.
Toll free: 1-800-662-6200
**www.infiniti.com**

**Isuzu Motors America, Inc.**
1400 S. Douglass Rd., Suite 100
Anaheim, CA 92806
714-935-9300
Toll free: 1-800-255-6727
**www.isuzu.com**

**Jaguar Cars** ↺
Customer Relationship Center
555 MacArthur Blvd.
Mahwah, NJ 07430-2327
Toll free: 1-855-524-8278
**www.jaguarusa.com**

**Jeep**
See: Chrysler Group, LLC
Toll free: 1-877-426-5337
**www.jeep.com/en**

**Kia Motors America, Inc.** ↺
PO Box 52410
Irvine, CA 92619-2410
Toll free: 1-800-333-4542
**www.kia.com**

**Land Rover** ↺
Customer Relationship Center
555 MacArthur Blvd.
Mahwah, NJ 07430
Toll free: 1-800-637-6837
**www.landroverusa.com**

**Lexus**
PO Box 2991
Mail Drop L201
Torrance, CA 90509-2991
Toll free: 1-800-255-3987

**Lincoln**
See: Ford Motor Company
Toll free: 1-800-521-4140
**www.lincoln.com**

◆ Provided financial support for the publication of the Consumer Action Handbook.

**Mazda North American Operations**
PO Box 19734
Irvine, CA 92623-9734
Toll free: 1-800-222-5500
www.mazdausa.com

**Mercedes Benz, USA, LLC**
Three Mercedes Dr.
Montvale, NJ 07645
Toll free: 1-800-367-6372
www.mbusa.com

**Mercury**
PO Box 6128
Dearborn, MI 48121
Toll free: 1-800-521-4140
www.mercuryvehicles.com

**Mitsubishi Motors North America, Inc.**
PO Box 6400
Cypress, CA 90630-998
Toll free: 1-888-648-7820
www.mitsubishicars.com

**Nissan North America, Inc.**
PO Box 685003
Franklin, TN 37068-5003
Toll free: 1-800-647-7261
www.nissanusa.com

**Oldsmobile**
PO Box 33171
Detroit, MI 48232-5171
Toll free: 1-800-442-6537
TTY: 1-800-833-9935
✉: cac@oldsmobile.com
www.oldsmobile.com

**Peugeot Motors of America, Inc.**
Overlook at Great Notch
150 Clove Rd.
Little Falls, NJ 07424
973-812-4444
✉: customerservice@peugeotusa.net
www.peugeot.com

**Pontiac**
See: GMC
Toll free: 1-800-762-2737
TTY: 1-800-833-9935
www.pontiac.com

**Porsche Cars North America, Inc.**
Owner Relations
980 Hammond Dr., Suite 1000
Atlanta, GA 30328
Toll free: 1-800-767-7243
www.porsche.com/usa

**Saab Automobile USA**
Toll free: 1-800-955-9007
www.saabusa.com

**Saturn**
Customer Service Center
PO Box 33173
Detroit, MI 48232-5173
Toll free: 1-800-553-6000
✉: cac@saturn.com
www.saturn.com

**Smart USA**
See: Mercedes Benz, USA, LLC
Toll free: 1-800-762-7887
www.smartusa.com

**Subaru of America, Inc.**
Subaru Plaza
PO Box 6000
Cherry Hill, NJ 08034-6000
Toll free: 1-800-782-2783
www.subaru.com

**Toyota Motor Sales U.S.A., Inc.**
Department WC 11
19001 S. Western Ave.
Torrance, CA 90501
310-468-4000
Toll free: 1-800-331-4331
www.toyota.com

**Volkswagen Group of America, Inc.**
3800 Hamlin Rd.
Auburn Hills, MI 48326
Toll free: 1-800-822-8987
www.vw.com

**Volvo Cars of North America**
One Volvo Dr.
PO Box 914
Rockleigh, NJ 07647
Toll free: 1-800-458-1552
www.volvocars.com

## Automotive Dispute Resolution Programs

### BBB AUTO LINE

Council of Better Business Bureaus, Inc.
3033 Wilson Blvd., Suite 600
Arlington, VA 22201-3863
703-276-0100
Toll free: 1-800-955-5100
✉: info@cbbb.bbb.org
**www.bbb.org**
Third-party dispute resolution program for automobile manufacturers.

### Consumer Financial Protection Bureau

PO Box 4503
Iowa City, IA 52244
Toll free: 1-855-411-2372
TTY: 1-855-729-2372
✉: info@consumerfinance.gov
**www.consumerfinance.gov**
The CFPB supervises and accepts complaints related to your vehicle loans and financing problems. Contact this agency if you encountered problems while shopping for or managing your vehicle loan.

### DOT Auto Safety Hotline

1200 New Jersey Ave., SE., West Bldg.
Washington, DC 20590
Toll free: 1-888-327-4236
TTY: 1-800-424-9153
**www.nhtsa.gov/Contact**
Consumers can contact the DOT Auto Safety Hotline to report safety defects in vehicles, tires, and child safety seats. Information is available about air bags, child safety seats, seat belts, and general highway safety. Consumers who experience a safety defect in their vehicle are encouraged to report the defect to the Hotline in addition to the dealer or manufacturer.

### Motorist Assurance Program (MAP)

201 Park Washington Ct.
Falls Church, VA 22046
703-538-3557
✉: map@motorist.org
**www.motorist.org**
MAP accredits those auto repair shops that apply and follow industry developed standards for inspecting vehicles as well as meet other requirements. MAP handles inquiries and disputes between accredited shops and customers. MAP also offers information to consumers about how to locate a repair shop, talk to a technician, and work successfully with auto repair shops.

### National Center for Dispute Settlement (NCDS)

43230 Garfield Rd., Suite 130
Clinton Township, MI 48038
586-226-2470
✉: info@ncdsusa.org
**www.ncdsusa.org**
NCDS is a neutral administrator of the dispute resolution process. NCDS facilitates the process under their rules, but is not the decision maker, rather the decision is made by an independent arbitrator.

### Contacting Automotive Dispute Resolution Programs

An automotive dispute resolution program is another resource to consult if you need to solve a problem with your car's manufacturer or dealership. If you have been unable to reach an agreement with your manufacturer, consider contacting the automotive dispute resolution resources listed here. The method used to resolve your dispute may be mediation, arbitration, or conciliation. Decisions of arbitrators are usually binding and must be accepted by both the customer and the business. Ask for a copy of the rules of the program before you file your case.

Read the contract that you signed when you purchased your car. Manufacturers and dealers may have included a clause that requires you to agree to mandatory arbitration, waiving your right to sue or settle a disagreement in a court of law.

## Council

**Arlington**
3033 Wilson Blvd., Suite 600
Arlington, VA 22201
703-276-0100

## Alabama

**Birmingham**
1210 S. 20th St.
Birmingham, AL 35205
205-558-2222

**Cullman**
202 1st Ave., SE, Suite I
Cullman, AL 35055
256-775-2917

**Dothan**
1971 S. Brannon Stand Rd., Suite 1
Dothan, AL 36305
334-794-0492

**Huntsville**
210A Exchange Pl.
Huntsville, AL 35806
256-533-1640

**Mobile**
960 S. Schillinger Rd., Suite I
Mobile, AL 36695
251-433-5494

**Montgomery**
4750 Woodmere Blvd., Suite D
Montgomery, AL 36107
334-273-5530

## Alaska

**Anchorage**
341 W. Tudor Rd., Suite 209
Anchorage, AK 99503
907-562-0704

## Arizona

**Phoenix**
4428 N. 12th St.
Phoenix, AZ 85014-4585
602-264-1721

**Prescott**
1569 W. Gurley St.
Prescott, AZ 86305
928-772-3410

**Tucson**
5151 E. Broadway Blvd., Suite 100
Tucson, AZ 85711
520-888-5353

### Contacting Your Local Better Business Bureau

Better Business Bureaus (BBBs) are non-profit organizations that encourage honest advertising and selling practices, and are supported primarily by local businesses. BBBs offer a variety of consumer services, including consumer education materials; business reports, particularly unanswered or unsettled complaints or other problems; mediation and arbitration services; and information about charities and other organizations that are seeking public donations. They also provide ratings (A, B, C, D, or F) of local companies to express the BBB's confidence that the company operates in a trustworthy manner and demonstrates a willingness to resolve customer concerns.

Complaints should be submitted in writing so that an accurate record exists of the dispute. The BBB will then present the complaint to the company involved. If the complaint is not resolved, the BBB may offer an alternative dispute settlement process. BBBs do not judge or rate individual products or brands, handle employer/employee wage disputes, or give legal advice.

If you need help with a consumer question or complaint, call your local BBB or visit its website.

BBB*OnLine* (www.bbb.org/online) provides Internet users an easy way to verify the legitimacy of online businesses. Companies carrying the BBB*OnLine* seal have been checked out by the BBB and agree to resolve customer concerns.

The Council of Better Business Bureaus, the umbrella organization for the BBBs, can assist with complaints about the truthfulness and accuracy of national advertising claims, including children's advertising; provide reports on national soliciting charities; and help to settle disputes with automobile manufacturers through the BBB Auto Line program (p. 66).

## Arkansas

**Little Rock**
12521 Kanis Rd.
Little Rock, AR 72211
501-664-7274

## California

**Bakersfield**
1601 H St., Suite 101
Bakersfield, CA 93301
661-322-2074

**Culver City**
6125 Washington Blvd., 3rd Floor
Culver City, CA 90232
310-945-3166

**Fresno**
4201 W. Shaw Ave., Suite 107
Fresno, CA 93722
559-222-8111

**Long Beach**
3363 Linden Ave., Suite A
Long Beach, CA 90807
562-216-9242

**Los Angeles**
315 N. La Cadena Dr.
Colton, CA 92324
909-825-7280

**Oakland**
1000 Broadway, Suite 625
Oakland, CA 94607
510-844-2000

**Placentia**
550 W. Orangethorpe Ave.
Placentia, CA 92870
714-985-8922

**Sacramento**
3075 Beacon Blvd.
West Sacramento, CA 95691
916-443-6843

**San Diego**
5050 Murphy Canyon Rd., Suite 110
San Diego, CA 92123
858-496-2131

**San Jose**
1112 S. Bascom Ave.
San Jose, CA 95128
408-278-7400

**Santa Barbara**
PO Box 129
Santa Barbara, CA 93101
805-963-8657

**Stockton**
11 S. San Joaquin St., 8th Floor
Stockton, CA 95202
209-948-4880

## Colorado

**Colorado Springs**
25 N. Wahsatch Ave.
Colorado Springs, CO 80903
719-636-1155

**Denver**
1020 Cherokee St.
Denver, CO 80204-4039
303-758-2100

**Fort Collins**
8020 S. County Rd. 5, #100
Fort Collins, CO 80528
970-484-1348

## Connecticut

**Wallingford**
94 S. Turnpike Rd.
Wallingford, CT 06492-4322
203-269-2700

## Delaware

**Wilmington**
60 Reads Way
New Castle, DE 19720
302-221-5255

## District Of Columbia

**Washington**
1411 K St., NW, Suite 1000
Washington, DC 20005-3404
202-393-8000

## Florida

**Clearwater**
2655 McCormick Dr.
Clearwater, FL 33759
727-535-5522

**Jacksonville**
4417 Beach Blvd., Suite 202
Jacksonville, FL 32207
904-721-2288

**Miami**
14750 N.W. 77 Ct., Suite 317
Miami Lakes, FL 33016
305-827-5363

**Orlando**
1600 S. Grant St.
Longwood, FL 32750
407-621-3300

**Pensacola**
912 E. Gadsden St.
Pensacola, FL 32501
850-429-0002

**Stuart**
101 E. Ocean Blvd., Suite 202
Stuart, FL 34994
772-223-1492

**West Palm Beach**
4411 Beacon Circle, Suite 4
West Palm Beach, FL 33407
561-842-1918

## Georgia

**Atlanta**
503 Oak Pl., Suite 590
Atlanta, GA 30349
404-766-0875

**Augusta**
1227 Augusta West Pkwy., Suite 15
Augusta, GA 30909
706-210-7676

**Columbus**
500 12th St.
Columbus, GA 31901
706-324-0712

**Macon**
277 Martin Luther King, Jr. Blvd.
Suite 102
Macon, GA 31201-3495
478-742-7999

**Savannah**
6555 Abercorn St., Suite 120
Savannah, GA 31405-5817
912-354-7521

## Hawaii

**Honolulu**
1132 Bishop St., Suite 615
Honolulu, HI 96813
808-536-6956

## Idaho

**Boise**
1200 N. Curtis Rd.
Boise, ID 83706
208-342-4649

**Idaho Falls**
453 River Pkwy.
Idaho Falls, ID 83402
208-523-9754

## Illinois

**Chicago**
330 N. Wabash Ave., Suite 3120
Chicago, IL 60611-7621
312-832-0500

**Peoria**
112 Harrison St.
Peoria, IL 61602
309-688-3741

**Rockford**
401 W. State St., Suite 500
Rockford, IL 61101
815-963-2222

## Indiana

**Evansville**
3101 N. Green River Rd., Suite 410
Evansville, IN 47715
812-473-0202

**Fort Wayne**
4011 Parnell Ave.
Fort Wayne, IN 46805
260-423-4433

**Indianapolis**
151 N. Delaware St., Suite 2020
Indianapolis, IN 46204-2599
317-488-2222

**Merriville**
7863 Broadway, Suite 124
Merriville, IN 46410
219-227-8400

**Osceola**
10775 McKinley Hwy., Suite B
Osceola, IN 46561
574-675-9315

## Iowa

**Bettendorf**
2435 Kimberly Rd., Suite 260 N
Bettendorf, IA 52722-4100
563-355-6344

**Des Moines**
505 5th Ave., Suite 950
Des Moines, IA 50309
515-243-8137

## Kansas

**Wichita**
345 N. Riverview St., Suite 720
Wichita, KS 67203
316-263-3146

## Kentucky

**Lexington**
1390 Olivia Ln., Suite 100
Lexington, KY 40511
859-259-1008

**Louisville**
844 S. 4th St.
Louisville, KY 40203
502-583-6546

## Louisiana

**Alexandria**
5220-C Rue Verdun
Alexandria, LA 71303
318-473-4494

**Baton Rouge**
748 Main St.
Baton Rouge, LA 70802
225-346-5222

**Houma**
801 Barrow St., Suite 400
Houma, LA 70360
985-868-3456

**Lafayette**
4007 W. Congress St., Suite B
Lafayette, LA 70506
337-981-3497

**Lake Charles**
2309 E. Prien Lake Rd.
Lake Charles, LA 70601
337-478-6253

**Monroe**
1900 N. 18th St., Suite 411
Monroe, LA 71201
318-387-4600

**New Orleans**
710 Baronne St., Suite C
New Orleans, LA 70113
504-581-6222

**Shreveport**
2006 E. 70th St.
Shreveport, LA 71105
318-797-1337

## Maryland

**Baltimore**
502 S. Sharp St., Suite 1200
Baltimore, MD 21201
410-347-3990

## Massachusetts

**Marlborough**
290 Donald Lynch Blvd., Suite 102
Marlborough, MA 01752
508-652-4800

**Worcester**
340 Main St., Suite 802
Worcester, MA 01608
508-755-2548

## Michigan

**Detroit**
26777 Central Park Blvd., Suite 100
Southfield, MI 48076-4163
248-223-9400

**Grand Rapids**
40 Pearl St., NW, Suite 354
Grand Rapids, MI 49503
616-774-8236

## Minnesota

**Minneapolis/ St. Paul**
220 S. River Ridge Circle
Burnsville, MN 55337
651-699-1111

## Mississippi

**Jackson**
505 Avalon Way, Suite B
Jackson, MS 39047
601-398-1700

## Missouri

**Kansas City**
8080 Ward Pkwy., Suite 401
Kansas City, MO 64114
816-421-7800

**Springfield**
430 S. Glenstone Ave., Suite A
Springfield, MO 65802
417-862-4222

**St. Louis**
211 N. Broadway, Suite 2060
St. Louis, MO 63102
314-645-3300

## Nebraska

**Lincoln**
3633 O St., Suite 1
Lincoln, NE 68510
402-436-2345

**Omaha**
11811 P St.
Omaha, NE 68137
402-391-7612

## Nevada

**Las Vegas**
6040 S. Jones Blvd.
Las Vegas, NV 89118
702-320-4500

**Reno**
4834 Sparks Blvd., Suite 102
Sparks, NV 89436
775-322-0657

## New Hampshire

**Concord**
48 Pleasant St.
Concord, NH 03301
603-224-1991

## New Jersey

**Trenton**
1700 Whitehorse-Hamilton Square Rd.
Suite D-5
Trenton, NJ 08690-3596
609-588-0808

## New Mexico

**Albuquerque**
2625 Pennsylvania St., NE, Suite 2050
Albuquerque, NM 87110-3658
505-346-0110

**Farmington**
308 N. Locke Ave.
Farmington, NM 87401-5855
505-326-6501

## New York

**Buffalo**
100 Bryant Woods S
Amherst, NY 14228
716-881-5222

**Farmingdale**
399 Conklin St., Suite 300
Farmingdale, NY 11735
212-533-6200

**New York**
30 E. 33rd St., 12th Floor
New York, NY 10016
212-533-6200

**Tarrytown**
150 White Plains Rd., Suite 107
Tarrytown, NY 10591-5521
212-533-6200

## North Carolina

**Asheville**
112 Executive Park
Asheville, NC 28801
828-253-2392

**Charlotte**
13860 Ballantyne Corporate Place
Suite 225
Charlotte, NC 28277
704-927-8611

**Greensboro**
3608 W. Friendly Ave.
Suite 212
Greensboro, NC 27410-4895
336-852-4240

**Raleigh**
5540 Munford Rd., Suite 130
Raleigh, NC 27612-2655
919-277-4222

**Winston-Salem**
500 W. 5th St., Suite 202
Winston-Salem, NC 27101-2728
336-725-8348

## Ohio

**Akron**
222 W. Market St.
Akron, OH 44303
330-253-4590

**Canton**
1434 Cleveland Ave., NW
Canton, OH 44703
330-454-9401

**Cincinnati**
Seven W. 7th St., Suite 1600
Cincinnati, OH 45202
513-421-3015

**Cleveland**
2800 Euclid Ave., 4th Floor
Cleveland, OH 44115
216-241-7678

**Columbus**
1169 Dublin Rd.
Columbus, OH 43215-1005
614-486-6336

**Dayton**
15 W. 4th St., Suite 300
Dayton, OH 45402-1830
937-222-5825

**Lima**
219 N. McDonel St.
Lima, OH 45801
419-223-7010

**Toledo**
Integrity Place
7668 King's Pointe Rd.
Toledo, OH 43617
419-531-3116

**Youngstown**
International Towers
25 Market St.
Youngstown, OH 44503
330-744-3111

## Oklahoma

**Oklahoma City**
17 S. Dewey St.
Oklahoma City, OK 73102-2400
405-239-6081

**Tulsa**
1722 S. Carson Ave., Suite 3200
Tulsa, OK 74119
918-492-1266

## Oregon

**Lake Oswego**
4004 S.W. Kruse Way Place, Suite 375
Lake Oswego, OR 97035
503-212-3022

## Pennsylvania

**Bethlehem**
50 W. North St.
Bethlehem, PA 18018-3907
610-866-8780

**Harrisburg**
1337 N. Front St.
Harrisburg, PA 17102
717-364-3250

**Philadelphia**
1880 John F. Kennedy Blvd., Suite 1330
Philadelphia, PA 19103
215-985-9313

**Pittsburgh**
400 Holiday Dr., Suite 220
Pittsburgh, PA 15220
412-456-2700

**Scranton/Wilkes-Barre**
4099 Birney Ave.
Moosic, PA 18507
570-342-5100

## Puerto Rico

**San Juan**
530 Avenida De La Constitucion, #206
San Juan, PR 00901
787-289-8710

## South Carolina

**Columbia**
2442 Devine St.
Columbia, SC 29205
803-254-2525

**Conway**
1121 3rd Ave.
Conway, SC 29526
843-488-2227

**Greenville**
408 N. Church St., Suite C
Greenville, SC 29601-2164
864-242-5052

## South Dakota

**Sioux Falls**
300 N. Phillips Ave., #100
Sioux Falls, SD 57104
605-271-2066

## Tennessee

**Chattanooga**
1010 Market St., Suite 200
Chattanooga, TN 37402
423-266-6144

**Clarksville**
214 Main St.
Clarksville, TN 37040
931-503-2222

**Columbia**
502 N. Garden St., Suite 201
Columbia, TN 38401
931-388-9222

**Cookeville**
18 N. Jefferson St.
Cookeville, TN 38501
931-520-0008

**Franklin**
367 Riverside Dr., Suite 110
Franklin, TN 37064
615-242-4222

**Knoxville**
255 N. Peters Rd., Suite A
Knoxville, TN 37923
865-692-1600

**Memphis**
3693 Tyndale Dr.
Memphis, TN 38125
901-759-1300

**Murfreesboro**
530 Uptown Square
Murfreesboro, TN 37129
615-242-4222

**Nashville**
201 4th Ave. N., Suite 100
Nashville, TN 37219
615-242-4222

## Texas

**Abilene**
3300 S. 14th St., Suite 307
Abilene, TX 79605-5052
325-691-1533

**Amarillo**
720 S. Tyler St., Suite B112
Amarillo, TX 79101
806-379-6222

**Austin**
1005 La Posada Dr.
Austin, TX 78752
512-445-2911

**Beaumont**
550 Fannin St., Suite 100
Beaumont, TX 77701-2011
409-835-5348

**College Station**
418 Tarrow St.
College Station, TX 77840-1822
979-260-2222

**Corpus Christi**
719 S. Shoreline, Suite 304
Corpus Christi, TX 78401
361-852-4949

**Dallas**
1601 Elm St., Suite 3838
Dallas, TX 75201-3093
214-220-2000

**El Paso**
720 Arizona Ave.
El Paso, TX 79902
915-577-0191

**Fort Worth**
101 Summit Ave., Suite 707
Fort Worth, TX 76102-5978
817-332-7585

**Harker Heights**
445 E. Central Texas Expy., Suite 1
Harker Heights, TX 76548
254-699-0694

**Houston**
1333 W. Loop South, Suite 1200
Houston, TX 77027
713-868-9500

**Longview**
2401 Judson Rd., #102
Longview, TX 75605
903-758-3222

**Lubbock**
3333 66th St.
Lubbock, TX 79413-5711
806-763-0459

**Midland**
10100 Liberator Ln.
Midland, TX 79711
432-563-1880

**San Angelo**
3134 Executive Dr., Suite A
San Angelo, TX 76904
325-949-2989

**San Antonio**
425 Soledad St., Suite 500
San Antonio, TX 78205
210-828-9441

**Tyler**
3600 Old Bullard Rd.
Building 1, Suite 101
Tyler, TX 75701
903-581-5704

**Weslaco**
502 E. Expressway 83, Suite C
Weslaco, TX 78596
956-968-3678

**Wichita Falls**
4245 Kemp Blvd., Suite 1012
Wichita Falls, TX 76308
940-691-1172

## Utah

**Salt Lake City**
5673 S. Redwood Rd., Suite 22
Salt Lake City, UT 84123-5322
801-892-6009

## Virginia

**Norfolk**
586 Virginian Dr.
Norfolk, VA 23505
757-531-1300

**Richmond**
720 Moorefield Park Dr., Suite 300
Richmond, VA 23236
804-648-0016

**Roanoke**
5115 Bernard Dr., Suite 202
Roanoke, VA 24018
540-342-3455

## Washington

**DuPont**
1000 Station Dr., Suite 222
DuPont, WA 98327
206-431-2222

**Spokane**
152 S. Jefferson St., Suite 200
Spokane, WA 99201
509-455-4200

## West Virginia

**Charleston**
1018 Kanawha Blvd. E, Suite 301
Charleston, WV 25301
304-345-7502

## Wisconsin

**Milwaukee**
10101 W. Greenfield Ave., Suite 125
West Allis, WI 53214
414-847-6000

## Contacting Corporate Consumer Affairs Departments

The following directory lists the addresses and phone numbers for hundreds of corporations. Many companies have a consumer affairs department that handles consumer questions and concerns. Consumer affairs offices are set up within companies because they want to hear from you. If you do not find the company you are looking for, try checking your public libraries for the following resources:

- *The Standard & Poor's Register of Corporations, Directors and Executives*
- *Trade Names Directory*
- *Standard Directory of Advertisers*
- *Dun & Bradstreet Directory*

To identify the name of a company that manufactures a specific product, check the product label and other documents given to you at the time of your purchase. *The Thomas Register of American Manufacturers*, another resource available at many public libraries, might also be helpful. It lists the manufacturers of thousands of products.

If you have a complaint about an item or service, it is usually best to go back to the seller BEFORE you contact the companies in this directory. Follow up with a letter, phone call, or e-mail message to the consumer affairs department of the company to let it know about your complaint and whether the seller was able to resolve your problem. You may express your complaint on a company's social media profile to get quick attention to your problem.

---

## A

**AAMCO Transmissions, Inc.**
Consumer Affairs
201 Gibraltar Rd.
Horsham, PA 19044
Toll free: 1-800-523-0401
www.aamco.com

**Abbott Nutrition Products Division**
Consumer Relations
625 Cleveland Ave.
Columbus, OH 43215-1754
Toll free: 1-800-227-5767
www.abbottnutrition.com

**ABC, Inc.**
Audience Relations Dept.
500 S. Buena Vista St.
Burbank, CA 91521-4551
818-460-7477
www.abc.com

**Abercrombie & Fitch**
Customer Service
200 Abercrombie Way
New Albany, OH 43054
614-219-5380
Toll free: 1-866-681-3115
✉: abercrombie@abercrombie.com
www.abercrombie.com

**Accor North America**
PO Box 326
Worthington, OH 43085
Toll free: 1-800-557-3435
www.accor-na.com

**Adidas USA**
Customer Service
5055 N. Greeley Ave.
Portland, OR 97217
Toll free: 1-800-448-1796
✉: consumer.relations@adidas.com
www.adidas.com

**Adobe Systems, Inc.**
345 Park Ave.
San Jose, CA 95110-2704
408-536-6000
Toll free: 1-800-833-6687 (Customer and Technical Support)
www.adobe.com

**Aetna, Inc.**
151 Farmington Ave.
Hartford, CT 06156
860-273-0123
www.aetna.com

**Aflac**
1932 Wynnton Rd.
Columbus, GA 31999
Toll free: 1-800-992-3522
www.aflac.com

**AirTran Airways**
Customer Relations
1800 Phoenix Blvd., Suite 104
Atlanta, GA 30349
Toll free: 1-866-247-2428
Toll free: 1-800-965-2107 ext. 8900 (Baggage)
www.airtran.com

**Alamo Rent A Car**
Customer Care
8420 St. John Industrial Dr.
Saint Louis, MO 63114
Toll free: 1-800-445-5664
TTY: 1-800-522-9292
www.alamo.com

**Alaska Airlines**
Customer Care
PO Box 24948-SEAGT
Seattle, WA 98124-0948
Toll free: 1-800-654-5669
Toll free: 1-877-815-8253 (Baggage)
TTY: 1-800-682-2221
www.alaskaair.com

**Alberto Culver Company**
See: Unilever
www.alberto.com

**Albertsons, Inc.**
Customer Service
157 S. Howard St.
Spokane, WA 99201
208-395-6200
Toll free: 1-877-932-7948 (Customer Service)
www.albertsons.com

**Alcon Laboratories, Inc.**
Technical Consumer Affairs
6201 South Fwy.
Fort Worth, TX 76134
Toll free: 1-800-862-5266
✉: consumeraffairs.ft.worth@alconlabs.com
www.alconlabs.com

**Allied Van Lines, Inc.**
Customer Service
700 Oakmont Ln.
Westmont, IL 60559
Toll free: 1-800-470-2851
✉: custsvc@alliedvan.com
www.allied.com

**Allstate Insurance Company**
PO Box 12055
1819 Electric Rd., SW
Roanoke, IL 24018
847-402-5000
Toll free: 1-800-255-7828 (Claims)
www.allstate.com

**Amana Appliances**
Customer Service
553 Benson Rd.
Benton Harbor, MI 49022
Toll free: 1-866-616-2664
www.amana.com

**Amazon.com, Inc.**
Customer Service
PO Box 81226
Seattle, WA 98108-1226
Toll free: 1-866-216-1072
www.amazon.com

**AMC Entertainment, Inc.**
PO Box 725489
Atlanta, GA 31139-9923
www.amctheatres.com

**America Online, Inc.**
Member Services
22000 AOL Way
Dulles, VA 20166
Toll free: 1-800-827-6364
TTY: 1-800-759-3323
www.aol.com

**American Airlines, Inc.**
Customer Relations
PO Box 619612 Mail Drop 2400
Dallas/Fort Worth Airport, TX
75261-9612
817-967-2000
Toll free: 1-800-535-5225 (Baggage)
www.aa.com

**American Automobile Association (AAA)**
Member Relations
1000 AAA Dr., Mail Space 61
Heathrow, FL 32746
407-444-8402
Toll free: 1-866-636-2377
www.aaa.com

**American Eagle Outfitters**
Customer Service
150 Thorn Hill Dr.
Warrendale, PA 15086
Toll free: 1-888-232-4535
✉: custserv@ae.com
www.ae.com

**American Express Company** ↻ ♦
Customer Service
PO Box 981540
El Paso, TX 79998-1540
Toll free: 1-800-528-4800
Toll free: 1-877-297-4438 (Gift Cards)
TTY: 1-800-221-9950
www.americanexpress.com

**American Girl**
PO Box 620497
Middleton, WI 53562-0497
Toll free: 1-800-360-1861
✉: im_cs@americangirl.com
www.americangirl.com

**American Greetings Corporation**
Consumer Relations
One American Rd.
Cleveland, OH 44144
Toll free: 1-800-777-4891
✉: consumer.relations@
amgreetings.com
www.americangreetings.com

**American Tourister**
See: Samsonite Corporation
Toll free: 1-800-765-2247
Toll free: 1-800-262-8282 (Warranty and Repair)
✉: Questions@
AmericanTourister.com
www.americantourister.com

**Amtrak**
Customer Relations
60 Massachusetts Ave., NE
Washington, DC 20002
Toll free: 1-800-872-7245
TTY: 1-800-523-6590
www.amtrak.com

**Amway Corporation**
Customer Service - North American Business Region
7575 Fulton St., E
Ada, MI 49355-0001
Toll free: 1-800-253-6500
Toll free: 1-800-529-8772
(Personalized Health)
TTY: 1-800-548-3878
www.amway.com

**Andersen Windows, Inc.** ↻
Window Care Call Center
100 4th Ave., N
Bayport, MN 55003-1096
Toll free: 1-888-888-7020 (Service)
www.andersenwindows.com

**Angie's List**
1030 E. Washington St.
Indianapolis, IN 46202
Toll free: 1-888-888-5478
www.angieslist.com

**Anheuser-Busch, Inc.** ↻
Customer Relationship Group
One Busch Pl.
St. Louis, MO 63118
Toll free: 1-800-342-5283
www.anheuser-busch.com

**Anthem**
2015 Staples Mills Rd.
Richmond, VA 23230
804-354-7000
www.anthem.com

**Apple Computer, Inc.**
One Infinite Loop
Cupertino, CA 95014
408-996-1010
Toll free: 1-800-676-2775
(Customer Service)
Toll free: 1-800-275-2273
(Technical Support)
TTY: 1-877-204-3930
www.apple.com

**Applebee's**
8140 Ward Pkwy.
Kansas City, MO 64114
Toll free: 1-888-592-7753
www.applebees.com

**Arby's Restaurant Group, Inc.**
1155 Perimeter Center W, 12th Floor
Atlanta, GA 30338
678-514-4100
✉: customerfeedback@arbys.com
www.arbys.com

**Atlas World Group, Inc.**
Customer Service
1212 Saint George Rd.
Evansville, IN 47711-2364
Toll free: 1-800-638-9797
www.atlasvanlines.com

**AT&T, Inc.**
Customer Relations
175 E. Houston St.
San Antonio, TX 78205
210-821-4105
Toll free: 1-800-464-7928
(Wireless Customer Service)
www.att.com

**Avis Rent-A-Car System**
Toll free: 1-800-352-7900
TTY: 1-800-331-2323
✉: custserv@avis.com
www.avis.com

**Avon Products, Inc.**
Customer Service
1345 Avenue of the Americas
New York, NY 10105
212-282-7000
Toll free: 1-800-367-2866
Toll free: 1-800-445-2866
(Product Information)
www.avon.com

## B

**Bacardi USA, Inc.** ⟲
Consumer Affairs
2701 S. Le Jeune Rd.
Coral Gables, FL 33134
Toll free: 1-800-222-2734
**www.bacardi.com**

**Bally Total Fitness Corporation**
Member Services
PO Box 96241
Washington, DC 20090-6241
Toll free: 1-866-402-2559
**www.ballyfitness.com**

**Banana Republic**
Customer Services
5900 N. Meadows Dr.
Grove City, OH 43123
Toll free: 1-888-277-8953
TTY: 1-888-906-1345
✉: custserv@bananarepublic.com
**www.bananarepublic.com**

**Bank of America Corporation**
PO Box 25118
Tampa, FL 33622-5118
Toll free: 1-800-432-1000
TTY: 1-800-288-4408
**www.bankofamerica.com**

**Barnes & Noble**
Toll free: 1-800-843-2665
**www.bn.com**

**Baskin-Robbins**
Toll free: 1-800-859-5339
✉: support@baskinrobbins.com
**www.baskinrobbins.com**

**Bassett Furniture**
3525 Fairystone Park Hwy.
PO Box 626
Bassett, VA 24055
Toll free: 1-877-308-7485
(Baby Furniture)
Toll free: 1-800-525-7070
✉: juvenile@bassettfurniture.com
**www.bassettfurniture.com**

**Bayer HealthCare, LLC** ⟲
Consumer Care
36 Columbia Rd.
PO Box 1910
Morristown, NJ 07962-1910
Toll free: 1-800-331-4536
**www.bayercare.com**

**Becton, Dickinson and Company**
Customer Service
One Becton Dr., Mail Code 376
Franklin Lakes, NJ 07417
201-847-6800
Toll free: 1-888-237-2762
**www.bd.com**

**Beech-Nut Nutrition Corporation**
Consumer Affairs
100 Hero Dr.
Amsterdam, NY 12010
314-436-7667
Toll free: 1-800-233-2468
✉: beech-nut@beech-nut.com
**www.beechnut.com**

**Beiersdorf, Inc.** ⟲
Consumer Relations
45 Danbury Rd.
Wilton, CT 06897
Toll free: 1-800-227-4703
**www.beiersdorf.us**

**Bellisio Foods, Inc.**
Consumer Affairs
PO Box 16630
Duluth, MN 55816
✉: info@bellisiofoods.com
**www.bellisiofoods.com**

**Ben & Jerrys Homemade, Inc.** ⟲
Consumer Services
30 Community Dr.
South Burlington, VT 05403-6828
802-846-1500
**www.benjerry.com**

**Benihana, Inc.**
Customer Relations
8750 N.W. 36th St., Suite 300
Miami, FL 33178
Toll free: 1-800-327-3369
✉: CustomerService@benihana.com
**www.benihana.com**

**Best Buy Company, Inc.** ⟲
Customer Care
PO Box 9312
Minneapolis, MN 55440-9312
Toll free: 1-888-237-8289
**www.bestbuy.com**

**Best Western International, Inc.**
Customer Service
PO Box 10203
Phoenix, AZ 85064
Toll free: 1-800-528-1238
TTY: 1-800-528-2222
✉: customerservice@
bestwestern.com
**www.bestwestern.com**

**BIC Corporation** ⟲
Consumer Affairs
One Bic Way, Suite 1
Shelton, CT 06484-6299
Toll free: 1-800-546-1111
**www.bicworld.com**

**Big Lot Stores, Inc.**
Customer Service
300 Phillipi Rd.
Columbus, OH 43228-5311
Toll free: 1-800-877-1253
✉: talk2us@biglots.com
**www.biglots.com**

**Birds Eye Foods, Inc.**
Consumer Relations
See: Pinnacle Foods Group, LLC
Toll free: 1-800-563-1786
(Birds Eye, Freshlike, Nalley or
Bersteins Products)
Toll free: 1-800-270-2743 (Other
Brands)
✉: consumerinsights@
pinnacle.speedymail.com
**www.birdseyefoods.com**

**Bissell Homecare, Inc.** ⟲
Customer Service
PO Box 3606
Grand Rapids, MI 49501
Toll free: 1-800-237-7691
**www.bissell.com**

**BJ's Wholesale Club, Inc.**
Member Care
25 Research Dr.
Westborough, MA 01581
Toll free: 1-800-257-2582
**www.bjs.com**

**Black & Decker, Inc.** ⟲
Customer Service
701 E. Joppa Rd.
Joppa, MD 21286
410-716-3900
Toll free: 1-800-544-6986
**www.blackanddecker.com**

**Blockbuster Entertainment
Corporation**
Customer Care
3000 Redbud Blvd.
McKinney, TX 75270
Toll free: 1-866-692-2789 (Blockbuster
Online)
Toll free: 1-800-406-6843 (In-Store)
✉: online.consumerrelations@
blockbuster.com
**www.blockbuster.com**

**Bloomingdales, Inc.**
Customer Service
PO Box 8215
Mason, OH 45040
Toll free: 1-800-777-0000
**www.bloomingdales.com**

**Blue Cross and Blue Shield Association (BCBSA)**
Consumer Affairs
1310 G St., NW
Washington, DC 20005
202-626-4780
www.bcbs.com

**Bob Evans Farms, Inc.**
Consumer Relations
3776 S. High St.
Columbus, OH 43207
Toll free: 1-800-939-2338
www.bobevans.com

**Bojangles Restaurants, Inc.**
Customer Relations
9432 Southern Pine Blvd.
Charlotte, NC 28273
Toll free: 1-888-300-4265
www.bojangles.com

**BP Corporation**
Consumer Relations
28301 Ferry Rd.
Warrenville, IL 60555
Toll free: 1-800-333-3991
✉: bpconsum@bp.com
www.bp.com

**Bridgestone Retail Operations, LLC**
Consumer Affairs
PO Box 6397
Bloomingdale, IL 60108
Toll free: 1-800-367-3872
✉: firestone_consumer_affairs@inspyresolutions.com
www.firestonecompleteautocare.com

**Brinker International**
6820 LBJ Freeway
Dallas, TX 75240
972-980-9917
www.brinker.com

**Brio Tuscan Grill**
Guest Feedback
777 Goodale Blvd., Suite 100
Columbus, OH 43212
Toll free: 1-888-452-7286
www.brioitalian.com

**Bristol-Myers Squibb Company**
Customer Relations
345 Park Ave.
New York, NY 10154
Toll free: 1-800-332-2056
✉: drug.information@bms.com
www.bms.com

**British Airways**
Customer Relations
PO Box 300686
Jamaica, NY 11430-0686
Toll free: 1-800-247-9297
Toll free: 1-800-828-8144 (Baggage Claims)
Toll free: 1-800-403-0882 (Online Support)
TTY: 1-866-393-0961
www.britishairways.com

**Brown Shoe Company, Inc.**
Consumer Care
8300 Maryland Ave.
St. Louis, MO 63105
Toll free: 1-800-766-6465
✉: info@brownshoe.com
www.brownshoe.com

**Brown-Forman Beverages Worldwide**
Consumer Support
850 Dixie Hwy.
Louisville, KY 40210
Toll free: 1-800-753-4567
www.brown-forman.com

**Buca di Beppo**
Guest Services
4700 Millenia Blvd., Suite 400
Orlando, FL 32839
✉: famiglia@bucainc.com
www.bucadibeppo.com

**Budget Rent A Car System, Inc.**
Customer Service
Six Sylvan Way
Parsippany, NJ 07054
Toll free: 1-800-214-6094
TTY: 1-800-826-5510
www.budget.com

**Bulova Corporation**
Customer Relations
One Bulova Ave.
Woodside, NY 11377
Toll free: 1-800-228-5682
✉: service@bulova.com
www.bulova.com

**Burger King Corporation**
Consumer Relations Department
5505 Blue Lagoon Dr.
Miami, FL 33126
Toll free: 1-866-394-2493
www.bk.com

**Burlington Coat Factory Direct Corporation**
Customer Relations Department
1830 Route 130 N
Burlington, NJ 08016
Toll free: 1-888-223-2628
www.burlingtoncoatfactory.com

**Bush Brothers Company** ⌒
Consumer Relations
PO Box 52330
Knoxville, TN 37950-2330
Toll free: 1-800-590-3797
✉: letters@bushbros.com
www.bushbeans.com

## C

**Calvin Klein**
See: Phillips-Van Heusen
Toll free: 1-866-214-6694
Toll free: 1-866-513-0513 (Website)
www.calvinklein.com

**Campbell Soup Company** ⌒
Consumer Affairs
One Campbell Pl.
Camden, NJ 08103-1701
Toll free: 1-800-257-8443
www.campbellsoup.com

**Canon USA, Inc.**
One Canon Plaza
Lake Success, NY 11042-1198
Toll free: 1-800-652-2666
TTY: 1-866-251-3752
www.usa.canon.com

**Capital One** ⌒
General Correspondence
PO Box 30285
Salt Lake City, UT 84130-0285
1-800-955-7070
TTY: 1-800-206-7986
✉: webinfo@capitalone.com
www.capitalone.com

**Captain D's Seafood**
1717 Elm Hill Pike, Suite A-1
Nashville, TN 37210
Toll free: 1-800-314-4819
www.captainds.com

**Carfax, Inc.**
Consumer Affairs
5860 Trinity Pkwy., Suite 600
Centerville, VA 20120
703-218-0340
✉: carfaxwebsupport@carfax.com
www.carfax.com/help

**Carnival Cruise Lines** ⌒
Guest Relations
3655 N.W. 87th Ave.
Miami, FL 33178-2428
Toll free: 1-800-929-6400
✉: guestcare@carnival.com
www.carnival.com

**Carrier Air Conditioning Company**
Customer Relations
PO Box 4808, Carrier Pkwy.
Syracuse, NY 13221-4808
Toll free: 1-800-227-7437
**www.residential.carrier.com**

**Carvel Corporation**
Retail Stores/Food Service
301 Congress Ave., Suite 1100
Austin, TX 78701
Toll free: 1-800-322-4848
**www.carvel.com**

**Casio, Inc.**
570 Mt. Pleasant Ave.
Dover, NJ 07801
973-361-5400
Toll free: 1-800-706-2534 (Repairs)
Toll free: 1-800-435-7732
(Technical Support)
✉: memberservices@casio.com
**www.casio.com**

**Casual Male Retail Group**
Customer Service
555 Turnpike St.
Canton, MA 02021
Toll free: 1-855-746-7395
✉: info@casualmale.com
**www.casual-male-big-and-tall.
destinationxl.com**

**The CBS Television Network** ⟲
Audience Services
524 W. 52nd St.
New York, NY 10019-6198
212-975-3247
✉: audsvcs@cbs.com
**www.cbs.com**

**Chanel, Inc.**
Consumer Relations
Nine W. 57th St., 44th Floor
New York, NY 10019
Toll free: 1-800-550-0005
✉: consumerrelations@
chanelusa.com
**www.chanel.com**

**Chase Bank
(J.P. Morgan Chase Bank)**
PO Box 36520
Louisville, KY 40233-6520
212-270-6000 (Corporate)
Toll free: 1-800-935-9935
(Checking and Savings)
TTY: 1-800-242-7383
**www.chase.com**

**Chattem, Inc.** ⟲
Consumer Affairs
PO Box 22219
Chattanooga, TN 37409
Toll free: 1-888-442-4464
**www.chattem.com**

**Check 'n Go**
7755 Montgomery Rd., Suite 400
Cincinnati, OH 45236
Toll free: 1-888-372-9329
✉: comments@checkngo.com
**www.checkngo.com**

**The Cheesecake Factory** ⟲
26901 Malibu Hills Rd.
Calabasas Hills, CA 91301
818-871-3000
**www.thecheesecakefactory.com**

**Chevron Corporation**
Consumer Connection Center
PO Box 4000
Bellaire, TX 77402-4000
**www.chevron.com**

**Chick-fil-A, Inc.**
Customer Feedback
PO Box 500367
Atlanta, GA 31150
404-765-8000
Toll free: 1-866-232-2040
**www.chick-fil-a.com**

**Children's Place** ⟲
Customer Service
500 Plaza Dr.
Secaucus, NJ 07094
Toll free: 1-877-752-2387
**www.childrensplace.com**

**Chili's Grill and Bar**
See: Brinker International
Toll free: 1-800-983-4637
(Guest Relations)
**www.chilis.com**

**Chipotle Mexican Grill, Inc.**
1401 Wynkoop St., Suite 500
Denver, CO 80202
303-595-4000
✉: customerservice@chipotle.com
**www.chipotle.com**

**Choice Hotels** ⟲
Guest Relations
6811 E. Mayo Blvd., Suite 100
Phoenix, AZ 85054
Toll free: 1-800-300-8800
**www.choicehotels.com**

**Church & Dwight Company, Inc.** ⟲
Consumer and Professional Relations
469 N. Harrison St.
Princeton, NJ 08540
609-683-5900
Toll free: 1-800-524-1328
**www.churchdwight.com**

**Citibank, Inc.** ⟲
Client Services
100 Citibank Dr.
San Antonio, TX 78245-9004
Toll free: 1-800-627-3999 (Banking)
Toll free: 1-800-950-5114 (Credit cards)
TTY: 1-800-788-0002
**www.citibank.com**

**The Clorox Company** ⟲
Consumer Services
Mail Stop 2334
1221 Broadway
Oakland, CA 94612-1888
Toll free: 1-800-835-4523 (GLAD)
Toll free: 1-800-227-1860
(Household Cleaners)
Toll free: 1-800-292-2200
(Laundry Brands)
Toll free: 1-800-426-6228 (Insecticides)
**www.thecloroxcompany.com**

**The Coca-Cola Company** ⟲
Industry and Consumer Affairs
PO Box 1734
Atlanta, GA 30301
Toll free: 1-800-438-2653
**www.thecocacolacompany.com**

**Coldwell Banker Real Estate
Corporation**
Customer Service
One Campus Dr.
Parsippany, NJ 07054
Toll free: 1-877-373-3829
**www.coldwellbanker.com**

**The Colgate-Palmolive
Company** ⟲ ♦
Consumer Affairs
300 Park Ave.
New York, NY 10022
Toll free: 1-800-468-6502
✉: colgate-palmolive_consumer_
affairs@colpal.com
**www.colgate.com**

**Colonial Penn Life Insurance**
Customer Service
399 Market St.
Philadelphia, PA 19181
Toll free: 1-877-877-8052
(General Questions)
Toll free: 1-800-523-9100
(Customer Service and Claims)
**www.colonialpenn.com**

**Combe, Inc.** ⟳
Consumer Resources
1101 Westchester Ave.
White Plains, NY 10604-3597
Toll free: 1-800-431-2610
**www.combe.com**

**Comcast Corporation**
One Comcast Center
Philadelphia, PA 19103
Toll free: 1-800-266-2278
Toll free: 1-800-934-6489 (Xfinity)
**www.comcast.com**

**ConAgra Foods** ⟳
Consumer Affairs
One ConAgra Dr.
Omaha, NE 68102
Toll free: 1-800-722-1344
✉: consumeraffairs@
conagrafoods.com
**www.conagrafoods.com**

**Conair Cuisinart Corporation**
Consumer Affairs
150 Milford Rd.
East Windsor, NJ 08520
203-351-9000
Toll free: 1-800-326-6247
(Personal Care)
Toll free: 1-800-334-4031 (Oral Care)
Toll free: 1-800-726-0190
✉: feedback@conair.com
**www.conair.com**

**Costco Wholesale Corporation**
Member Service
PO Box 34331
Seattle, WA 98124
Toll free: 1-800-774-2678
Toll free: 1-800-955-2292
(Online Members)
**www.costco.com**

**Coty Inc.** ⟳
Consumer Affairs
118 American Rd.
Morris Plains, NJ 10016
Toll free: 1-800-715-4023
Toll free: 1-800-953-5080 (Sally Hansen,
N.Y.C., and LaCross brands)
**www.coty.com**

**Cox Communications**
1550 W. Deer Valley Rd.
Phoenix, AZ 85027
ww2.cox.com

**craigslist, Inc.**
222 Sutter St.
San Francisco, CA 94108
**www.craigslist.org**

**Crate and Barrel**
Customer Service Department
1860 W. Jefferson Ave.
Naperville, IL 60540-3918
Toll free: 1-800-967-6696
✉: customer_service@
crateandbarrel.com
**www.crateandbarrel.com**

**Crayola, LLC** ⟳
Consumer Affairs
PO Box 431
Easton, PA 18044-0431
Toll free: 1-800-272-9652
**www.crayola.com**

**Cricket Wireless**
See: Leap Wireless International
Toll free: 1-800-274-2538
**www.mycricket.com**

**Crowne Plaza**
See: InterContinental
Hotels Group, PLC
Toll free: 1-800-465-2680
**www.crowneplaza.com**

**Curves International**
100 Ritchie Rd.
Waco, TX 76712
Toll free: 1-800-848-1096
**www.curves.com**

**CVS Corporation**
Customer Relations Department
One CVS Dr.
Woonsocket, RI 02895
401-765-1500
Toll free: 1-800-746-7287
Toll free: 1-888-607-4287 (Website)
✉: customercare@cvs.com
**www.cvs.com**

---

**D**

**Dairy Queen Corporation** ⟳
Customer Relations
7505 Metro Blvd.
Minneapolis, MN 55439
952-830-0200
**www.dairyqueen.com**

**The Dannon Company, Inc.** ⟳
Consumer Response Center
PO Box 90296
Allentown, PA 18109-0296
Toll free: 1-877-326-6668
**www.dannon.com**

**Darden Restaurants** ⟳
PO Box 695011
Orlando, FL 32859-5011
407-245-4000
✉: dardeninfo@darden.com
**www.darden.com**

**Days Inns Worldwide, Inc.**
PO Box 4090
Aberdeen, SD 57401
Toll free: 1-800-441-1618
**www.daysinn.com**

**Dean & DeLuca**
Customer Care
4115 E. Harry St.
Wichita, KS 67218
316-821-3200
Toll free: 1-800-221-7714
✉: customercare@deandeluca.com
**www.deandeluca.com**

**Del Monte Foods Company** ⟳
Consumer Affairs
PO Box 80
Pittsburgh, PA 15230-0080
415-247-3000
Toll free: 1-800-543-3090
**www.delmonte.com**

**Dell, Inc.**
Customer Service
One Dell Way
Round Rock, TX 78682
Toll free: 1-800-624-9897
(Customer Service)
Toll free: 1-866-243-9297
(Technical Support)
TTY: 1-877-335-5889
**www.dell.com**

**Delta Air Lines, Inc.** ⟳
Customer Care
PO Box 20980
Department 980
Atlanta, GA 30320-2980
404-773-0305
404-209-3434 (Disability assistance)
Toll free: 1-800-325-8224 (Baggage)
**www.delta.com**

**Delta Faucets Company**
55 E. 111th St.
Indianapolis, IN 46280
317-848-1812
Toll free: 1-800-345-3358
✉: customerservice@
deltafaucet.com
www.deltafaucet.com

**Denny's Corporation**
Call Center
203 E. Main St. P-8-6
Spartanburg, SC 29319
Toll free: 1-800-733-6697
(Customer Service)
www.dennys.com

**Dial Corporation** ⌕
See: The Henkel Corporation
Toll free: 1-800-258-3425
www.dialsoap.com

**Diamond Foods, Inc.** ⌕
Consumer Affairs
1050 S. Diamond St.
Stockton, CA 95205-7087
209-467-6000
www.diamondfoods.com

**Dick's Sporting Goods**
345 Court St.
Coraopolis, PA 15108
Toll free: 1-877-846-9997
✉: customersupport@
dickssportinggoods.com
www.dickssportinggoods.com

**Dillard's, Inc.**
Customer Service Department
PO Box 486
Little Rock, AR 72203
501-376-5200
Toll free: 1-800-345-5273
TTY: 1-800-444-1732
✉: questions@dillards.com
www.dillards.com

**Diners Club International**
Customer Service
PO Box 6101
Carol Stream, IL 60197-6101
Toll free: 1-800-234-6377
www.dinersclubus.com

**DIRECTV Enterprises, Inc.**
PO Box 6550
Greenwood Village, CO 80155-6550
Toll free: 1-800-531-5000
TTY: 1-800-779-4388
www.DIRECTV.com

**Discover Financial Services, Inc.**
Card Customer Service
PO Box 30943
Salt Lake City, UT 84130-0943
224-405-0900 (Headquarters)
801-902-3100
Toll free: 1-800-347-2683
TTY: 1-800-347-7449
www.discoverfinancial.com

**Dish Network**
Toll free: 1-888-333-3474
✉: feedback@customermail.
dishnetwork.com
www.dishnetwork.com

**Dole Food Company, Inc.** ⌕
Consumer Center
PO Box 5700
Thousand Oaks, CA 91359-5700
Toll free: 1-800-356-3111
✉: Dole.Consumer.Center@dole.com
www.dole.com

**Dollar Rent A Car, Inc.**
Customer Service 2W2
PO Box 33167
Tulsa, OK 74153-1167
918-669-3000
Toll free: 1-800-800-5252 (Customer Service)
✉: rhelpdesk@dollar.com
www.dollar.com

**Domino's Pizza, Inc.** ⌕
Customer Service
30 Frank Lloyd Wright Dr.
PO Box 997
Ann Arbor, MI 48106
734-930-3030
Toll free: 1-888-366-4667
www.dominos.com

**Doubletree**
See: Hilton Hospitality, Inc.
Toll free: 1-800-222-8733
TTY: 1-800-368-1133
www.doubletree.com

**Dr. Pepper/Snapple Group, Inc.** ⌕
Consumer Relations
PO Box 869077
Plano, TX 75086-9077
972-673-7000
Toll free: 1-800-696-5891
www.drpeppersnapplegroup.com

**DSW**
Customer Service
810 DSW Dr.
Columbus, OH 43219
Toll free: 1-866-379-7463
www.dsw.com

**Dunkin Donuts**
Consumer Care
130 Royall St.
Canton, MA 02021
Toll free: 1-800-859-5339
www.dunkindonuts.com

**DuPont Company**
Corporate Information Center
Chestnut Run Plaza 705/GS38
PO Box 80705
Wilmington, DE 19880-0705
Toll free: 1-800-441-7515
✉: info@dupont.com
www.dupont.com

**Duracell North America**
Consumer Relations
Berkshire Corporate Park
Bethel, CT 06801
Toll free: 1-800-551-2355
www.duracell.com

## E

**E. & J. Gallo Winery** ⌕
Consumer Relations
600 Yosemite Blvd.
Modesto, CA 95354-2760
Toll free: 1-877-687-9463
✉: consumerrelations@ejgallo.com
www.gallo.com

**Eagle Family Foods**
Consumer Response
One Strawberry Ln.
Orrville, OH 44667
Toll free: 1-888-656-3245
www.eaglebrand.com

**Eastman Kodak Company**
Kodak Information Center/
Consumer Contact Center
343 State St.
Rochester, NY 14650
Toll free: 1-800-235-6325
(Digital Cameras, Printer Docks, Photo Printers)
Toll free: 1-800-242-2424
www.kodak.com

**e-Bay, Inc.**
2065 Hamilton Ave.
San Jose, CA 95125
Toll free: 1-800-322-9266
www.eBay.com

**Eddie Bauer, Inc.**
Customer Satisfaction Center
PO Box 7001
Groveport, OH 43125
Toll free: 1-800-426-8020
TTY: 1-800-462-6757
✉: CustomerCare@
csc.eddiebauer.com
**www.eddiebauer.com**

**eHarmony**
Customer Care
PO Box 3640
Santa Monica, CA 90408
Toll free: 1-800-951-2023
**www.eharmony.com**

**The Electrolux Group**
Consumer Assistance Center
2715 Washington Rd.
Augusta, GA 30909
Toll free: 1-877-435-3287
**www.electrolux.com**

**Eli Lilly & Company** ↄ
Consumer Communications
Lilly Corporate Center
Indianapolis, IN 46285
317-276-2000
Toll free: 1-800-545-5979
**www.lilly.com**

**Elizabeth Arden, Inc.** ↄ
Consumer Affairs
309 South St.
New Providence, NJ 07974
Toll free: 1-800-326-7337
✉: consumer@elizabetharden.com
**www.elizabetharden.com**

**Embassy Suites**
See: Hilton Hospitality, Inc.
Toll free: 1-800-362-2779
**www.embassysuites.com**

**Enterprise Rent-a-Car**
600 Corporate Park Dr.
Saint Louis, MO 63105-4211
Toll free: 1-800-264-6350
✉: customerservice@enterprise.com
**www.enterprise.com**

**Equifax**
Office of Consumer Affairs
PO Box 740241
Atlanta, GA 30374
Toll free: 1-800-685-1111
**www.equifax.com**

**The Estee Lauder
Companies, Inc.** ↄ
Consumer Care
767 5th Ave.
New York, NY 10153
212-572-4200
Toll free: 1-888-378-3359
✉: consumercare-us@
gcc.elc.estee.com
**www.elcompanies.com**

**Ethan Allen, Inc.**
PO Box 1966
Danbury, CT 06813
Toll free: 1-888-324-3571
✉: orders@ethanallen.com
**www.ethanallen.com**

**The Eureka Company**
Consumer Service Department
PO Box 3900
Peoria, IL 61701
Toll free: 1-800-282-2886
**www.eureka.com**

**Expedia, Inc.** ↄ
Customer Support
333 108th Ave., NE
Bellevue, WA 98004
Toll free: 1-800-787-7186
**www.expedia.com**

**Experian**
National Consumer Assistance Center
PO Box 2002
Allen, TX 75013
Toll free: 1-888-397-3742
✉: support@experiandirect.com
**www.experian.com**

**Express Scripts**
Toll free: 1-800-631-7780
**www.express-scripts.com**

**Exxon Mobil**
Customer Relations
PO Box 1049
Buffalo, NY 14240-1049
Toll free: 1-800-243-9966
**www.exxonmobil.com**

## F

**Facebook, Inc.**
1601 S. California Ave.
Palo Alto, CA 94304
650-543-4800
✉: info@facebook.com
**www.facebook.com**

**Fairfield Inn**
See: Marriott International, Inc.
Toll free: 1-800-721-7033
**www.fairfieldinn.com**

**Farmers Insurance**
4680 Wilshire Blvd.
Los Angeles, CA 90010
Toll free: 1-800-435-7764
TTY: 1-888-891-1660
**www.farmers.com**

**FedEx Corporation** ↄ
Customer Relations
3875 Airways Blvd.
Module H3 Department 4634
Memphis, TN 38116
Toll free: 1-800-463-3339
**www.fedex.com**

**Fingerhut Direct Marketing, Inc.**
Customer Service
6250 Ridgewood Rd.
St. Cloud, MN 56303
Toll free: 1-800-208-2500
✉: customerservice@fingerhut.com
**www.fingerhut.com**

**Fisher-Price**
Consumer Affairs
636 Girard Ave.
East Aurora, NY 14052
716-687-3000
Toll free: 1-800-432-5437
TTY: 1-800-382-7470
✉: fpconaff@fisher-price.com
**www.fisher-price.com**

**Florsheim, Inc.**
Customer Service
333 W. Estabrook Blvd.
Glendale, WI 53212
Toll free: 1-866-454-0449
✉: us.consumers@florsheim.com
**www.florsheim.com**

**Flowers Foods, Inc.** ↄ
1919 Flowers Circle
Thomasville, GA 31757
229-226-9110
**www.flowersfoods.com**

**Food Lion, Inc.**
Customer Relations
PO Box 1330
Salisbury, NC 28145-1330
Toll free: 1-800-210-9569
**www.foodlion.com**

**Forever 21**
Customer Service
3880 N. Mission Rd.
Los Angeles, CA 90031
213-741-5100
Toll free: 1-888-494-3837
**www.forever21.com**

**Fortune Brands**
Corporate Affairs Department
520 Lake Cook Rd.
Deerfield, IL 60015
847-484-4400
✉: mail@fortunebrands.com
**www.fortunebrands.com**

**Frigidaire Home Products**
2715 Washington Rd.
Augusta, GA 30909
Toll free: 1-800-374-4432
**www.frigidaire.com**

**Frito-Lay**
Consumer Affairs
PO Box 660634
Dallas, TX 75266-6234
972-334-7000
Toll free: 1-800-352-4477
**www.fritolay.com**

**Frontier Airlines, Inc.**
Customer Relations
7001 Tower Rd.
Denver, CO 80249-7312
Toll free: 1-800-432-1359
TTY: 1-800-872-3608
**www.frontierairlines.com**

**FTD, Inc.**
Customer Service
3113 Woodcreek Dr.
Downers Grove, IL 60515
630-719-7756
Toll free: 1-800-736-3383
**www.ftd.com**

**Fuji Photo Film USA, Inc.**
Consumer Information Service Center
1100 King George Post
Edison, NJ 08837
Toll free: 1-800-800-3854
**www.fujifilm.com**

## G

**Gap, Inc.**
Customer Relations
100 Gap Online Dr.
Grove City, OH 43123-8605
Toll free: 1-800-427-7895
TTY: 1-888-906-1104
✉: custserv@gap.com
**www.gap.com**

**Gateway, Inc.**
Customer Service
PO Box 6137
Temple, TX 76503
**www.gateway.com**

**GEICO**
One GEICO Plaza
Washington, DC 20076
Toll free: 1-877-418-1312 (Car)
Toll free: 1-888-395-1200 (Home)
Toll free: 1-888-532-5433 (Life)
TTY: 1-800-833-8255
**www.geico.com**

**General Electric Company**
3135 Easton Turnpike
Fairfield, CT 06828
203-373-2211
Toll free: 1-800-626-2005
**www.ge.com**

**General Mills, Inc.** ↄ
Consumer Services
PO Box 9452
Minneapolis, MN 55440
Toll free: 1-800-248-7310
**www.generalmills.com**

**Georgia-Pacific Corporation**
Consumer Affairs
133 Peachtree St., NE
Atlanta, GA 30303
Toll free: 1-800-283-5547
(Consumer Products)
TTY: 1-800-283-5547 ext. 5
**www.gp.com**

**Gerber Products Company**
Consumer Affairs
445 State St.
Fremont, MI 49413-0001
Toll free: 1-800-284-9488
**www.gerber.com**

**Giant Food, Inc.**
8301 Professional Pl., Suite 115
Landover, MD 20785
301-341-4322
Toll free: 1-888-469-4426
TTY: 301-200-8995
**www.giantfood.com**

**GlaxoSmithKline Consumer
Healthcare** ↄ
Consumer Information
PO Box 13398
Five Moore Dr.
Research Triangle Park, NC 27709
412-200-4000
Toll free: 1-888-825-5249
(Prescription Drugs)
Toll free: 1-800-245-1040
(Non-Prescription)
✉: consumer.communications@
gsk.com
**www.gsk.com**

**The Golden Grain Company**
PO Box 049003
Chicago, IL 60604-9003
Toll free: 1-800-421-2444
**www.ricearoni.com**

**Gold's Gym International**
Customer Care Department
125 E. John Carpenter Fwy., Suite 1300
Irving, TX 75062
214-574-4653
**www.goldsgym.com**

**Goodrich Corporation**
Consumer Relations Department
PO Box 19001
Greenville, SC 29602-9001
Toll free: 1-877-788-8899
**www.bfgoodrichtires.com**

**The Goodyear Tire
Rubber Company**
Department 728
1144 E. Market St.
Akron, OH 44316-0001
330-769-2121
Toll free: 1-800-321-2136
✉: consumer_relations@
goodyear.com
**www.goodyear.com**

**Google.com**
1600 Amphitheatre Pkwy.
Mountain View, CA 94043
650-253-0000
**www.google.com**

**Graco Children's Products, Inc.**
Consumer Services
150 Oaklands Blvd.
Exton, PA 19341
Toll free: 1-800-345-4109
**www.gracobaby.com**

**Greyhound Lines, Inc.**
PO Box 660362
Dallas, TX 75266-0362
214-849-8000
214-849-6246 (Baggage)
Toll free: 1-800-231-2222
(Fares/Schedules)
TTY: 1-800- 345-3109
**www.greyhound.com**

**Guess? Inc.**
Customer Service
1444 S. Alameda St.
Los Angeles, CA 90021
213-765-3100
Toll free: 1-877-444-8377
**www.guess.com**

◆ Provided financial support for the publication of the Consumer Action Handbook.

**Guinness Company**
801 Main Ave.
Norwalk, CT 06851
203-229-2100
Toll free: 1-800-521-1591
✉: guinness@consumer-care.net
www.guinness.com

## H

**H & R Block, Inc.**
Customer Support
One H & R Block Way
Kansas City, MO 64105
Toll free: 1-800-472-5625
www.hrblock.com

**Hallmark Cards, Inc.**
Consumer Affairs
PO Box 419034
Mail Drop #216
Kansas City, MO 64141
Toll free: 1-800-425-5627
www.hallmark.com

**Hampton Inn & Suites**
See: Hilton Hospitality, Inc.
Toll free: 1-800-426-7866
www.hamptoninn.com

**Hanes Hosiery**
Consumer Relations
PO Box 3013
Winston-Salem, NC 27102
Toll free: 1-800-225-4872
www.haneshosiery.com

**Harry & David**
Customer Service
2500 South Pacific Hwy.
Medford, OR 97501-2675
541-864-2121
Toll free: 1-877-322-1200
✉: service@harryanddavid.com
www.harryanddavid.com

**Hartz Mountain Corporation** ⌇
Consumer Affairs
400 Plaza Dr.
Secaucus, NJ 07094
Toll free: 1-800-275-1414
www.hartz.com

**Hasbro, Inc.**
Consumer Affairs
PO Box 200
Dept. C-847
Pawtucket, RI 02862-0200
401-727-6899
Toll free: 1-800-255-5516
✉: customersupport@hasbro.com
www.hasbro.com

**Heinz North America** ⌇
Consumer Resource Center/
Consumer Affairs
PO Box 57
Pittsburgh, PA 15230
Toll free: 1-800-255-5750
✉: heinzconsumeraffairs@
us.hjheinz.com
www.heinz.com

**Henkel Consumer Goods** ⌇
19001 N. Scottsdale Rd.
Scottsdale, AZ 85255
480-754-3425
Toll free: 1-800-258-3425
www.henkelna.com

**Hershey Food Corporation** ⌇
Consumer Relations
100 Crystal A Dr.
Hershey, PA 17033
Toll free: 1-800-468-1714
www.hersheys.com

**Hertz Corporation**
Customer Relations
PO Box 26120
Oklahoma City, OK 73126
Toll free: 1-800-654-4173
TTY: 1-800-654-2280
www.hertz.com

**Hewlett-Packard Company** ⌇
3000 Hanover St.
Bldg. 6A. Mail Stop 1247
Palo Alto, CA 94304
650-857-1501
Toll free: 1-800-474-6836
www.hp.com

**Hillshire Brands**
Consumer Affairs
PO Box 3901
Neenah, WI 61612
Toll free: 1-800-323-7117 (Desserts)
Toll free: 1-800-925-3326 (Meats)
www.hillshirebrands.com

**Hilton Garden Inn**
See: Hilton Hospitality, Inc.
Toll free: 1-877-782-9444
www.hiltongardeninn.com

**Hilton Hospitality, Inc.**
Guest Assistance
755 Crossover Ln.
Memphis, TN 38117
901-374-5000
Toll free: 1-800-445-8667
TTY: 1-800-368-1133
www.hilton.com

**Hitachi America Ltd.**
Customer Services
PO Box 99652
Troy, MI 48099
✉: customerservice.ce@
hal.hitachi.com
Toll free: 1-800-448-2244

**Holiday Inn/Holiday Inn Express**
See: InterContinental Hotels Group
Toll free: 1-800-465-4329
www.holiday-inn.com

**Home Depot, Inc.**
Customer Care
2455 Paces Ferry Rd.
Atlanta, GA 30339-4024
Toll free: 1-800-466-3337
Toll free: 1-800-430-3376
(Website Questions)
✉: customercare@homedepot.com
www.homedepot.com

**Home Goods**
See: TJX Companies, Inc.
Toll free: 1-800-888-0776
www.homegoods.com

**Home Shopping Network**
Customer Service
PO Box 9090
Clearwater, FL 33758
Toll free: 1-800-284-3900
(Phone Orders)
Toll free: 1-800-933-2887
(Online Orders)
www.hsn.com

**Homewood Suites**
See: Hilton Hospitality Inc.
Toll free: 1-800-225-5466
www.homewoodsuites.com

**Hoover Company**
TTI Floor Care North America
7005 Cochran Rd.
Glenwillow, OH 44139
Toll free: 1-800-944-9200
www.hoover.com

**Hormel Foods Company** ⌇
Consumer Affairs
One Hormel Pl.
Austin, MN 55912
Toll free: 1-800-523-4635
www.hormel.com

**Howard Johnson, Inc.**
PO Box 4090
Aberdeen, SD 57401
Toll free: 1-800-544-9881
www.hojo.com

**Humana, Inc.**
PO Box 14601
Lexington, KY 40512-4601
502-580-1000
Toll free: 1-800-448-6262
www.humana.com

**Hyatt Hotels & Resorts** ℃
Consumer Affairs
9805 Q St.
Omaha, NE 68127
402-592-6465
Toll free: 1-800-323-7249
www.hyatt.com

## I

**IBM Corporation** ℃
One New Orchard Rd.
Armonk, NY 10504-1722
914-499-1900
Toll free: 1-800-426-4968
(Customer Service)
TTY: 1-800-426-3383
✉: askibm@vnet.ibm.com
www.ibm.com

**Ikea**
Customer Relations
420 Alan Wood Rd.
Conshohocken, PA 19428
Toll free: 1-800-434-4532
www.ikea.com

**Intel**
Consumer Relations
2200 Mission College Blvd.
Santa Clara, CA 95054
408-765-8080 (Headquarters)
www.intel.com

**InterContinental Hotels Group PLC** ℃
Guest Relations
PO Box 30321
Salt Lake City, UT 84130-321
Toll free: 1-800 621-0555
www.ihgplc.com

## J

**Jack In The Box**
Guest Relations
9330 Balboa Ave.
San Diego, CA 92123-1516
858-571-2121
Toll free: 1-800-955-5225
www.jackinthebox.com

**Jackson Hewitt Tax Service, Inc.**
Three Sylvan Way, Suite 301
Parsippany, NJ 07054
Toll free: 1-800-234-1040
www.jacksonhewitt.com

**JanSport, Inc.**
2601 Harbor Bay Pkwy.
Alameda, CA 94577
501-614-4000
Toll free: 1-800-558-3600
www.jansport.com

**Janssen Pharmaceuticals, Inc.** ℃
PO Box 200
Titusville, NJ 08560
Toll free: 1-800-526-7736
www.ortho-mcneil.com

**Jarden Consumer Solutions, Inc.** ℃
Consumer Affairs
2381 Executive Center Dr.
Boca Raton, FL 34331
Toll free: 1-800-458-8407
www.jardencs.com

**JCPenney Company, Inc.**
Corporate Customer Relations
PO Box 10001
Dallas, TX 75301-7311
Toll free: 1-800-322-1189
www.jcpenney.com

**J. Crew**
Customer Relations
One Ivy Crescent
Lynchburg, VA 24513-1001
Toll free: 1-800-562-0258
✉: contactus@jcrew.com
www.jcrew.com

**Jenny Craig, Inc.**
Customer Care
5770 Fleet St.
Carlsbad, CA 92008
760-696-4000 (Headquarters)
Toll free: 1-800-536-6922
✉: WebCustomerService@
jennycraig.com
www.jennycraig.com

**JetBlue Airways Corporation**
Customer Relations
PO Box 17435
Salt Lake City, UT 84117-7435
Toll free: 1-800-538-2583
TTY: 1-800-336-5530
✉: promise@jetblue.com
www.jetblue.com

**Jiffy Lube International, Inc.**
Customer Service
PO Box 4427
Houston, TX 77210-4458
Toll free: 1-800-344-6933
www.jiffylube.com

**John Hancock Financial Services, Inc.**
601 Congress St.
Boston, MA 02210-2805
617-572-6000
Toll free: 1-800-732-5543
TTY: 1-800-832-5282
www.johnhancock.com

**Johnson & Johnson Consumer Products, Inc.** ℃
PO Box 726
Langhorne, PA 19047-0726
732-524-0400
Toll free: 1-800-526-3967
www.jnj.com

**Johnson Publishing Company, Inc.**
820 S. Michigan Ave.
Chicago, IL 60605
312-322-9200
www.johnsonpublishing.com

**Just Born, Inc** ℃
Consumer Relations
1300 Stefko Blvd.
Bethlehem, PA 18017
610-867-7568
Toll free: 1-888-645-3453
✉: consumerrelations@justborn.com
www.justborn.com

**JVC Company of America** ℃
Customer Care
1700 Valley Rd.
Wayne, NJ 07470
Toll free: 1-800-252-5722
www.jvcservice.com

## K

**Kao Brands Company** ℃
Consumer Relations Department
2535 Spring Grove Ave.
Cincinnati, OH 45214
www.kaobrands.com

**Kawasaki Motor Corporation, USA**
Consumer Services
PO Box 25252
Santa Ana, CA 92799-5252
949-460-5688
www.kawasaki.com

**Kellogg Company** ℃◆
Consumer Affairs
PO Box CAMB
Battle Creek, MI 49016
Toll free: 1-800-962-1413
www.kelloggcompany.com

◆ Provided financial support for the publication of the Consumer Action Handbook.

**KFC**
PO Box 725489
Atlanta, GA 31139
Toll free: 1-800-225-5532
www.kfc.com

**Kimberly-Clark Corporation** ⌣
Consumer Services
Dept. INT
PO Box 2020
Neenah, WI 54957-2020
Toll free: 1-888-525-8388
www.kimberly-clark.com

**The Kirby Company**
Customer Relations
1920 W. 114th St.
Cleveland, OH 44102
Toll free: 1-800-494-8586
✉: consumer@kirbywhq.com
www.kirby.com

**KitchenAid**
See: Whirlpool Corporation
Toll free: 1-800-422-1230
(Large Appliances)
Toll free: 1-800-541-6390
(Small Appliances)
www.kitchenaid.com

**Kmart Corporation**
Customer Service
Toll free: 1-866-562-7848
✉: help@customerservice.kmart.com
www.kmart.com

**Kohler Company**
444 Highland Dr.
Kohler, WI 53044
920-457-4441
Toll free: 1-800-456-4537
www.kohler.com

**Kohls Corporation** ⌣
Customer Service
N56 W. 17000 Ridgewood Dr.
Menomonee Falls, WI 53051
262-703-7000
Toll free: 1-866-887-8884
Toll free: 1-800-564-5740 (Credit)
✉: customer.service@kohls.com
www.kohls.com

**Kona Grill, Inc.**
7150 E. Camelback Rd., #220
Scottsdale, AZ 85251
480-922-8100
www.konagrill.com

**Kraft Foods, Inc.** ⌣
Consumer Relations
One Kraft Court
Glenview, IL 60025
Toll free: 1-877-535-5666
www.kraftfoods.com

**Kroger Company**
1014 Vine St.
Cincinnati, OH 45202-1100
Toll free: 1-800-576-4377
www.kroger.com

## L

**LA Fitness International, LLC**
Member Services
PO Box 54170
Irvine, CA 92619-1300
www.lafitness.com

**Land O'Lakes, Inc.** ⌣
Consumer Affairs
PO Box 64050
St. Paul, MN 55164-9784
Toll free: 1-800-328-4155
Toll free: 1-800-328-9680 (Corporate)
www.landolakes.com

**Lands End, Inc.**
Customer Service
One Lands End Ln.
Dodgeville, WI 53595
Toll free: 1-800-963-4816
TTY: 1-800-541-3459
✉: landsend@landsend.com
www.landsend.com

**Lane Bryant**
777 S. State Rd. 7
Margate, FL 33068
Toll free: 1-866-886-4731
www.lanebryant.com

**Lane Furniture**
Consumer Services
PO Box 1627
Hwy. 145 South
Tupelo, MS 38802
Toll free: 1-877-405-3745
✉: service@lanefurniture.com
www.lanefurniture.com

**La-Z-Boy, Inc.**
Consumer Services
1284 N. Telegraph Rd.
Monroe, MI 48162-3309
Toll free: 1-800-375-6890
✉: cservice@la-z-boy.com
www.la-z-boy.com

**LeapFrog Enterprises, Inc.**
Customer Support
6401 Hollis St., Suite 100
Emeryville, CA 94608-1071
Toll free: 1-800-701-5327
Toll free: 1-866-334-5327
(Online Support)
✉: support@leapfrog.com
www.leapfrog.com

**Leap Wireless International, Inc.**
5887 Copley Dr.
San Diego, CA 92111
858-882-6000
Toll free: 1-800-274-2538
www.leapwireless.com

**Lee Jeans**
Consumer Services
9001 W. 67th St.
Merriam, KS 66202
Toll free: 1-800-453-3348
www.lee.com

**L'eggs Products**
Consumer Services
PO Box 3013
Winston-Salem, NC 27102
Toll free: 1-800-925-4872
www.leggs.com

**LEGO Systems Inc**
Consumer Affairs
555 Taylor Rd.
PO Box 1138
Enfield, CT 06083-1138
Toll free: 1-800-838-9647
Toll free: 1-877-518-5346
(Shop at Home)
www.lego.com

**Lennox Industries, Inc.** ⌣
Consumer Affairs
PO Box 799900
Dallas, TX 75379
Toll free: 1-800-953-6669
www.lennox.com

**LensCrafters**
4000 Luxottica Pl.
Mason, OH 45040
Toll free: 1-877-753-6727
www.lenscrafters.com

**Levi Strauss & Company** ⌣
1155 Battery St.
San Francisco, CA 94111
Toll free: 1-866-860-8907
✉: customerservice@levisstore.com
www.levi.com

**Lexmark International, Inc.**
740 W. New Circle Rd.
Lexington, KY 40550
Toll free: 1-800-539-6275
www.lexmark.com

**LG Electronics, Inc** ⌣
Customer Service
PO Box 240007
201 James Record Rd.
Huntsville, AL 35813
Toll free: 1-800-243-0000 (Appliances)
www.lge.com

**Liberty Mutual Insurance Group** ⟲
Customer Service
100 Liberty Way
Dover, NH 03820
Toll free: 1-800-398-8924
✉: Liberty.Service@
libertymutual.com
**www.libertymutual.com**

**Lillian Vernon Corporation**
Customer Service
PO Box 35980
Colorado Springs, CO 80935-5980
Toll free: 1-800-901-9291
✉: custservice@lillianvernon.com
**www.lillianvernon.com**

**Limited Brands, Inc.**
Customer Service
Three Limited Pkwy.
Columbus, OH 43230
614-415-7000
Toll free: 1-800-945-5088
**www.limitedbrands.com**

**LinkedIn Corporation**
2029 Stierlin Ct.
Mountain View, CA 94043
**www.linkedin.com**

**Little Tikes**
Consumer Services
2180 Barlow Rd.
Hudson, OH 44236
Toll free: 1-800-321-0183
✉: littletikes.cares@
littletikescare.com
**www.littletikes.com**

**L.L. Bean, Inc.**
Dept. CFM
Freeport, ME 04033-0001
207-552-3028
Toll free: 1-800-441-5713
TTY: 1-800-545-0090
**www.llbean.com**

**Loehmann's**
Customer Service
2500 Halsey St.
Bronx, NY 10461
1-855-563-4626
✉: customerservice@
loehmanns.com
**www.loehmanns.com**

**Longhorn Steakhouse**
See: Darden Restaurants
407-245-4000
**www.longhornsteakhouse.com**

**Long John Silver's Restaurants, Inc.**
✉: LJScares@LJSilvers.com
**www.ljsilvers.com**

**L'Oreal USA** ⟲
575 5th Ave.
New York, NY 10017
212-818-1500 (Headquarters)
Toll free: 1-800-322-2036
**www.lorealusa.com**

**Lowe's**
Customer Care
PO Box 1111
North Wilkesboro, NC 28656
Toll free: 1-800-445-6937
✉: customercare@lowes.com
**www.lowes.com**

## M

**MAACO Enterprises, Inc.**
610 Freedom Business Center
Suite 200
King of Prussia, PA 19406
610-265-6606
Toll free: 1-800-523-1180
**www.maaco.com**

**Macy's** ⟲
Customer Service
PO Box 8113
Mason, OH 45040
Toll free: 1-800-526-1202
Toll free: 1-877-493-9207 (Credit)
**www.macys.com**

**Magic Chef**
Customer Service
777 Mark St.
Wood Dale, IL 49022
Toll free: 1-888-775-0202
**www.magicchef.com**

**Magnavox**
Toll free: 1-800-705-2000
**www.magnavox.com**

**Marriott International, Inc.**
Guest Relations
1818 N. 90th St.
Omaha, NE 68114-1315
Toll free: 1-800-535-4028
✉: customer.care@marriott.com
**www.marriott.com**

**Mars Chocolate North America** ⟲
800 High St.
Hackettstown, NJ 07840
908-852-1000
✉: askus@masterfoodsusa.com
**www.masterfoods.com**

**Marshalls, Inc.**
See: TJX Companies, Inc.
Toll free: 1-888-627-7425
**www.marshallsonline.com**

**Massachusetts Mutual Insurance Company (Mass Mutual)**
Customer Relations
1295 State St.
Springfield, MA 01111-0001
Toll free: 1-800-272-2216
(Life Insurance)
Toll free: 1-800-505-8952
(Long Term Insurance)
**www.massmutual.com**

**MasterCard Worldwide**
Consumer Inquiries
(Contact your issuing bank first)
2000 Purchase St.
Purchase, NY 10577
Toll free: 1-800-307-7309
✉: Consumer_Inquiries@
mastercard.com
**www.mastercard.com**

**Match.com, LLC**
PO Box 25472
Dallas, TX 75225
**www.match.com**

**Mattel, Inc.**
Worldwide Consumer Affairs
333 Continental Blvd.
El Segundo, CA 90245-5012
310-252-2000
Toll free: 1-800-524-8697
TTY: 1-800-382-7470
**www.mattel.com**

**Maybelline, Inc.**
Consumer Affairs
PO Box 1010
Clark, NJ 07066
Toll free: 1-800-944-0730
**www.maybelline.com**

**Mayflower Transit, LLC**
One Mayflower Dr.
St. Louis, MO 63026
636-305-4000
Toll free: 1-800-241-1321
Toll free: 1-800-325-9970 (Claims)
**www.mayflower.com**

**Maytag**
Customer Service
553 Benson Rd.
Benton Harbor, MI 49022
Toll free: 1-800-344-1274
**www.maytag.com**

**McCormick & Company, Inc.** ⟲
Consumer Affairs
211 Schilling Circle
Hunt Valley, MD 21031
410-527-6000
Toll free: 1-800-632-5847
**www.mccormick.com**

**McCormick & Schmicks Seafood Restaurants**
1510 W. Loop South
Houston, TX 77027
713-850-1010
Toll free: 1-800-552-6379
**www.mccormickandschmicks.com**

**McDonald's Corporation** ⟲
Customer Satisfaction Dept.
2111 McDonalds Dr.
Oak Brook, IL 60523
Toll free: 1-800-244-6227
**www.mcdonalds.com**

**McKee Foods Corporation** ⟲
PO Box 750
Collegedale, TN 37315
Toll free: 1-800-522-4499
**www.mckeefoods.com**

**Meineke Car Care Centers, Inc.**
Customer Service
128 S. Tryon St., Suite 900
Charlotte, NC 28202
704-377-8855
Toll free: 1-800-447-3070
**www.meineke.com**

**The Mentholatum Company, Inc.**
Consumer Affairs
707 Sterling Dr.
Orchard Park, NY 14127
716-677-2500
Toll free: 1-800-688-9046
**www.mentholatum.com**

**Merck & Co., Inc.**
One Merck Dr.
PO Box 100
Whitehouse Station, NJ 08889-0100
908-423-1000
Toll free: 1-800-444-2080
Toll free: 1-800-727-5400
(Patient Assistance)
**www.merck.com**

**Merrill Lynch Company, Inc.**
(Contact local branch manager first)
4 World Financial Center
250 Vesey St.
New York, NY 10080
Toll free: 1-800-637-7455
TTY: 1-800-657-3323
✉: general_askml@ml.com
**www.merrilllynch.com**

**Merry Maids**
See: Service Master Company
Toll free: 1-800-637-7962
✉: info@merrymaids.com
**www.merrymaids.com**

**MetLife, Inc.**
1095 Avenue of the Americas
New York, NY 10036
Toll free: 1-800-638-5433
**www.metlife.com**

**Michelinas**
See: Bellisio Foods, Inc.
218-723-5555
✉: michelinas@bellisiofoods.com
**www.michelinas.com**

**Michelin North America, Inc.**
Consumer Care Department
PO Box 19001
Greenville, SC 29602-9001
Toll free: 1-866-866-6605
**www.michelinman.com**

**Microsoft Corporation**
Customer Service
1 Microsoft Way
Redmond, WA 98052-6399
425-882-8080
Toll free: 1-800-642-7676
TTY: 1-800-892-5234
**www.microsoft.com**

**Midas, Inc.** ⟲
Consumer Relations
823 Donald Ross Rd.
Juno Beach, FL 33408
Toll free: 1-800-621-8545
**www.midas.com**

**MillerCoors** ⟲
Consumer Affairs
250 S. Wacker Dr.
Chicago, IL 60606-5888
Toll free: 1-800-645-5376
✉: contact@millercoors.com
**www.millercoors.com**

**Mitsubishi Digital Electronics America, Inc.**
Consumer Relations Department
9351 Jeronimo Rd.
Irvine, CA 92618
Toll free: 1-800-332-2119
✉: tvsupport@mevsa.com
**www.mitsubishi-tv.com**

**Money Management International** ♦
14141 Southwest Fwy.
Suite 1000
Sugar Land, TX 77478-3494
Toll free: 1-866-889-9347
**www.moneymanagement.org**

**Morgan Stanley**
Client Advocate
1585 Broadway
New York, NY 10036
Toll free: 1-800-869-3326
✉: clientadvocate@
morganstanley.com
**www.morganstanley.com**

**Motel 6**
Guest Relations
PO Box 326
Worthington, OH 43085
614-601-4089
Toll free: 1-800-557-3435
**www.motel6.com**

**Motorola, Inc.**
Corporate Communications
600 N. US Highway 45
Libertyville, IL 60048
847-523-5000
Toll free: 1-800-734-5870
TTY: 1-888-390-6456
**www.motorola.com**

**Motts, Inc.**
Consumer Relations
PO Box 869077
Plano, TX 75086-9077
Toll free: 1-800-426-4891
**www.motts.com**

**Movado Group, Inc.**
650 From Rd., Suite 375
Paramus, NJ 07652-3556
201-267-8000
Toll free: 1-800-810-2311
**www.movadogroupinc.com**

**Mutual of Omaha Insurance Company**
Customer Service
Mutual of Omaha Plaza
Omaha, NE 68175
402-342-7600
Toll free: 1-800-228-7104
Toll free: 1-800-775-1000 (Claims)
✉: individualclaims@
mutualofomaha.com
**www.mutualofomaha.com**

**Myspace.com**
8391 Beverly Blvd., #349
Los Angeles, CA 90048
✉: info@myspace.com
**www.myspace.com**

## N

**Nabisco Foods Group**
See: Kraft Foods, Inc.
Toll free: 1-800-622-4726
www.nabiscoworld.com

**National Amusements, Inc.**
Customer Service
PO Box 9108
846 University Ave.
Dedham, MA 02062-9108
✉: customer_service@
national-amusements.com
www.showcasecinemas.com

**National Car Rental System, Inc.**
Customer Service
8420 St. John Industrial Dr.
St. Louis, MO 63114
Toll free: 1-800-468-3334
TTY: 1-800-328-6323
www.nationalcar.com

**Nationwide Mutual Insurance Company**
Customer Advocacy
One Nationwide Plaza
Columbus, OH 43215-0220
Toll free: 1-877-669-6877
(Auto and Property Insurance)
Toll free: 1-800-882-2822
(General Inquiries)
Toll free: 1-800-848-6331 (Investments)
www.nationwide.com

**NaturaLawn of America**
One E. Church St.
Fredrick, MD 21701
301-694-5440
Toll free: 1-800-989-5444
✉: natural@nl-amer.com
www.nl-amer.com

**Nautica Enterprises, Inc.**
Consumer Relations
40 W. 57th St.
New York, NY 10019
Toll free: 1-866-376-4184
www.nautica.com

**NBC Universal, Inc.**
Viewer Relations
30 Rockefeller Plaza
New York, NY 10112
212-664-2333
✉: nbcshows@nbcuni.com
www.nbc.com

**The Neiman-Marcus Group, Inc.** ⟲
Customer Relations
PO Box 650589
Dallas, TX 75265-0589
214-761-2660
Toll free: 1-888-888-4757
www.neimanmarcus.com

**Nestle Purina PetCare Company** ⟲
Office of Consumer Affairs
Checkerboard Square
St. Louis, MO 63164
314-982-1000
Toll free: 1-800-778-7462
www.purina.com

**Nestle USA** ⟲
Consumer Services Center
800 N. Brand Blvd.
Glendale, CA 91203
Toll free: 1-800-225-2270
www.nestle.com

**Nestle Waters North America, Inc.** ⟲
900 Long Ridge Rd., Bldg. 2
Stamford, CT 06902-1138
203-531-4100
Toll free: 1-866-676-1672
www.nestle-watersna.com

**Netflix**
Customer Service
100 Winchester Circle
Los Gatos, CA 95032
Toll free: 1-866-579-7172
www.netflix.com

**Neutrogena Corporation**
Consumer Affairs
199 Grandview Rd.
Skillman, NJ 08558
Toll free: 1-800-582-4048
✉: ntgweb@neuus.jnj.com
www.neutrogena.com

**New England Financial**
See: MetLife, Inc.
Toll free: 1-800-388-4000
www.nefn.com

**New York and Company**
Customer Service
450 W. 33rd St., 5th Floor
New York, NY 10001
Toll free: 1-800-723-5333
Toll free: 1-800-961-9906 (Website)
✉: service@nyandcompany.com
www.nyandcompany.com

**New York Life Insurance Company**
Corporate Compliance Department
One Rockwood Rd.
Sleepy Hollow, NY 10591
Toll free: 1-800-710-7945
www.newyorklife.com

**Nexxus Products Company**
See: Unilever
Toll free: 1-800-444-6399
www.nexxus.com

**Nickelodeon**
1515 Broadway
New York, NY 10036
212-846-2543
www.nick.com

**Nike, Inc.** ⟲
Consumer Services
One Bowerman Dr.
Beaverton, OR 97005
503-671-6453
Toll free: 1-800-806-6453
www.nike.com

**Nikon, Inc.**
Consumer Affairs
1300 Walt Whitman Rd.
Melville, NY 11747-3064
631-547-4200
310-414-8107 (Parts)
Toll free: 1-800-645-6687
(Technical and Service Repair)
www.nikonusa.com

**Nine West Group, Inc.**
Customer Relations
Nine West Plaza
1129 Westchester Ave.
White Plains, NY 10604
914-640-6400
Toll free: 1-800-999-1877
www.ninewest.com

**Nintendo** ⟲
4600 150th Ave., NE
Redmond, WA 98052
Toll free: 1-800-255-3700
www.nintendo.com

**Nokia USA**
Customer Contact Center
6021 Connection Dr.
Irving, TX 75039
Toll free: 1-888-665-4228
TTY: 1-800-246-6542
✉: customercare@nokia.com
nokiausa.com

♦ Provided financial support for the publication of the Consumer Action Handbook.

**Nordstrom, Inc.**
Customer Service
1700 7th Ave., Suite 300
Seattle, WA 98101
Toll free: 1-888-282-6060
**www.nordstrom.com**

**North American Van Lines**
North American Claims Department
PO Box 988
Ft. Wayne, IN 46801-0988
Toll free: 1-800-348-2111
**www.navl.com**

**The North Face, Inc.**
Customer Service
2013 Farallon Dr.
San Leandro, CA 94577
Toll free: 1-800-863-1968
Toll free: 1-855-500-8639 (Warranties)
✉: tnfsupport@vfc.com
**www.thenorthface.com**

**Northwestern Mutual Life
Insurance Company**
Corporate Relations
720 E. Wisconsin Ave.
Milwaukee, WI 53202-4797
414-271-1444
**www.northwesternmutual.com**

**Norwegian Cruise Lines**
Guest Relations
7665 Corporate Center Dr.
Miami, FL 33126
Toll free: 1-866-625-1164
Toll free: 1-866-584-9756
(Special Needs)
**www.ncl.com**

**Novartis Pharmaceuticals
Corporation** ∽
Customer Interaction Center
One Health Plaza
East Hanover, NJ 07936-1080
862-778-8300
Toll free: 1-888-669-6682
**www.pharma.us.novartis.com**

**The NutraSweet Company**
Customer Service
10 S. Wacker Dr.
Chicago, IL 60606
Toll free: 1-800-323-5321
**www.nutrasweet.com**

**NutriSystem, Inc.**
Customer Service
600 Office Center Dr.
Fort Washington, PA 19034
215-706-5300
Toll free: 1-800-585-5483
✉: customerservice@
nutrisystem.com.
**www.nutrisystem.com**

## O

**Ocean Spray Cranberries, Inc.** ∽
Consumer Affairs Department
One Ocean Spray Dr.
Lakeville-Middleboro, MA 02349
Toll free: 1-800-662-3263
**www.oceanspray.com**

**Office Depot, Inc.**
6600 N. Military Trail
Boca Raton, FL 33496
Toll free: 1-800-463-3768
**www.officedepot.com**

**OfficeMax, Inc.**
Customer Service
263 Shuman Blvd.
Naperville, IL 60563
630-438-7800
Toll free: 1-800-283-7674
✉: online@officemax.com
**www.officemax.com**

**Old Navy**
Customer Relations
200 Old Navy Ln.
Grove City, OH 43123-8605
Toll free: 1-800-653-6289
TTY: 1-800-449-4253
✉: custserv@oldnavy.com
**www.oldnavy.com**

**Olive Garden**
PO Box 695017
Orlando, FL 32869
Toll free: 1-800-331-2729
**www.olivegarden.com**

**Olympus America**
3500 Corporate Pkwy.
PO Box 610
Center Valley, PA 18034-0610
Toll free: 1-800-622-6372
Toll free: 1-888-553-4448
(Digital Cameras)
**www.olympusamerica.com**

**Omni Hotels**
Guest Relations
420 Decker Dr.
Irving, TX 75062
Toll free: 1-800-809-6664
**www.omnihotels.com**

**1-800-FLOWERS**
Customer Satisfaction Department
One Old Country Rd., Suite 500
Carle Place, NY 11514
Toll free: 1-800-356-9377
Toll free: 1-800-716-4851
(Customer Service)
**www.1800flowers.com**

**On the Border**
See: Brinker International
Toll free: 1-800-682-6882
**www.ontheborder.com**

**Orbitz, Inc.** ∽
Customer Service
500 W. Madison St., Suite 1000
Chicago, IL 60661
Toll free: 1-888-656-4546
**www.orbitz.com**

**Orkin**
Customer Care Center
2170 Piedmont Rd., NE
Atlanta, GA 30324
Toll free: 1-888-675-4662
**www.orkin.com**

**Oster**
See: Jarden Consumer Solutions, Inc.
Toll free: 1-800-334-0759
**www.oster.com**

**Outback Steakhouse**
2202 N. West Shore Blvd., Suite 500
Tampa, FL 33607-5761
813-282-1225
✉: newsoutback@outback.com
**www.outback.com**

**Overstock.com**
Customer Service
6350 S. 3000 E
Salt Lake City, UT 84121
Toll free: 1-800-843-2446
**www.overstock.com**

**Owens Corning**
Consumer Relations
One Owens Corning Pkwy.
Toledo, OH 43659
Toll free: 1-800-438-7465
✉: answers@
answers.owenscorning.com
**www.owenscorning.com**

## P

**Panasonic Corporation
of North America**
Customer Experience Department
661 Independence Pkwy.
Chesapeake, VA 23320
Toll free: 1-800-211-7262
**www.panasonic.com**

**Panera Bread**
6710 Clayton Rd.
Richmond Heights, MO 63117
314-633-7100
Toll free: 1-800-301-5566
**www.panerabread.com**

**Papa John's International, Inc.**
PO Box 99900
Louisville, KY 40269-9990
Toll free: 1-877-547-7272
**www.papajohns.com**

**Pathmark Stores, Inc.**
Customer Relations
Two Paragon Dr.
Montvale, NJ 07645
Toll free: 1-866-443-7374
✉: customers@pathmark.com
**www.pathmark.com**

**Payless ShoeSource**
Customer Service
3231 S.E. 6th Ave.
Topeka, KS 66607
Toll free: 1-877-474-6379
✉: CustomerService@
csr.payless.com
**www.payless.com**

**PayPal.com**
2211 N. 1st St.
San Jose, CA 95131
Toll free: 1-888-221-1161
**www.paypal.com**

**PearleVision**
Customer Service
4000 Luxottica Pl.
Mason, OH 45040
Toll free: 1-800-937-3937
**www.pearlevision.com**

**Pennzoil**
See: Shell Oil Company
713-546-4000
Toll free: 1-800-237-8645
✉: generalpublicenquiries-us@
shell.com
**www.pennzoil.com**

**Pep Boys Auto**
3111 W. Allegheny Ave.
Philadelphia, PA 19132
Toll free: 1-800-737-2697
✉: custserv@pepboys.com
**www.pepboys.com**

**Pepperidge Farm, Inc.** ⟲
Consumer Affairs
595 Westport Ave.
Norwalk, CT 06851
Toll free: 1-888-737-7374
**www.pepperidgefarm.com**

**Pepsi-Cola Company** ⟲
Consumer Relations
One Pepsi Way
Somers, NY 10589
Toll free: 1-800-433-2652
**www.pepsico.com**

**Perdue Farms, Inc.** ⟲
Consumer Relations
PO Box 1656
Horsham, PA 19044-6656
Toll free: 1-800-473-7383
**www.perdue.com**

**Petco**
Toll free: 1-877-738-6742
**www.petco.com**

**PetSmart, Inc.**
Customer Service
Toll free: 1-888-839-9638
✉: customercare@petsmart.com
**www.petsmart.com**

**P.F. Chang's China Bistro, Inc.**
7676 E. Pinnacle Peak Rd.
Scottsdale, AZ 85255
Toll free: 1-866-732-4264
**www.pfchangs.com**

**Pfizer, Inc.**
Consumer Affairs
235 E. 42nd St.
New York, NY 10017
212-733-2323
Toll free: 1-800-879-3477
(Customer Response)
Toll free: 1-800-438-1985
(Medical Questions)
**www.pfizer.com**

**Pharmavite Corporation** ⟲
Consumer Affairs
PO Box 9606
Mission Hills, CA 91346-9606
818-221-6200
Toll free: 1-800-276-2878 (Nature Made)
Toll free: 1-888-676-9569 (Soy Joy)
**www.pharmavite.com**

**Philip Morris USA**
Quality Department
PO Box 18583
Pittsburgh, PA 15236
804-274-2000
Toll free: 1-800-343-0975
**www.philipmorrisusa.com**

**Philips Consumer Electronics North America**
Customer Service
3000 Minuteman Rd., Mail Stop 109
Andover, MA 01810
Toll free: 1-888-744-5477
**www.philips.com**

**Phillips-Van Heusen Corporation**
Customer Services
1001 Frontier Rd., Mail Stop # 44
Bridgewater, NJ 08807
Toll free: 1-800-388-9122 (Van Heusen)
Toll free: 1-800-950-2277 (Bass)
Toll free: 1-800-866-7292 (Izod)
Toll free: 1-866-214-6694 (Calvin Klein)
**www.pvh.com**

**Pinnacle Foods Group LLC** ⟲
Consumer Relations
PO Box 3900
Peoria, IL 61612
**pinnaclefoods.com**

**Pioneer Electronics Service, Inc.**
Customer Service
Toll free: 1-800-228-7221(Parts)
Toll free: 1-800-421-1404 (General Service)
**www.pioneerelectronics.com**

**Pirelli Tire Corporation**
100 Pirelli Dr.
Rome, GA 30161
Toll free: 1-800-747-3554
**www.us.pirelli.com**

**Pizza Hut** ⟲
7100 Corporate Dr.
Plano, TX 75024
972-338-7700
Toll free: 1-800-948-8488
**www.pizzahut.com**

**Playskool**
Toll free: 1-800-752-9755
✉: customersupport@hasbro.com
**www.hasbro.com/playskool**

**Playstation**
See: Sony Corporation of America
Toll free: 1-800-345-7669
**www.us.playstation.com**

**Playtex Products, Inc.**
Consumer Affairs
890 Mountain Ave.
New Providence, NJ 07974
Toll free: 1-888-310-4290
**www.playtexproductsinc.com**

**Polaroid Corporation**
Customer Care Center
4400 Baker Ave.
Minnetonka, MN 55343
Toll free: 1-800-765-2764
(Product Support)
Toll free: 1-888-312-2615
(Order Support)
✉: info@polaroid.com
**www.polaroid.com**

**Polo/Ralph Lauren Corporation**
Consumer Relations
625 Madison Ave., 11th Floor
New York, NY 10022
Toll free: 1-888-475-7674
✉: customerassistance@
ralphlauren.com
**www.polo.com**

**Popeyes Louisiana Kitchen**
Guest Hospitality
PO Box 725489
Atlanta, GA 31139
Toll free: 1-877-767-3937
✉: popeyescommunications@
popeyes.com
**www.popeyes.com**

**Prestige Brands** ⌣
Office of Consumer Affairs
90 N. Broadway
Irvington, NY 10533
Toll free: 1-800-443-4908
**www.prestigebrandsinc.com**

**Price Chopper Supermarkets** ⌣
Consumer Services
461 Nott St.
Schenectady, NY 12308
518-355-5000
Toll free: 1-800-666-7667
**www.pricechopper.com**

**Priceline**
800 Connecticut Ave.
Norwalk, CT 06854
Toll free: 1-877-477-5807
**www.priceline.com**

**Princess Cruise Lines**
Customer Relations
24305 Town Center Dr.
Santa Clarita, CA 91355
Toll free: 1-800-774-6237
✉: customerrelations@
princesscruises.com
**www.princess.com**

**The Procter & Gamble
Company** ⌣◆
Consumer Relations
PO Box 599
Cincinnati, OH 45201
513-983-1100
Toll free: (Toll free numbers
appear on all labels)
**www.pg.com**

**The Progressive Corporation**
Customer Service
6300 Wilson Mills Rd.
Mayfield Village, OH 44143
440-461-5000 (Corporate)
Toll free: 1-800-776-4737
**www.progressive.com**

**Prudential Financial, Inc.**
Policyowner Relations Dept.
One Corporate Dr.
Shelton, CT 06484
Toll free: 1-800-778-2255 (Insurance)
Toll free: 1-888-778-2888 (Annuities)
Toll free: 1-800-732-0416
(Long-Term Care)
TTY: 1-800-526-8061
**www.prudential.com**

**Publishers Clearing House** ⌣
Consumer Affairs
101 Winners Circle
Port Washington, NY 11050
Toll free: 1-800-459-4724
Toll free: 1-800-392-4190 (Sweepstakes scams using PCH name)
✉: pchconsumeraffairs@pch.com
**www.pch.com**

**Publix** ⌣
Consumer Relations
PO Box 407
Lakeland, FL 33802-0407
Toll free: 1-800-242-1227
**www.publix.com**

## Q

**Qdoba Mexican Grill**
4865 Ward Rd., Suite 500
Wheat Ridge, CO 80033-1902
720-898-2300
Toll free: 1-888-497-3622
✉: info@qdoba.com
**www.qdoba.com**

**The Quaker Oats Company**
Consumer Response/QTG
PO Box 049003
Chicago, IL 60604-9003
312-821-1000
Toll free: 1-800-367-6287
**www.quakeroats.com**

**QuikTrip Corporation**
PO Box 3475
Tulsa, OK 74101
918-615-7700
Toll free: 1-800-848-1966
**www.quiktrip.com**

**Quiznos**
1001 17th St., Suite 200
Denver, CO 80202
720-359-3300 (Headquarters)
Toll free: 1-866-486-2783
(Customer Comments)
**www.quiznos.com**

**QVC, Inc.**
Customer Service
1200 Wilson Drive at Studio Park
West Chester, PA 19380
Toll free: 1-800-345-5788
TTY: 1-800-544-3316
✉: QVCcares@QVC.com
**www.qvc.com**

## R

**Radio Shack Corporation**
Customer Care
Riverfront Campus
Mail Stop #CF4-216
300 Radio Shack Circle
Fort Worth, TX 76102-1964
817-415-3011
Toll free: 1-800-843-7422
✉: RadioShack.Customer.Care@
RadioShack.com
**www.radioshack.com**

**Radisson Hotels Resorts**
11340 Blondo St., Suite 100
Omaha, NE 68164
Toll free: 1-800-615-7253
**www.radisson.com**

**Ramada Inn**
See: Wyndham Hotel Group
Toll free: 1-800-828-6644
**www.ramada.com**

**Rayovac Corporation**
Consumer Service
PO Box 44960
Madison, WI 53744
Toll free: 1-800-237-7000
✉: consumers@rayovac.com
**www.rayovac.com**

**Readers Digest Association, Inc.**
Customer Service
Readers Digest Rd.
Pleasantville, NY 10570-7000
914-238-1000
Toll free: 1-800-304-2807
TTY: 1-800-735-4327
✉: letters@rd.com
**www.readersdigest.com**

**Reckitt Benckiser, Inc.**
Consumer Relations
PO Box 224
Parsippany, NJ 07054-0224
Toll free: 1-800-228-4722
✉: corpcomms@
reckittbenckiser.com
**www.reckittbenckiser.com**

**Red Lobster**
Guest Relations
1000 Darden Center Dr.
Orlando, FL 32837
407-245-4000
Toll free: 1-800-562-7837
**www.redlobster.com**

**Regal Ware, Inc.**
Consumer Service
1675 Reigle Dr.
Kewaskum, WI 53040
262-626-2121
✉: info@regalware.com
**www.regalware.com**

**Remington Products Company**
Consumer Services
PO Box 1
DeForest, WI 53532
Toll free: 1-800-392-6544
✉: ContactUs@
remingtonproducts.com
**www.remington-products.com**

**Rent-A-Center**
Customer Service
5501 Headquarters Dr.
Plano, TX 75024
Toll free: 1-800-422-8186
**www.rentacenter.com**

**Residence Inn**
See: Marriott International, Inc.
Toll free: 1-800-228-2800
**www.residenceinn.com**

**Rich Products**
Consumer Relations
PO Box 20670
127 Airport Rd.
St. Simons Island, GA 31522
912-638-5000
Toll free: 1-888-732-7251
✉: rsp-consumer.relations@rich.com

**Rite Aid Corporation**
Customer Support
PO Box 3165
Harrisburg, PA 17105
717-761-2633
Toll free: 1-800-748-3243
Toll free: 1-888-213-9920 (Rebates)
TTY: 1-800-821-1833
**www.riteaid.com**

**Rolex Watch U.S.A., Inc.**
665 5th Ave., 5th Floor
New York, NY 10022
212-758-7700
**www.rolex.com**

**Roto-Rooter Corporation**
225 E. 5th St.
Cincinnati, OH 45202
513-762-6690
Toll free: 1-800-438-7686
**www.roto-rooter.com**

**Royal Caribbean International**
Corporate Guest Relations
1050 Caribbean Way
Miami, FL 33132
Toll free: 1-800-256-6649
Toll free: 1-800-398-9819 (Website)
**www.royalcaribbean.com**

**Rubbermaid**
Consumer Services
3320 W. Market St.
Fairlawn, OH 44333
Toll free: 1-888-895-2110
**www.rubbermaid.com**

**Ruths Chris Steakhouse**
Ruths Hospitality Group, Inc.
1030 W. Canton Ave., Suite 100
Winter Park, FL 32789
407-333-7440
**www.ruthschris.com**

## S

**Safe Auto Insurance**
Customer Service
PO Box 182109
Columbus, OH 43218-2109
Toll free: 1-800-723-3288
✉: csd@safeauto.com

**Safeway, Inc.**
Customer Service Center
MS 10501
PO Box 29093
Phoenix, AZ 85038-9093
Toll free: 1-877-723-3929
**www.safeway.com**

**Saks Fifth Avenue**
Customer Relations
PO Box 10327
Jackson, MS 39289
212-940-5027
Toll free: 1-877-551-7257
✉: service@saks.com
**www.saks.com**

**Sam's Club**
Member Service
2101 S.E. Simple Savings Dr.
Bentonville, AR 72716-0745
Toll free: 1-888-746-7726
**www.samsclub.com**

**Samsonite Corporation**
Customer Service
575 West St., Suite 110
Mansfield, MA 02048
Toll free: 1-800-765-2247
Toll free: 1-800-262-8282 (Warranty)
✉: questions@samsonite.com
**www.samsonite.com**

**Samsung Electronics America**
Customer Service and
Technical Support
85 Challenger Rd.
Ridgefield Park, NJ 07660
Toll free: 1-800-726-7864
Toll free: 1-888-987-4357
(Mobile Phones)
TTY: 1-888-899-7608
**www.samsung.com**

**Sanofi-Aventis**
55 Corporate Dr.
Bridgewater, NJ 08807-2854
Toll free: 1-800-981-2491
**www.sanofi-aventis.us**

**Sargento Foods Inc.** ☙
Consumer Affairs
One Persnickety Pl.
Plymouth, WI 53073
920-893-8484 (Corporate)
Toll free: 1-800-243-3737
**www.sargento.com**

**Sara Lee Foods**
See: Hillshire Brands
**saralee.com**

**SC Johnson and Son, Inc.** ☙
1525 Howe St.
Racine, WI 53403
Toll free: 1-800-494-4855
**www.scjohnsonwax.com**

**The Scotts Company** ☙
Help Center
14111 Scottslawn Rd.
Marysville, OH 43041
Toll free: 1-888-270-3714
**www.scotts.com**

**Seabourn Cruise Line**
Guest Relations
300 Elliott Ave., W
Seattle, WA 98119
206-626-9179
Toll free: 1-866-755-5619
✉: guestrelations@seabourn.com
**www.seabourn.com**

**Sealy Corporation**
Consumer Support
One Office Parkway at Sealy Dr.
Trinity, NC 27370
Toll free: 1-800-697-3259
**www.sealy.com**

◆ Provided financial support for the publication of the Consumer Action Handbook.

**Sears**
Executive Customer Relations
3333 Beverly Rd.
Mail Stop RR
Hoffman Estates, IL 60179
847-286-2500
Toll free: 1-800-549-4505 (Retail)
Toll free: 1-800-697-3277 (Online)
TTY: 1-800-659-7017
**www.sears.com**

**Seiko Instruments USA, Inc.**
Customer Service
2990 Lomita Blvd.
Torrance, CA 90505
Toll free: 1-800-757-1011
**www.seikoinstruments.com**

**Seneca Foods Corporation**
Consumer Affairs
3736 S. Main St.
Marion, NY 14505
315-926-8100
Toll free: 1-800-872-1110
**www.senecafoods.com**

**Serta, Inc.**
Customer Service
Three Golf Center #392
Hoffman Estates, IL 60169
847-645-0200
Toll free: 1-888-557-3782
✉: customer.service@serta.com
**www.serta.com**

**Service Master Company**
860 Ridge Lake Blvd.
Memphis, TN 38120
**www.servicemaster.com**

**7-Eleven, Inc**
Customer Relations
Location 231
PO Box 711
Dallas, TX 75221-0711
972-828-7011
Toll free: 1-800-255-0711
**www.7-Eleven.com**

**Sharp Electronics Corporation**
Customer Service
Sharp Plaza
Mahwah, NJ 07495
Toll free: 1-800-237-4277
**www.sharpusa.com**

**Shell Oil Company**
Customer Care
PO Box 2463
Houston, TX 77252
713-241-6161 (Headquarters)
Toll free: 1-888-467-4355
Toll free: 1-800-331-3703 (Shell Card)
✉: ShellCustomerCare@shell.com
**www.shellus.com**

**Sheraton Hotels**
See: Starwood Hotels & Resorts
Worldwide, Inc.
Toll free: 1-800-325-3535
**www.sheraton.com**

**Sherwin-Williams Company**
Midland Building
101 Prospect Ave., NW
PO Box 647
Cleveland, OH 44115
Toll free: 1-800-474-3794
**www.sherwin-williams.com**

**Shoneys, Inc.**
Guest Relations
1717 Elm Hill Pike, Suite B-1
Nashville, TN 37210
615-391-5395
Toll free: 1-877-377-2233
✉: helpdesk@shoneys.com
**www.shoneys.com**

**Simmons Bedding Company**
Consumer Service
One Concourse Pkwy., Suite 800
Atlanta, GA 30328-6188
Toll free: 1-877-399-9397
✉: customerassistance@
simmons.com
**www.simmons.com**

**Slim-Fast Foods Company**
Consumer Services Dept.
920 Sylvan Ave., 2nd Floor
Englewood Cliffs, NJ 07632
Toll free: 1-800-754-6327
✉: support@slimfast.com
**www.slimfast.com**

**Sonesta International Hotels Corporation**
255 Washington St.
Newton, MA 02458
617-421-5447
Toll free: 1-800-766-3782
✉: info@sonesta.com
**www.sonesta.com**

**Sony Corporation of America**
Consumer Information Service Center
12451 Gateway Blvd.
Fort Myers, FL 33913
239-768-7547 (Consumer Eletronics)
Toll free: 1-800-345-7669 (Playstation)
**www.sony.com**

**Southwest Airlines**
Customer Relations Department
PO Box 36647-1CR
Dallas, TX 75235
214-932-0333
Toll free: 1-800-435-9792
TTY: 1-800-533-1305
**www.southwest.com**

**Spiegel Brands, Inc**
Customer Satisfaction
One Spiegel Ave.
Hampton, VA 23630-5367
Toll free: 1-800-222-5680
✉: clientservices@spiegel.com
**www.spiegel.com**

**Spirit Airlines**
2800 Executive Way
Miramar, FL 33025
Toll free: 1-800-772-7117
✉: customer@spirit.com
**www.spiritair.com**

**Springs Global U.S., Inc.**
Public Relations Dept. of
Corporate Communication
PO Box 70
Fort Mill, SC 29716
803-547-1500
Toll free: 1-888-926-7888
Toll free: 1-800-221-6352
(Window Products)
**www.springs.com**

**Sprint Nextel**
KSOPHT0101-Z4300
6391 Sprint Pkwy.
Overland Park, KS 66251-4300
Toll free: 1-888-211-4727
(Sprint Phones)
Toll free: 1-800-639-6111
(Nextel Phones)
Toll free: 1-800-877-4646
(Wireline Service)
**www.sprint.com**

**Stanley Hardware (Division of the Stanley Works)**
Customer Service
480 Myrtle St.
New Britain, CT 06053
Toll free: 1-800-622-4393
**www.stanleyhardware.com**

**Staples, Inc.**
Consumer Affairs
500 Staples Dr.
Framingham, MA 01702
Toll free: 1-800-378-2753
**www.staples.com**

**Starbucks**
Customer Relations
PO Box 3717
Seattle, WA 98124-3717
Toll free: 1-800-782-7282
**www.starbucks.com**

**Starwood Hotels & Resorts Worldwide, Inc.** ↄ
Customer Service
PO Box 6020
Lancaster, CA 93539
Toll free: 1-800-625-5144
✉: customercare@
starwoodhotels.com
**www.starwoodhotels.com**

**State Farm**
Customer Service
One State Farm Plaza
Bloomington, IL 61710
309-766-2311
Toll free: 1-800-782-8332
✉: info@statefarm.com
**www.statefarm.com**

**SteinMart**
1200 Riverplace Blvd.
Jacksonville, FL 32207
904-346-1500
Toll free: 1-888-783-4662
✉: e-customerservice@
steinmart.com
**www.steinmart.com**

**Stop & Shop Supermarket Company, Inc.**
Customer Service Dept.
1385 Hancock St.
Quincy, MA 02169
Toll free: 1-800-767-7772
**www.stopandshop.com**

**StubHub, Inc.**
199 Fremont St., Suite 300
San Francisco, CA 94105
✉: customerservice@stubhub.com
**www.stubhub.com**

**Subway**
325 Bic Dr.
Milford, CT 06461
Toll free: 1-800-888-4848
**www.subway.com**

**Suntrust**
PO Box 85024
Richmond, VA 23285-5024
Toll free: 1-800-786-8787
TTY: 1-800-854-8965
**www.suntrust.com**

**Symantec Corporation**
Customer Service
350 Ellis St.
Mountain View, CA 94043
Toll free: 1-800-721-3934
**www.symantec.com**

## T

**Taco Bell**
Customer Relations
One Glen Bell Way
Irvine, CA 92618
Toll free: 1-800-822-6235
**www.tacobell.com**

**Talbots**
Customer Service Department
One Talbots Dr.
Hingham, MA 02043
781-741-4028
Toll free: 1-800-992-9010
TTY: 1-800-624-9179
✉: customerservice@talbots.com
**www.talbots.com**

**Target Stores** ↄ
Guest Relations and Quality Assurance
PO Box 9350
Minneapolis, MN 55440
Toll free: 1-800-440-0680
✉: guest.relations@target.com
**www.target.com**

**TEAC America, Inc.** ↄ
Customer Service
7733 Telegraph Rd.
Montebello, CA 90640
323-726-0303
323-727-7627 (Service)
✉: custser@teac.com
**www.teac.com**

**Teleflora**
PO Box 60910
Los Angeles, CA 90060-0910
Toll free: 1-800-835-3356
✉: service@teleflora.com
**www.teleflora.com**

**Terminix**
See: Service Master Company
Toll free: 1-800-837-6464
✉: terminixcares@terminix.com
**www.terminix.com**

**Texas Instruments, Inc.**
Consumer Relations
PO Box 660199
Dallas, TX 75266-0199
972-995-2011
Toll free: 1-800-842-2737
**www.ti.com**

**T.G.I. Fridays**
Guest Relations
4201 Marsh Ln.
Carrollton, TX 75007
Toll free: 1-800-374-4297 (Option 1)
**www.tgifridays.com**

**3M**
Customer Relations
3M Center
St. Paul, MN 55144-1000
651-737-6501
Toll free: 1-800-364-3577
**www.3m.com**

**Thrifty Car Rental**
PO Box 35250
Tulsa, OK 74153
918-669-2168
Toll free: 1-800-847-4389
TTY: 1-888-332-3677
✉: customercare@thrifty.com
**www.thrifty.com**

**TicketMaster**
Attn: Fan Support
1000 Corporate Landing
Charleston, WV 25311
Toll free: 1-800-653-8000
**www.ticketmaster.com**

**Time, Inc.**
Consumer Affairs
3000 University Center Dr.
Tampa, FL 33612-6408
813-979-6625
Toll free: 1-866-550-6934
✉: subsvcs@time.customersvc.com
**www.time.com**

**Time Warner, Inc.**
One Time Warner Center
New York, NY 10019
212-484-8000
**www.timewarner.com**

**Timex Corporation**
Customer Service
1302 Pike Ave.
North Little Rock, AR 72114
501-372-1111
Toll free: 1-800-448-4639
✉: custserv@timex.com
**www.timex.com**

**TJ Maxx**
See: TJX Companies, Inc.
508-390-3000
Toll free: 1-800-926-6299
**www.tjmaxx.com**

**TJX Companies, Inc.**
770 Cochituate Rd.
Framingham, MA 01701
508-390-1000
Toll free: 1-800-926-6299 (TJ Maxx)
Toll free: 1-800-888-0776
(Home Goods)
Toll free: 1-888-627-7425 (Marshalls)
www.tjx.com

**T-Mobile Wireless ⌣**
Customer Relations
PO Box 37380
Albuquerque, NM 87176-7380
Toll free: 1-877-453-1304
(Customer Care)
Toll free: 1-800-866-2453
(Product Questions)
TTY: 1-877-296-1018
www.tmobile.com

**Top-Flite Professional Golf Company**
See: Dick's Sporting Goods
www.topflite.com

**The Toro Company ⌣**
Consumer Customer Care
8111 Lyndale Ave., S
Bloomington, MN 55420
Toll free: 1-888-384-9939
✉: consumer.service@toro.com
www.toro.com

**Toshiba America**
Digital Products Division
9740 Irvine Blvd.
Irvine, CA 92618-1697
Toll free: 1-800-631-3811
Toll free: 1-800-457-7777 (Computers)
✉: customer_support@tacp.com
www.tacp.toshiba.com

**Totes/Isotoner**
Customer Service
9655 International Blvd.
Cincinnati, OH 45246-5658
513-682-8200 (Warranties)
Toll free: 1-800-762-8712
Toll free: 1-800-281-4535
(Online Purchases)
✉: customeraffairs@totes.com
www.totes.com

**Toys R Us**
Guest Relations
One Geoffrey Way
Wayne, NJ 07470
973-617-3500
Toll free: 1-800-869-7787
✉: contactus@toysrus.com
www.toysrus.com

**Trader Joe's**
PO Box 5049
Monrovia, CA 91016
626-599-3817
www.traderjoes.com

**Trane**
Residential Customer Relations
One Centennial Ave.
Piscataway, NJ 08854
903-581-3660
www.trane.com

**TransUnion, LLC**
Consumer Solutions
PO Box 2000
Chester, PA 19022
Toll free: 1-800-888-4213
(Obtain a Report)
Toll free: 1-800-916-8800 (Disputes)
Toll free: 1-800-680-7289 (Frauds)
✉: fvad@transunion.com
(Fraud Victims)
www.transunion.com

**Travelers Companies, Inc.**
Consumer Affairs
One Tower Square 8MS
Hartford, CT 06183
Toll free: 1-866-336-2077
(Customer Advocacy)
Toll free: 1-800-252-4633
(Claim Inquiry)
www.travelers.com

**Travelocity.com LP**
Customer Service
11603 Crosswinds Way, Suite 125
San Antonio, TX 78233
Toll free: 1-888-872-8356
TTY: 1-800-555-7585
✉: travelocity@travelocity.com
www.travelocity.com

**Travelodge**
See: Wyndham Hotel Group
Toll free: 1-800-835-2424
www.travelodge.com

**True Value Company**
Customer Service
8600 W. Bryn Mawr Ave.
Chicago, IL 60631-3505
Toll free: 1-877-502-4641
www.truevalue.com

**TruGreen Lawn Care**
See: Service Master Company
Toll free: 1-877-905-5147
✉: customercare@trugreenmail.com
www.trugreen.com

**Turtle Wax, Inc.**
Consumer Affairs
PO Box 247
Willowbrook, IL 60559-0247
Toll free: 1-800-887-8539
www.turtlewax.com

**TV Guide**
Customer Relations
1800 N. Highland Ave., 7th Floor
New York, CA 90028
Toll free: 1-800-866-1400
✉: feedback@tvguide.com
www.tvguide.com

**Twitter.com**
1355 Market St., Suite 900
San Francisco, CA 94103
www.twitter.com

**Tyson Foods ⌣**
Consumer Relations CP631
2200 Don Tyson Pkwy.
Springdale, AR 72762
Toll free: 1-800-643-3410
www.tyson.com

## U

**U-Haul International**
Customer Service
2727 N. Central Ave.
Phoenix, AZ 85004
Toll free: 1-800-789-3638
www.uhaul.com

**Uniden America Corporation**
Customer Service
4700 Amon Carter Blvd.
Fort Worth, TX 76155
817-858-3300
Toll free: 1-800-297-1023
TTY: 1-800-874-9314
✉: cservice@uniden.com
www.uniden.com

**Unilever ⌣**
Consumer Services
920 Sylvan Ave., 2nd Floor
Englewood Cliffs, NJ 07632
Toll free: 1-800-298-5018
✉: comments@unilever.com
www.unilever.com

**Uniroyal Tires**
Consumer Care Department
PO Box 19001
Greenville, SC 29602-9001
Toll free: 1-877-458-5878
www.uniroyal.com

**United Airlines** ↺
Customer Care
900 Grand Plaza NHCCR
Houston, TX 77067-4323
Toll free: 1-800-864-8331
Toll free: 1-800-335-2247 (Baggage)
TTY: 1-800-323-0170
✉: customervoice9@united.com
www.ual.com

**United Healthcare**
Customer Service
PO Box 740815
Atlanta, GA 30374-0815
Toll free: 1-888-545-5205
www.uhc.com

**United Online, Inc.**
LNR Warner Center
21301 Burbank Blvd.
Woodland Hills, CA 91367
www.unitedonline.com

**United Parcel Service (UPS)**
Customer Service
55 Glenlake Pkwy., NE
Atlanta, GA 30328
Toll free: 1-800-742-5877
TTY: 1-800-833-0056
www.ups.com

**United Van Lines, Inc.**
Claim Department
One United Dr.
St. Louis, MO 63026
Toll free: 1-800-948-4885
www.unitedvanlines.com

**Uno Chicago Grill**
100 Charles Park Rd.
Boston, MA 02132
617-323-9200
Toll free: 1-866-600-8667
✉: mail@unos.com
www.unos.com

**US Airways**
Customer Relations
4000 E. Sky Harbor Blvd.
Phoenix, AZ 85034
480-693-0800
Toll free: 1-800-428-4322
TTY: 1-800-245-2966
www.usairways.com

**US Bancorp**
US Bancorp Center
800 Nicollet Mall
Minneapolis, MN 55402
Toll free: 1-800-872-2657
TTY: 1-800-685-5065
www.usbank.com

## V

**The Valvoline Company**
Customer Service
PO Box 14000
Lexington, KY 40512
Toll free: 1-800-832-6825
www.valvoline.com

**Verizon Communications, Inc.**
(Contact the Verizon office in your
geographic area)
Toll free: 1-800-837-4966
Toll free: 1-800-922-0204
(Wireless Service)
TTY: 1-800-974-6006
www.verizon.com

**Viacom, Inc.**
1515 Broadway
New York, NY 10036
212-258-6000
www.viacom.com

**Victoria's Secret Stores**
Customer Service
North American Office
PO Box 16589
Columbus, OH 43216-6589
Toll free: 1-800-411-5116
TTY: 1-800-695-1788
✉: customercare@
victoriassecret.com
www.victoriassecret.com

**Virgin Atlantic Airways, Ltd.**
PO Box 570
Canton, MA 02021
Toll free: 1-800-821-5438
TTY: 1-800-847-4641
✉: customer.relations.us@
fly.virgin.com
www.virgin-atlantic.com

**Virgin Mobile USA, LLP**
Customer Resolutions
10 Independence Blvd.
Warren, NJ 07059
Toll free: 1-888-322-1122
✉: ourteam@virginmobileusa.com
www.virginmobileusa.com

**Visa USA, Inc.**
(Contact your issuing bank first)
PO Box 194607
San Francisco, CA 94119-4607
Toll free: 1-800-847-2911
✉: askvisausa@visa.com
www.visa.com

**Vonage**
Customer Care
23 Main St.
Holmdel, NJ 07733
Toll free: 1-866-243-4357
www.vonage.com

**The Vons Companies, Inc.**
See: Safeway, Inc.
Toll free: 1-877-723-3929
www.vons.com

## W

**Wal-Mart Stores, Inc.** ↺
Customer Relations
702 S.W. 8th St.
Bentonville, AR 72716
Toll free: 1-800-925-6278
Toll free: 1-800-966-6546
(Website Questions)
www.wal-mart.com

**Walgreens**
Consumer Relations
200 Wilmot Rd.
Deerfield, IL 60015
Toll free: 1-800-925-4733 (In-store)
Toll free: 1-877-250-5823 (Online)
www.walgreens.com

**Walter Drake, Inc.**
Customer Service
PO Box 3680
Oshkosh, WI 54903-3680
Toll free: 1-855-202-7393
wdrake.com

**Wegman's Food Markets**
Consumer Affairs
1500 Brooks Ave.
PO Box 30844
Rochester, NY 14603-0844
Toll free: 1-800-934-6267
www.wegmans.com

**Weight Watchers International** ↺
Corporate Affairs
11 Madison Ave., 17th Floor
New York, NY 10010
Toll free: 1-800-651-6000
✉: customerservice@
weightwatchers.com
www.weightwatchers.com

**Wells Fargo Company** ↺
Customer Service
PO Box 560948
Charlotte, NC 28256
Toll free: 1-800-869-3557 (General)
TTY: 1-800-877-4833
www.wellsfargo.com

**Wendy's International, Inc.**
One Dave Thomas Blvd.
Dublin, OH 43017
614-764-3100 ext. 2032
Toll free: 1-800-443-7266
**www.wendys.com**

**Western Union Financial Services, Inc.**
Customer Advocate Dept.
PO Box 6036
Englewood, CO 80112
Toll free: 1-800-222-5598
Toll free: 1-800-448-1492 (Fraud)
✉: customeradvocatedept@
westernunion.com
**www.westernunion.com**

**Westin**
See: Startwood Hotels
& Resorts Worldwide, Inc.
Toll free: 1-800-937-8461
**www.westin.com**

**Whirlpool Corporation**
Customer Service
553 Benson Rd.
Benton Harbor, MI 49022
Toll free: 1-800-688-2002
Toll free: 1-800-344-1274 (Maytag)
Toll free: 1-800-422-1230 (KitchenAid)
✉: whirlpool_customerexperience@
whirlpool.com
**www.whirlpool.com**

**Whole Foods Markets, Inc.**
550 Bowie St.
Austin, TX 78703
512-542-0878
✉: customer.questions@
wholefoods.com
**www.wholefoods.com**

**W Hotels**
See: Starwood Hotels & Resorts
Worldwide, Inc.
**www.whotels.com**

**Williams-Sonoma, Inc.**
10000 Covington Cross Dr.
Las Vegas, NV 89144
Toll free: 1-877-812-6235
✉: CustomerService@
williams-sonoma.com
**www.williams-sonoma.com**

**Winn-Dixie Stores, Inc.**
Customer Service
PO Box B
Jacksonville, FL 32203-0297
Toll free: 1-866-946-6349
✉: Svc_WDCustResp@
winn-dixie.com
**www.winn-dixie.com**

**Winnebago Industries**
Owner Relations
PO Box 152
Forest City, IA 50436-0152
641-585-3535
Toll free: 1-800-537-1885
✉: info@winnabagoind.com
**www.winnebagoind.com**

**Wrangler**
Consumer Relations
PO Box 21488
Greensboro, NC 27420-1488
Toll free: 1-888-784-8571
✉: wranglerweb@vfc.com
**www.wrangler.com**

**Wyndham Hotel Group**
Customer Service
1910 8th Ave. NE
Aberdeen, SD 57401
Toll free: 1-800-347-7559
**www.wyndhamworldwide.com**

## X

**Xbox**
See: Microsoft Corporate
Toll free: 1-800-469-9269
TTY: 1-866-740-9269
**www.xbox.com**

**Xerox Corporation**
Customer Relations
PO Box 4505
45 Glover Ave.
Norwalk, CT 06856
203-968-3000
Toll free: 1-877-979-8498
(Customer Relations)
Toll free: 1-888-339-7887  (Billing)
Toll free: 1-800-821-2797
(Customer Technical Support)
Toll free: 1-800-275-9376
✉: webmaster@xerox.com
**www.xerox.com**

## Y

**Yahoo! Online**
Customer Care
701 1st Ave.
Sunnyvale, CA 94089
408-349-5070 (Customer Care)
Toll free: 1-866-562-7219
(Customer Care)
✉: cc-advoc@yahoo-inc.com
**www.yahoo.com**

**Yamaha Motor Corporation**
Customer Relations
6555 Katella Ave.
Cypress, CA 90630
714-761-7435
Toll free: 1-800-962-7926
(Customer Relations)
Toll free: 1-800-252-5265
(Yamaha Card)
**www.yamaha-motor.com**

**YUM! Brands, Inc.**
Customer Relations
1900 Colonel Sanders Ln.
Louisville, KY 40213
Toll free: 1-800-225-5532 (KFC)
Toll free: 1-800-948-8488 (Pizza Hut)
Toll free: 1-800-822-6235 (Taco Bell)
**www.yum.com**

## Z

**Zales Jewelers**
Customer Service
PO Box 152771
Irving, TX 75038-1003
Toll free: 1-800-311-5393
✉: customersupport@zales.com
**www.zales.com**

**Zappos.com**
Customer Loyalty
2280 Corporate Circle, Suite 100
Henderson, NV 89074
Toll free: 1-800-927-7671
✉: cs@zappos.com
**www.zappos.com**

**Zenith Electronics Corp.**
Customer Service
2000 Millbrook Dr.
Lincolnshire, IL 60069
Toll free: 1-877-993-6484
**www.zenith.com**

## Contacting Federal Agencies

Many federal agencies have enforcement and/or complaint-handling duties for products and services used by the general public. Others act for the benefit of the public, but do not resolve individual consumer problems. Agencies also create printed publications, and websites that may be helpful when making purchase decisions or dealing with consumer problems. Some agencies provide timely information to citizens through profile pages and videos on social media outlets, blogs, text messages, and news feeds. If you need help in deciding which federal agency to contact, check the index at the end of this book or call 1-800-333-4636.

## Commission on Civil Rights

624 9th St., NW
Washington, DC 20425
202-376-8128 (Publications)
Toll free: 1-800-552-6843 (Complaint Referrals)
TTY: 1-800-877-8339 (Nationwide Complaint Referral)
✉: referrals@usccr.gov
**www.usccr.gov**
The U.S. Commission on Civil Rights is an independent, bipartisan agency charged with monitoring federal civil rights enforcement.

## Consumer Financial Protection Bureau (CFPB)

1700 G St., NW
Washington, DC 20552
Toll free: 1-855-411-2372
TTY: 1-855-729-2372
✉: info@consumerfinance.gov
**www.consumerfinance.gov**
The CFPB ensures that financial products and services work for consumers. The Bureau helps consumers by providing educational materials and accepts complaints. They supervise banks, lenders, as well as large non bank entities, such as credit reporting agencies and debt collection companies. CFPB also works to make credit card, mortgage, and other loan disclosures clearer so consumers can understand their rights and responsibilities.

## Consumer Product Safety Commission (CPSC) ◆

4330 East West Hwy.
Bethesda, MD 20814
Toll free: 1-800-638-2772 (8:00 am - 5:30 pm, ET)
TTY: 1-800-638-8270
✉: info@cpsc.gov
**www.cpsc.gov**
**www.recalls.gov** (Government Recalls)
**www.saferproducts.gov** (Report incidents, injuries or safety concerns)
The CPSC protects the public from unreasonable risks of serious injury or death from thousands of types of consumer products under its jurisdiction, including products that pose a fire, electrical, chemical, or mechanical hazard or can injure children.

## Department of Agriculture (USDA)

### Center for Nutrition Policy and Promotion (CNPP)
3101 Park Center Dr., 10th Floor
Alexandria, VA 22302-1594
703-305-7600
**www.cnpp.usda.gov**
**www.choosemyplate.gov** (Dietary Guidelines)
The CNPP works to improve the health and well-being of Americans by developing and promoting dietary guidance that links scientific research to the nutrition needs of consumers.

### Food and Nutrition Service (FNS)
3101 Park Center Dr.
Alexandria, VA 22302
1-800-424-9121
TTY: 202-690-1202
**www.fns.usda.gov**
FNS provides children and low-income people access to food, a healthful diet, and nutrition education. The agency works to achieve this goal through several programs, including the Supplemental Nutrition Assistance Program (SNAP), school meals, and Women, Infants and Children (WIC).

### Meat and Poultry Hotline
Food Safety and Inspection Service
Toll free: 1-888-674-6854 (10:00 am - 4:00 pm, ET, English and Spanish)
TTY: 1-800-256-7072
✉: mphotline.fsis@usda.gov
**www.fsis.usda.gov**
This toll free service helps prevent foodborne illness by answering questions about the safe storage, handling, and preparation of meat, poultry, and egg products.

### National Institute of Food and Agriculture (NIFA)
1400 Independence Ave., SW
Mail Stop 2201
Washington, DC 20250-2215
202-720-4423
**www.nifa.usda.gov**
**www.eXtension.org** (Information from extension educators)
NIFA responds to issues that are critical to daily life (health, nutrition, parenting, personal finances) by sharing relevant, research-based information through a network of county extension offices. The educators in extension offices conduct workshops, and create and distribute publications. To find your local Cooperative Extension office, consult the county government listings in your local telephone directory or visit www.csrees.usda.gov/Extension.

## Department of Commerce (DOC)

### Seafood Inspection Program
National Oceanic and Atmospheric Administration (NOAA)
1315 East West Hwy.
Silver Spring, MD 20910
301-713-2355
Toll free: 1-800-422-2750
✉: NMFS.Seafood.Services@noaa.gov
**www.seafood.nmfs.noaa.gov**
NOAA oversees fisheries management in the United States and provides a voluntary inspection service to the industry. The NOAA Seafood Inspection Program offers product quality evaluation, grading, and certification services. NOAA provides official marks to eligible products, such as U.S. Grade A, Processed Under Federal Inspection (PUFI), and Lot Inspection.

### United States Patent and Trademark Office (USPTO)
PO Box 1450
Alexandria, VA  22313-1450
Toll free: 1-800-786-9199
TTY: 571-272-9950
✉: usptoinfo@uspto.gov
**www.uspto.gov**
The USPTO grants patents for intellectual property and trademarks for brand names and symbols, protecting the rights of inventors and designers.

### Weights and Measures Division (WMD)
Public Inquiries Unit
National Institute of Standards and Technology
100 Bureau Dr., Stop 2600
Gaithersburg, MD 20899-2600
301-975-4004
✉: owm@nist.gov
**www.nist.gov/pml/wmd/index.cfm**
The WMD promotes uniformity in U.S. weights and measures laws, regulations, and standards to achieve equity between buyers and sellers in the marketplace.

## Department of Education (ED)

### The Education Publications Center (EDPUBS)
PO Box 22207
Alexandria, VA 22304
Toll free: 1-877-433-7827 (9:00 am - 6:00 pm, ET, English and Spanish)
TTY: 1-877-576-7734
✉: edpubs@edpubs.ed.gov
**www.edpubs.gov**
This office helps consumers identify and order free publications and resources from the U.S. Department of Education.

### Federal Student Aid Information Center
PO Box 84
Washington, DC 20044-0084
319-337-5665
Toll free: 1-800-433-3243 (English and Spanish)
TTY: 1-800-730-8913 (English and Spanish)
✉:FederalStudentAidCustomerService@ed.gov
**www.studentaid.ed.gov**
Federal Student Aid provides over $150 billion in grants, work-study, and federal loans for students attending career and trade schools, community colleges, and four-year colleges or universities. Visit the website to learn about planning and paying for your postsecondary education and to apply for federal student aid. The website also provides federal student loan information such as descriptions of repayment plans and actions to take if you are having trouble making loan payments.

### Office for Civil Rights (OCR)
400 Maryland Ave., SW
Washington, DC 20202-1100
202-245-6700
Toll free: 1-800-421-3481
TTY: 1-877-521-2172
✉: ocr@ed.gov
**www.ed.gov/ocr**
This office works to ensure equal access to education and resolve complaints of discrimination.

### Office of Postsecondary Education (OPE)
1990 K St., NW
Washington, DC 20006
202-502-7750
**www2.ed.gov/about/offices/list/ope/index.html**
**www.ope.ed.gov/accreditation**
(Searchable Accreditation Database)
OPE develops programs to increase access to postsecondary education. This office works with state accreditation agencies to recognize institutions of higher learning that provide quality education.

### Office of Special Education and Rehabilitative Services (OSERS)
400 Maryland Ave., SW
Washington, DC 20202-7100
202-245-7468
Toll free: 1-800-872-5327 (English and Spanish)
TTY: 202-205-4208
**www.ed.gov/about/offices/list/osers/index.html**
**www.ed.gov/about/offices/list/osers/osep/index.html** (Office of Special Education Programs)
**www.ed.gov/about/offices/list/osers/rsa/index.html** (Rehabilitation Services Administration)
**www.ed.gov/about/offices/list/osers/nidrr/index.html** (National Institute of Disability & Rehabilitation Research)
OSERS provides support to parents and individuals, school districts and states in three main areas: special education, vocational rehabilitation, and research.

**Office of Vocational and Adult Education (OVAE)**
400 Maryland Ave., SW
Washington, DC 20202-7100
202-245-7700
Toll free: 1-800-872-5327 (English and Spanish)
✉: ovae@ed.gov
**www2.ed.gov/about/offices/list/ovae/index.html**
OVAE administers and coordinates programs that are
related to adult education and literacy, career and technical
education, and community colleges.

## Department of Energy (DOE)

**Public Affairs**
1000 Independence Ave., SW
Washington, DC 20585
202-586-5575
Toll free: 1-800-342-5363
TTY: 1-800-877-8339
**www.doe.gov**
**www.energy.gov/public-services**

**Energy Efficiency and Renewable Energy (EERE)**
Office of the Assistant Secretary
Mail Stop EE-1
Department of Energy
Washington, DC 20585
202-586-9220
✉: eereic@ee.doe.gov
**www.energysavers.gov**
EERE provides tips and information on products, services,
rebates, and tax credits to help consumers save money and
energy.

## Department of Health and Human Services (HHS)

**AIDS.gov**
Room 443H
Washington, DC 20201
Toll free: 1-800-448-0440
✉: cdcinfo@cdc.gov
**www.aids.gov**
AIDS.gov works to increase HIV testing and care for
people at-risk or living with HIV.

**Health Resources and Services Administration (HRSA)**
5600 Fishers Ln.
Rockville, MD 20857
Toll free: 1-888-275-4772 (8:30 am - 5:00 pm, ET)
TTY: 1-877-489-4772 (8:30 am - 5:00 pm, ET)
**www.hrsa.gov**
**findahealthcenter.hrsa.gov/Search_HCC.aspx**
(Find a local health center)
HRSA is responsible for improving access to health care
services for people that are uninsured and medically
vulnerable.

**HHS-TIPS Fraud Hotline**
Office of Inspector General
Attn: Hotline
PO Box 23489
Washington, DC 20026
Toll free: 1-800-447-8477
TTY: 1-800-377-4950
**www.oig.hhs.gov**
**Stopmedicarefraud.gov** (Report Medicare Fraud)
The Office of Inspector General (OIG) protects the
integrity of HHS programs, as well as the health and
welfare of the beneficiaries of those programs.

**National Health Information Center**
PO Box 1133
Washington, DC 20013-1133
301-565-4167
Toll free: 1-800-336-4797
✉: healthfinder@nhic.org
**www.health.gov/nhic**
**www.healthfinder.gov**
**www.healthfinder.gov/espanol** (in Spanish)
NHIC is a health information referral service that links
consumers and health professionals with organizations
best able to provide answers to their health-related
questions.

**Office for Civil Rights (OCR)**
200 Independence Ave., SW
Room 509F, HHH Building
Washington, DC 20201
Toll free: 1-800-368-1019
TTY: 1-800-537-7697
✉: OCRMail@hhs.gov
**www.dhhs.gov/ocr**
OCR helps protect people from discrimination in certain
health care and social service programs.

**Substance Abuse and Mental Health Services Administration (SAMHSA)**
PO Box 2345
Rockville, MD 20847-2345
Toll free: 1-877-726-4727
Toll free: 1-800-662-4357 (Treatment referral hotline)
TTY: 1-800-487-4889
✉: SAMHSAInfo@samhsa.hhs.gov
**www.samhsa.gov**
SAMHSA helps people living with mental illness or dealing
with substance abuse. The agency works to connect
mental health professionals and treatment centers with
people who need their services through a referral hotline
and provides an online treatment center locator.

## Administration for Children & Families (ACF)

370 L'Enfant Promenade, SW
Washington, DC 20447
Toll free: 1-888-289-8442 (Fraud Alert Hotline)
**www.acf.hhs.gov**
The ACF funds state, territory, local, and tribal organizations to provide family assistance (welfare), child support, child care, Head Start, child welfare, and other programs relating to children and families.

### Child Welfare Information Gateway

Administration for Children & Families (ACF)
Children's Bureau / ACYF
1250 Mayland Ave., SW, 8th Floor
Washington, DC 20024
Toll free: 1-800-394-3366 (8:30 am - 5:30 pm, ET)
✉: info@childwelfare.gov
**www.childwelfare.gov**
Child Welfare Information Gateway connects child welfare and related professionals to comprehensive information and resources to help protect children and strengthen families.

### Childcare.gov

Administration for Children & Families
370 L'Enfant Promenade, SW
Washington, DC 20447
**www.childcare.gov**

Childcare.gov is a comprehensive website designed to link parents, child care providers, and the general public to government sponsored child care and early learning information.

### National Runaway Switchboard (NRS)

Administration for Children & Families (ACF)
3080 N. Lincoln Ave.
Chicago, IL 60657
773-880-9860
Toll free: 1-800-786-2929 (24 hrs./7 days a week)
✉: info@1800RUNAWAY.org
**www.1800runaway.org**
NRS helps keep America's runaway and at-risk youth safe and off the streets. The organization serves as the federally designated national communication system for runaway and homeless youth.

### Office of Child Support Enforcement (OCSE)

Administration for Children & Families (ACF)
370 L'Enfant Promenade, SW
Washington, DC 20447
202-401-9373
**www.acf.hhs.gov/programs/cse**
The OCSE assures that assistance in obtaining support (both financial and medical) is available to children through locating parents, establishing paternity and support obligations, and enforcing those obligations.

## Administration for Community Living (ACL)

### Administration on Aging (AoA)

One Massachusetts Ave., NW
Washington, DC 20001
202-619-0724
✉: aoainfo@aoa.hhs.gov
**www.aoa.gov**
AoA is the federal focal point and advocate agency for older persons and their concerns. In this role, AoA works to heighten awareness among other federal agencies, organizations, groups, and the public about the valuable contributions that older Americans make to the nation. AoA also alerts others to the needs of vulnerable older people. Through information, referral and outreach efforts at the community level, AoA educates older people and their caregivers about the benefits and services available to help them.

### Eldercare Locator

Administration on Aging (AoA)
Toll free: 1-800-677-1116 (M-F, 9:00 am - 8:00 pm, ET)
TTY: 1-800-677-1116
✉: eldercarelocator@n4a.org
**www.eldercare.gov**
The Eldercare Locator is the first step to finding resources for older adults in any U.S. community. It is a free national service of the Administration on Aging that provides an instant connection to resources that enable older persons to live independently in their communities and offers support for caregivers. The Eldercare Locator is administered by The National Association of Area Agencies on Aging (n4a).

## Centers for Disease Control and Prevention (CDC)

1600 Clifton Rd.
Atlanta, GA 30333
Toll free: 1-800-232-4636 (24 hrs./7 days a week)
TTY: 1-888-232-6348
✉: cdcinfo@cdc.gov
**www.cdc.gov**
**www.cdc.gov/spanish** (in Spanish)
CDC collaborates to create the expertise, information, and tools that people and communities need to protect their health through health promotion, prevention of disease, injury and disability, and preparedness for new health threats.

### CDC National STD Hotline

Toll free: 1-800-232-4636 (24 hrs./7 days a week, in English and Spanish)
TTY: 1-888-232-6348 (in English and Spanish)
✉: cdcinfo@cdc.gov
**www.cdc.gov/std**
**www.cdc.gov/std/Spanish** (in Spanish)

## HIV/AIDS Prevention

Toll free: 1-800-232-4636 (24 hrs./7 days a week, in English and Spanish)
TTY: 1-888-232-6348
✉: cdcinfo@cdc.gov
**www.cdc.gov/hiv**
**www.cdc.gov/hiv/spanish** (in Spanish)
The Division of HIV/AIDS Prevention provides national leadership and support for HIV prevention research and the development, implementation, and evaluation of evidence-based HIV prevention programs serving persons affected by, or at risk for, HIV infection.

## Centers for Medicare & Medicaid Services (CMS)

Office of External Affairs
7500 Security Blvd.
Baltimore, MD 21244-1850
TTY: 1-877-486-2048
**www.cms.gov**

### Center for Medicaid and CHIP Services (CMCS)

Toll free: 1- 877-267-2323
**www.medicaid.gov**
**www.insurekidsnow.gov**
CMCS is the federal agency responsible for Medicaid and Child Health Insurance Programs (CHIP). Medicaid and CHIP provide health insurance for people with lower incomes, disabilities, children, pregnant women, and the elderly. Eligibility is determined by each state. Visit Medicaid.gov to find the requirements in your state.

### Medicare Service Center

Toll free: 1-800-633-4227
Toll free: 1-800-447-8477 (Medicare Fraud Hotline)
TTY: 1-877-486-2048
**www.medicare.gov**
**www.mymedicare.gov** (Personalized Medicare Benefits)
Medicare is a government sponsored health care program for people 65 years of age and older, some younger people with disabilities, and those with permanent kidney failure. The Medicare Service Center answers your questions about Medicare topics, manages your orders of Medicare publications, provides detailed information about the Medicare managed care plans in your area, and helps locate health care providers that participate in Medicare. Use mymedicare.gov, a free, secure online service, to access personalized information regarding your Medicare benefits, claims, and services.

## Food and Drug Administration (FDA)

10903 New Hampshire Ave.
Silver Spring, MD 20993-0002
Toll free: 1-888-463-6332
**www.fda.gov**
The FDA is responsible for protecting the public's health by assuring the safety, efficacy, and security of human and veterinary drugs, biological products, medical devices, our nation's food supply, cosmetics, and products that emit radiation. The FDA also provides accurate, science-based health information to the public.

## Center for Food Safety and Applied Nutrition Information Line (CFSAN)

Food and Drug Administration (FDA)
Outreach and Information Center
10903 New Hampshire Ave.
Silver Spring, MD 20993-0002
Toll free: 1-888-723-3366 (M-F, 10:00 am - 4:00 pm, ET)
**www.fda.gov/Food**
The CFSAN Information Line is a general information line for questions pertaining to food safety and applied nutrition.

## National Institutes of Health (NIH)

9000 Rockville Pike
Bethesda, MD 20892
301-496-4000
TTY: 301-402-9612
✉: NIHinfo@od.nih.gov
**www.nih.gov**
**www.salud.nih.gov** (in Spanish)
The National Institutes of Health (NIH) is the primary federal agency responsible for conducting and supporting medical research.

### AIDSinfo

National Institutes of Health (NIH)
PO Box 6303
Rockville, MD 20849-6303
301-315-2816
Toll free: 1-800-448-0440 (12:00 pm - 5:00 pm, ET, English and Spanish)
TTY: 1-888-480-3739
✉: ContactUs@aidsinfo.nih.gov
**www.aidsinfo.nih.gov**
**www.aidsinfo.nih.gov/infoSIDA** (in Spanish)
**www.aidsinfo.nih.gov/LiveHelp/default.aspx**
(Real time, online assistance M-F, 12:00 pm - 4:00 pm ET.. Spanish-speaking agents available)
AIDSinfo offers the latest federally approved information on HIV/AIDS clinical research, treatment and prevention, and medical practice guidelines for people living with HIV/AIDS, their families and friends, health care providers, scientists, and researchers.

### National Cancer Institute (NCI)

National Institutes of Health
NCI Office of Communications and Education
6116 Executive Blvd., Suite 300
Bethesda, MD 20892-8322
Toll free: 1-800-422-6237 (M-F, 8:00 am - 8:00 pm ET, English and Spanish)
✉: cancergovstaff@mail.nih.gov
**www.cancer.gov**
**www.cancer.gov/espanol** (in Spanish)
NCI coordinates the National Cancer Program, which conducts and supports research, training, health information dissemination, and other programs with respect to the cause, diagnosis, prevention, and treatment of cancer, rehabilitation from cancer, and the continuing care of cancer patients and the families of cancer patients.

◆ Provided financial support for the publication of the Consumer Action Handbook.

**National Institute of Allergy and Infectious Diseases (NIAID)**
6610 Rockledge Dr.
MSC 6612
Bethesda, MD 20892-6612
301-496-5717
Toll free: 1-866-284-4107
TTY: 1-800-877-8339
✉: ocpostoffice@niaid.nih.gov
**www.niaid.nih.gov**
NIAID provides health information on allergic, infectious, and immunologic diseases. Diseases include food allergy, sinusitis, and genital herpes. Consumers can call or write to the institute with questions and can order publications over the phone or on the website.

**National Institute of Mental Health (NIMH)**
National Institutes of Health (NIH)
6001 Executive Blvd.
Room 8184, MSC 9663
Bethesda, MD 20892-9663
301-443-4513
Toll free: 1-866-615-6464
TTY: 301-443-8431, 1-866-415-8051
✉: nimhinfo@nih.gov
**www.nimh.nih.gov**
NIMH is the federal agency that conducts and supports research that seeks to understand, treat, and prevent mental illness. Contact NIMH for information on the symptoms, diagnosis and treatment of mental disorders, clinical trials and research. A publication ordering system is available on the NIMH website. Some publications are available in Spanish.

## Department of Homeland Security (DHS)

Washington, DC 20528
202-282-8000
202-282-8495 (Comment Line)
**www.dhs.gov**
The mission of DHS is to ensure a homeland that is safe, secure, and resilient against terrorism and other hazards.

**Transportation Security Administration (TSA)**
601 S. 12th St.
Arlington, VA 20598-6002
Toll free: 1-866-289-9673
✉: TSA-ContactCenter@dhs.gov
**www.tsa.gov**
The TSA can assist you with questions or concerns about travel tips, permitted and prohibited items, and information on filing a claim for items that were damaged or lost during a TSA screening.

**U.S. Citizenship and Immigration Services (USCIS)**
Information and Customer Service Division
111 Massachusetts Ave., NW
Mail Stop 2260
Washington, DC 20529-2260
Toll free: 1-800-375-5283 (National Customer Service Center, M-F, 8:00 am - 8:00 pm, ET)
TTY: 1-800-767-1833
**www.uscis.gov**
**www.uscis.gov/portal/site/uscis-es** (in Spanish)
The USCIS is responsible for processing immigration and naturalization applications and establishing policies regarding immigration services.

**U.S. Customs and Border Protection**
1300 Pennsylvania Ave., NW
Washington, DC 20229
703-526-4200
Toll free: 1-877-227-5511 (General inquiries, M-F, 8:30 am - 5:00 pm, ET)
TTY: 1-866-880-6582
**www.cbp.gov**
CBP prevents individuals from entering the country illegally or bringing harmful and illegal substances into the US. They also protect agricultural products from pests and American businesses from theft of their intellectual property.

## Federal Emergency Management Agency (FEMA)

500 C St., SW
Washington, DC 20472
Toll free: 1-800-621-3362
TTY: 1-800-462-7585
**www.fema.gov**
**www.fema.gov/esp** (in Spanish)
**www.ready.gov** (Disaster Preparedness)
**www.listo.gov** (Disaster Preparedness, in Spanish)
**www.disasterassistance.gov** (Disaster Assistance)
FEMA supports citizens and emergency personnel to build, sustain, and improve the nation's capability to prepare for, protect against, respond to, recover from, and mitigate all hazards.

**FEMA Disaster Assistance**
PO Box 10055
Hyattsville, MD 20782-8055
Toll free: 1-800-621-3362
TTY: 1-800-462-7585
**www.fema.gov/assistance**
**www.disasterassistance.gov**
FEMA Disaster Assistance provides information about how you can get help before, during, or after a disaster and apply for assistance from the federal government. This office also provides information to help you prepare for, respond to, and recover from disasters.

**National Flood Insurance Program (NFIP)**
Federal Emergency Management Agency
500 C St., SW
Washington, DC 20472
Toll free: 1-888-379-9531
TTY: 1-800-427-5593
✉: FloodSmart@dhs.gov
**www.floodsmart.gov**
NFIP provides a means for property owners to financially protect themselves. The NFIP offers flood insurance to homeowners, renters, and business owners if their community participates in the NFIP.

## Department of Housing and Urban Development (HUD)

**Office of Fair Housing and Equal Opportunity (FHEO)**
451 7th St., SW, Room 5204
Washington, DC 20410-2000
202-708-4252
Toll free: 1-800-669-9777
(Complaints Hotline, English and Spanish)
TTY: 1-800-927-9275
**www.hud.gov/complaints/housediscrim.cfm**
**www.hud.gov/offices/fheo**
FHEO enforces federal laws and establishes policies that make sure all Americans have equal access to the housing of their choice. If you believe that you have been the victim of housing discrimination, file a complaint with this office.

## Department of Housing

451 7th St., SW
Washington, DC 20410
Toll free: 1-800-569-4287
(Find a HUD-approved housing counselor)
**portal.hud.gov/portal/page/portal/HUD/program_
offices/housing**
The Department of Housing provides public services through its nationally administered programs. It oversees the Federal Housing Administration mortgage insurance program and regulates the housing industry business. This division oversees single family and multifamily housing, helping qualified consumers find public housing, or buy a home.

**Federal Housing Administration (FHA)**
451 7th St., SW
Washington, DC 20410
Toll free: 1-800-225-5342 (English and Spanish)
TTY: 1-877-833-2483
✉: info@fhaoutreach.com
**portal.hud.gov/hudportal/HUD?src=/federal_
housing_administration**
FHA provides mortgage insurance on single-family, multifamily, and manufactured homes made by FHA-approved lenders throughout the United States and its territories.

**Interstate Land Sales Division**
451 7th St., SW, Room 9154
Washington, DC 20410
202-708-0502
TTY: 202-708-1455
**www.hud.gov/offices/hsg/sfh/ils/ilshome.cfm**
The Interstate Land Sales program protects consumers from fraud and abuse when buying or selling land from developers.

**Office of Manufactured Housing Programs**
Office of Deputy Assistant Secretary for Regulatory Affairs and Manufactured Housing
451 7th St., SW, Room 9164
Washington, DC 20410-8000
202-708-1112
Toll free: 1-800-927-2891 (English and Spanish)
TTY: 202-708-1455
✉: mhs@hud.gov
**www.hud.gov/offices/hsg/sfh/mhs/mhshome.cfm**
The Manufactured Housing Program is a consumer protection program that regulates the construction of certain factory-built housing units called "manufactured homes." HUD works with 23 states to respond to consumer complaints.

## Department of the Interior (DOI)

**Fish and Wildlife Service**
1849 C St., NW
Mail Stop 3351
Washington, DC 20240
Toll free: 1-800-344-9453
**www.fws.gov**
The Fish and Wildlife Service works to conserve, protect, and enhance fish, wildlife and plants and their habitats.

**National Park Service (NPS)**
1849 C St., NW
Room 7012
Washington, DC 20240
202-208-3818
**www.nps.gov**
**www.recreation.gov** (Federal recreational activities and reservations)
NPS preserves the nation's national parks and historic landmarks so that individuals may enjoy the natural environment for years to come.

## Department of Justice (DOJ)

**Americans with Disabilities Act (ADA)**
**Information Line**
950 Pennsylvania Ave., NW
Disability Rights Section-NYAV
Washington, DC 20530
Toll free: 1-800-514-0301 (M-W and F, 10:30 am - 4:30 pm, ET, Th, 12:30 pm - 4:30 pm, ET)
TTY: 1-800-514-0383
**www.ada.gov**
This service permits businesses, state and local governments, or others to call and ask questions about general or specific ADA requirements including questions about the ADA Standards for Accessible Design.

**U.S. Trustee Program**
Executive Offices for U.S. Trustees
20 Massachusetts Ave., NW, Suite 8000
Washington, DC 20530
202-307-1399
✉: ustrustee.program@usdoj.gov
**www.justice.gov/ust**
**www.justice.gov/ust/eo/bapcpa/ccde/cc_approved.htm** (Find approved credit counseling agencies)
The Trustee Program protects the integrity of the Federal bankruptcy system. The Program monitors the conduct of bankruptcy parties and private estate trustees. It also identifies and helps investigate bankruptcy fraud and abuse. The Program also approves credit counseling agencies and debtor education providers, both of which are required for persons that are going through the bankruptcy process.

## Department of Labor (DOL)

**Employee Benefits Security Administration (EBSA)**
Office of Participant Assistance
Department of Labor, Room N5623
200 Constitution Ave., NW
Washington, DC 20210
Toll free: 1-866-444-3272
TTY: 1-877-889-5627
**www.dol.gov/ebsa**
EBSA provides information and assistance on private sector, employer-sponsored retirement benefit and health benefit plans. The agency educates plan participants, beneficiaries, and sponsors to ensure that they have access to documents related to their benefit plan.

**Job Corps**
200 Constitution Ave., NW, Suite N4463
Washington, DC 20210
202-693-3000
Toll free: 1-800-733-5627
TTY: 1-877-889-5627
✉: national_office@jobcorps.gov
**www.jobcorps.gov**
Job Corps is a no-cost education and vocational training program that helps young people (ages 16 to 24) improve the quality of their lives through vocational and academic training.

**National Contact Center**
Toll free: 1-866-487-2365
TTY: 1-877-889-5627
**www.dol.gov**
The Department of Labor National Contact Center provides employees and employers a reliable resource to receive consistent, accurate, and current information assistance for all DOL programs.

**Occupational Safety and Health Administration (OSHA)**
U.S. Department of Labor
200 Constitution Ave., NW
Washington, DC 20210
Toll free: 1-800-321-6742
TTY: 1-877-889-5627
**www.osha.gov**
OSHA ensures safe and healthful working conditions by setting and enforcing standards and by providing training, outreach, education, and assistance.

**Office of Disability Employment Policy (ODEP)**
200 Constitution Ave., NW, Room S1303
Washington, DC 20210
202-693-7880
Toll free: 1-866-633-7365
TTY: 202-693-7881, 1-877-889-5627
**www.dol.gov/odep**
**www.disability.gov** (Portal for disability programs)
ODEP works to create policies to ensure that people with disabilities are fully integrated in the workforce.

**Veteran's Employment and Training Service (VETS)**
Department of Labor, Room S1325
200 Constitution Ave., NW
Washington, DC 20210
Toll free: 1-866-487-2365
TTY: 1-877-889-5627
✉: VETS-Public@dol.gov
**www.dol.gov/vets**
VETS provides resources to prepare and assist veterans obtain meaningful careers and maximize their employment opportunities.

## Department of State (DOS)

**National Passport Information Center (NPIC)**
Toll free: 1-877-487-2778 (M-F, 8:00 am - 10:00 pm, ET)
TTY: 1-888-874-7793
✉: NPIC@state.gov
**travel.state.gov/passport**
Contact the NPIC for information on U.S. passports, including the status of pending applications, as well as the locations of the over 9,400 passport acceptance facilities.

**Overseas Citizens Services**
Bureau of Consular Affairs
2201 C St., NW
Washington, DC 20520
202-501-4444 (from overseas, M-F, 8:00 am - 8:00 pm, ET)
202-647-4000 (After hours emergencies, Sundays, and holidays. Ask for the duty officer)
Toll free: 1-888-407-4747 (Emergencies and non-emergencies, M-F, 8:00 am - 8:00 pm, ET, except federal holidays)
**travel.state.gov/travel**
Contact the State Department for help with emergencies and non-emergencies affecting private Americans abroad. This office can also assist with sending money through US embassies to friends and family overseas that have emergencies while abroad.

**Visa Services**
Washington, DC 20520
202-663-1225 (M-F, 8:30 am - 5:00 pm, ET)
202-647-1512 (Emergency after hours)
✉: usvisa@state.gov
**travel.state.gov/visa**
Contact Visa Services for information on U.S. visas for foreigners.

## Department of Transportation (DOT)

**Aviation Consumer Protection Division (ACPD)**
Office of Aviation Enforcement and Proceedings
1200 New Jersey Ave., SE
Washington, DC 20590
202-366-2220 (Airline Service Complaints)
Toll free: 1-800-778-4838
(Air travelers with disabilities hotline)
TTY: 1-800-455-9880
✉: airconsumer@dot.gov
**airconsumer.ost.dot.gov/problems.htm**
**airconsumer.ost.dot.gov/spanish** (in Spanish)
The ACPD receives complaints from members of the public regarding air travel consumer issues. It verifies compliance with the Department's aviation consumer protection requirements and provides guidance to the industry and members of the public on consumer protection matters.

**Federal Aviation Administration (FAA)**
800 Independence Ave., SW
Washington, DC 20591
202-366-4000
Toll free: 1-866-835-5322
**www.faa.gov**
The FAA works to ensure that all air travel is safe.

**Federal Motor Carrier Safety Administration (FMCSA)**
1200 New Jersey Ave., SE
Suite W60-300
Washington, DC 20590
202-366-2519
Toll free: 1-800-832-5660 (Information Line)
TTY: 1-800-877-8339
**www.fmcsa.dot.gov**
**www.protectyourmove.gov** (Interstate moving)
The FMCSA provides information about your rights when moving across state lines (interstate moves). Consumers should submit household goods commercial complaints or dangerous safety violations involving a commercial truck or passenger bus to this agency.

**National Highway Traffic Safety Administration (NHTSA)**
1200 New Jersey Ave., SE
West Building
Washington, DC 20590
Toll free: 1-888-327-4236 (Vehicle Safety Hotline)
TTY: 1-800-424-9153
**www.nhtsa.dot.gov**
**www.vehiclehistory.gov** (Searchable database)
**www.safercar.gov**
NHTSA wants to hear from consumers regarding potential defects in their cars. NHTSA's hotline has information on safety recalls, crash test ratings, child safety seats, bicycles, air bags, distracted driving, and impaired driving prevention.

## Department of the Treasury

**Bureau of the Public Debt**
Treasury Direct
PO Box 7015
Parkersburg, WV 26106-7015
Toll free: 1-800-722-2678
**www.publicdebt.treas.gov**
**www.treasurydirect.gov** (Treasury bonds)
This agency borrows moneys to make sure that the federal government continues to operate. You can contact them to purchase bonds or to check on the maturity of bonds you have already purchased.

♦ Provided financial support for the publication of the Consumer Action Handbook.

## Internal Revenue Service (IRS)
Toll free: 1-800-829-1040 (Help for Individuals)
Toll free: 1-800-829-4933 (Help for Businesses)
Toll free: 1-800-829-4477 (Refund Status)
TTY: 1-800-829-4059
**www.irs.gov**
Free tax help is available from the Internal Revenue Service at www.irs.gov 24 hours a day, seven days a week. Numerous on-line applications, resources and taxpayer assistance services are available. Learn about electronic filing options, look up the status of your refund, print tax forms and instructions, look for preparers who can electronically file tax returns and find ways to connect with the IRS through New Media. If your personal tax questions require face-to-face assistance may visit the Taxpayer Assistance Centers closest to you. Locations are listed on irs.gov.

## Office of the Comptroller of the Currency (OCC)
Customer Assistance Group
1301 McKinney St., Suite 3450
Houston, TX 77010
Toll free: 1-800-613-6743 (M-F, 7:00 am-7:00 pm, CST)
TTY: 1-800-877-8339
**www.helpwithmybank.gov**
The Office of the Comptroller of the Currency (OCC) charters, regulates, and supervises all national banks and federal savings associations. It also supervises the federal branches and agencies of foreign banks.

## United States Mint
Customer Service Center
2799 Reeves Rd.
Plainfield, IN 46168
1-800-872-6468
TTY: 1-888-321-6468 (M-F, 8:30 am - 5:00 pm, ET)
**www.usmint.gov**
The Mint produces the coins that circulate throughout the US. They also produce special edition coinage that can be purchased for coin collections.

## Department of Veterans Affairs (VA) ♦

1722 I St., NW
Washington, DC 20421
Toll free: 1-800-827-1000
TTY: 1-800-829-4833
**www.va.gov**
**www.myhealth.va.gov** (Veteran health and wellness)
The VA oversees and administers benefits for veterans and their families. Some programs include home loans, life insurance policies, financing education through the GI bill, job training, and health resources. For information about VA medical care or benefits, write, call or visit your nearest VA facility.

## National Cemetery Administration (NCA)
810 Vermont Ave., NW
Washington, DC 20420
202-461-6240
TTY: 1-800-829-4833
**www.cem.va.gov**
Contact the NCA for information about burials, headstones or markers, the State Cemetery Grants Program, and presidential memorial certificates for veterans.

## Veterans Benefits Administration (VBA)
810 Vermont Ave., NW
Washington, DC 20420
202-461-9763 (Publications Only)
Toll free: 1-800-827-1000
TTY: 1-800-829-4833
**www.vba.va.gov/VBA**
The VBA helps veterans receive benefits, such as educational and financial resources.

## Veterans Health Administration (VHA)
810 Vermont Ave., NW
Washington, DC 20420
Toll free: 1-877-222-8387
**www.va.gov/health**
VHA serves the needs of America's veterans by providing primary care, specialized care, and related medical and social support services.

## Environmental Protection Agency (EPA)

### ENERGY STAR Program
Room 6202J
Washington, DC 20460
703-412-3086
Toll free: 1-888-782-7937 (M-F, 9:00 am - 5:00 pm, ET)
✉: hotline@energystar.gov
**www.energystar.gov**
The ENERGY STAR label is awarded to products for the home and office that are highly energy-efficient. The program encourages the use of energy efficient products that both protect the environment and save consumers money.

### Indoor Environments Division
1200 Pennsylvania Ave., NW
Mail Code 6609J
Washington, DC 20460
202-343-9370
Toll free: 1-800-438-4318
✉: IAQINFO@aol.com
**www.epa.gov/iaq/index.html**
This agency is a central source of information on indoor air quality. It is responsible for implementing the Indoor Environments Program, a voluntary (non-regulatory) program to address indoor air pollution.

**National Pesticide Information Center (NPIC)**
Oregon State University
333 Weniger Hall
Corvallis, OR 97331-6502
Toll free: 1-800-858-7378 (7:30 am - 3:30 pm, PT, Multiple languages)
✉: npic@ace.orst.edu
**npic.orst.edu**
NPIC is a service that provides objective, science-based information about a wide variety of pesticide-related subjects, including pesticide products, pesticide poisonings, toxicology, and environmental chemistry.

**National Service Center for Environmental Publications (NSCEP)**
PO Box 42419
Cincinnati, OH 45242-0419
Toll free: 1-800-490-9198
✉: nscep@bps-lmit.com
**www.epa.gov/nscep**
NSCEP distributes EPA's publications to the public. Consumers can order copies by phone, email, and postal mail or download digital versions of the publications.

**Office of Pollution Prevention and Toxics (OPPT)**
1200 Pennsylvania Ave., NW
Mail Code 7401-M
Washington, DC 20460
✉: oppt.homepage@epa.gov
**www.epa.gov/oppt**
**www.epa.gov/dfe** (Design for the Environment labeling program for household chemicals)
OPPT promotes environmental stewardship and manages the risk of chemicals in the marketplace to keep pollutants out of the environment. OPPT also creates tools and provides information to the public so that they can make smart chemical choices.

**Safe Drinking Water Hotline**
1200 Pennsylvania Ave., NW 4606M
Washington, DC 20460
703-412-3330
Toll free: 1-800-426-4791 (10:00 am - 4:00 pm, ET, English and Spanish)
**www.epa.gov/safewater/hotline**
The Office of Ground Water and Drinking Water helps protect public health by ensuring safe drinking water and protecting ground water.

## Equal Employment Opportunity Commission (EEOC)

131 M St., NE
Washington, DC 20507
202-663-4900
Toll free: 1-800-669-4000
TTY: 202-663-4494
✉: info@eeoc.gov
**www.eeoc.gov**
The EEOC enforces laws that make discrimination illegal in the workplace. The commission oversees all types of work situations including hiring, firing, promotions, harassment, training, wages, and benefits.

## Federal Communications Commission (FCC)

**Consumer and Governmental Affairs Bureau (CGB)**
445 12th St., SW
Washington, DC 20554
Toll free: 1-888-225-5322 (English and Spanish)
TTY: 1-888-835-5322
✉: fccinfo@fcc.gov
**www.fcc.gov/consumer-governmental-affairs-bureau**
**www.fcc.gov/consumers** (Consumer information)
The CGB develops and implements FCC's consumer policies and serves as the agency's connection to consumers. FCC accepts public inquiries, informal complaints, and questions regarding cable, radio, satellite, telephone, television and wireless services.

## Federal Deposit Insurance Corporation (FDIC) ♦

**Division of Depositor and Consumer Protection**
Consumer Response Center
1100 Walnut St., Box #11
Kansas City, MO 64106
Toll free: 1-877-275-3342 (M-F, 8:00 am - 8:00 pm, ET; Sat-Sun, 9:00 am - 5:00 pm, ET)
TTY: 1-800-925-4618
**www.fdic.gov**
**www2.fdic.gov/STARSMAIL/index.asp** (Online Consumer Assistance Form)
FDIC responds to questions about federal deposit insurance coverage and handles complaints and inquiries about FDIC-insured state banks, which are not members of the Federal Reserve System.

## Federal Maritime Commission (FMC)

**Office of Consumer Affairs and Dispute Resolution Services**
800 N. Capitol St., NW
Washington, DC 20573
202-523-5807
Toll free: 1-866-448-9586
✉: Complaints@fmc.gov
**www.fmc.gov**
FMC assists consumers engaged in disputes with transporting carriers, ocean transportation intermediaries, and cruise operators.

## Federal Reserve System

**Federal Reserve Consumer Help**
PO Box 1200
Minneapolis, MN 55480
Toll free: 1-888-851-1920 (8:00 am - 6:00 pm, CT)
TTY: 1-877-766-8533 (8:00 am - 6:00 pm, CT)
✉: consumerhelp@federalreserve.gov
**www.federalreserveconsumerhelp.gov**
This division receives and tracks consumer complaints and questions regarding practices by banks and other financial institutions supervised by the Board of Governors of the Federal Reserve System.

♦ Provided financial support for the publication of the Consumer Action Handbook.

## Federal Trade Commission (FTC) ♦

**Bureau of Consumer Protection**
Consumer Response Center
600 Pennsylvania Ave., NW
Washington, DC 20580
Toll free: 1-877-382-4357
TTY: 1-866-653-4261
**www.ftc.gov**
**www.consumer.gov** (Consumer protection basics)
**www.consumer.ftc.gov** (Consumer information)
**www.consumidor.gov** (Consumer protection basics,
in Spanish)
**www.OnGuardOnline.gov** (Online security tips)
**www.Admongo.gov** (Advertising literacy for kids)
The FTC works for the consumer to prevent fraudulent,
deceptive, and unfair business practices in the marketplace
and to provide information to help consumers spot,
stop, and avoid them. To file a complaint or to get free
information on consumer issues, visit ftc.gov or call the toll
free number above. The FTC records consumer complaints
(Internet, telemarketing, identity theft, and other fraud-
related complaints) into the Consumer Sentinel Network, a
secure, online database and investigative tool available to
hundreds of civil and criminal law enforcement agencies.
The FTC does not investigate individual consumer
complaints, but will investigate trends that they see from
the complaints they receive.

## General Services Administration (GSA) ♦

**Federal Citizen Information Center (FCIC) ♦**
Office of Citizen Services and Innovative Technologies
1800 F St., NW, 2nd Floor
Washington, DC 20405
For Catalog Orders: Send your name and address to:
Catalog, Pueblo, CO 81009
202-501-1794
Toll free: 1-800-333-4636 (8:00 am - 8:00 pm, ET, in English
and Spanish)
**www.USA.gov** (U.S. government's official web portal)
**www.Publications.USA.gov** (View, download,
and order government publications)
**www.kids.gov** (Government websites for kids)
**www.GobiernoUSA.gov** (USA.gov in Spanish)
FCIC publishes the free *Consumer Information Catalog*,
which lists more than 150 free and Federal booklets on a
wide variety of consumer topics, and maintains a family of
websites to help provide free, timely, and useful information
to citizens. Consumers can get the information they need
in three ways: through printed publications, by calling toll
free 1-800-333-4636, or by visiting www.USA.gov, the U.S.
government's official web portal. You can also follow FCIC
on social media on Facebook: www.facebook.com/USAgov
and on Twitter: @USAgov.

**Surplus Federal Property Sales**
1800 F St., NW
Washington, DC 20405
Toll free: 1-866-333-7472 option 3
**www.gsaauctions.gov**
GSA helps federal agencies dispose of unneeded property
by selling directly to the public. It sells personal property,
real estate, and vehicles to the public through online
auctions.

## National Council on Disability (NCD)

1331 F St., NW
Suite 850
Washington, DC 20004
202-272-2004
TTY: 202-272-2074
✉: ncd@ncd.gov
**www.ncd.gov**
The NCD is an independent federal agency making
recommendations to the President and Congress on
policies affecting Americans with disabilities. NCD works
to empower individuals with disabilities and to promote
equal opportunity.

## National Credit Union Administration (NCUA)

1775 Duke St.
Alexandria, VA 22314-3428
703-518-6300
Toll free: 1-800-827-9650 (Fraud Hotline)
✉: consumerassistance@ncua.gov
**www.ncua.gov**
**www.mycreditunion.gov** (Consumer education)
NCUA is the federal agency that charters and supervises
federal credit unions and insures savings in all federal and
most state-chartered credit unions across the country
through the National Credit Union Share Insurance Fund.

## Office of Personnel Management (OPM)

1900 E St., NW
Washington, DC 20415
202-606-1800
TTY: 202-606-2532
✉: general@opm.gov
**www.opm.gov**
**www.usajobs.gov** (Federal Employment Information)
**www.fedshirevets.gov** (Veterans Employment)
OPM manages the civil service of the federal government,
coordinates recruiting of new government employees, and
manages their health insurance and retirement benefits
programs. OPM also provides resources for locating
student jobs, summer jobs, scholarships, and internships.

## Pension Benefit Guaranty Corporation (PBGC)

**Customer Contact Center**
PO Box 151750
Alexandria, VA 22315-1750
Toll free: 1-800-400-7242 (M-F, 8:00 am - 7:00 pm, ET)
TTY: 1-800-877-8339 (Federal Relay Service, ask to be connected to 1-800-400-72420)
✉: mypension@pbgc.gov
**www.pbgc.gov**
**www.pbgc.gov/about/contact.html**
The PBGC protects the retirement incomes of workers in private sector defined pension benefit plans. When you call, it helps to have your Social Security number and your plan's name or number.

## Securities and Exchange Commission (SEC) ♦

**Office of Investor Education and Advocacy (OIEA)**
100 F St., NE
Washington, DC 20549-0213
Toll free: 1-800-732-0330
✉: help@sec.gov
**www.sec.gov**
**www.sec.gov/complaint.shtml** (Complaint Form)
**www.investor.gov** (Investor Information)
OIEA serves individual investors and is ready to help resolve investor complaints and answer questions.

## Small Business Administration (SBA)

409 3rd St., SW, Suite 7600
Washington, DC 20416
202-205-6740
Toll free: 1-800-827-5722 (Information)
TTY: 1-800-877-8339
✉: answerdesk@sba.gov
**www.sba.gov**
**www.business.usa.gov**
The SBA helps Americans start, build and grow businesses. Through an extensive network of field offices and partnerships the SBA aids, counsels, assists and protects the interests of small business concerns.

## Social Security Administration (SSA)

**Office of Public Inquiries**
6401 Security Blvd.
Baltimore, MD 21235
Toll free: 1-800-772-1213
TTY: 1-800-325-0778 (M-F, 7:00 am - 7:00 pm, ET)
**www.socialsecurity.gov**
**www.socialsecurity.gov/espanol** (in Spanish)
**www.socialsecurity.gov/myaccount** (Social Security earnings records)
The Social Security Administration provides retirement, survivors and disability benefits, as well as administers Supplemental Security Income (SSI) payments.

## U.S. Commodity Futures Trading Commission (CFTC)

**Office of External Affairs**
Three Lafayette Center
1155 21st St., NW
Washington, DC 20581
202-418-5000
TTY: 202-418-5514
✉: questions@cftc.gov
**www.cftc.gov**
CFTC protects market users and the public from fraud, manipulation, and abusive practices related to the sale of commodity and financial futures and options, and to foster open, competitive, and financially sound futures and option markets. In pursuit of its mission, the CFTC investigates and prosecutes commodities fraud, including foreign currency schemes, energy manipulation and hedge fund fraud, and works with other federal and state agencies to bring criminal and other actions. The CFTC also engages in public education and outreach by participating in consumer groups and issuing Consumer Advisories and other educational materials.

## U.S. Postal Service (USPS)

Toll free: 1-800-275-8777
**www.usps.com**
The USPS is the federal agency responsible for the delivery of mail across the nation. You can your visit your local post office to ship packages, purchase money orders, and apply for a passport (at select locations). The USPS has also made many of their services available online, such as purchasing and printing postage, tracking packages, and changing you address.

**United States Postal Inspection Service**
Criminal Investigations Service Center
Attn: Mail Fraud
433 W. Harrison St., Room 3255
Chicago, IL 60699-3255
Toll free: 1-877-876-2455
**postalinspectors.uspis.gov**
If you believe you have been the victim of a crime involving the U.S. mail or need assistance with postal-related problems of a law enforcement nature, you should contact your nearest Postal Inspection Service office. Addresses and telephone numbers can be found in the government pages of your telephone book or by visiting the Postal Inspection Service website.

## AARP

601 E St., NW
Washington, DC 20049
Toll free: 1-888-687-2277
Toll free: 1-800-646-2283 (Fraud Fighter Call Center)
TTY: 1-877-434-7598
✉: member@aarp.org
**www.aarp.org**
AARP is committed to addressing those consumer problems and issues that especially impact the financial security of people 50 years and older. Through advocacy at the federal and state levels, AARP works to make the marketplace safer for all consumers. AARP also employs a variety of strategies to help AARP members protect themselves from fraud and deceptive practices.

## American Council on Consumer Interests (ACCI)

PO Box 2528
Tarpon Springs, FL 34688
**www.consumerinterests.org**
ACCI is a consumer policy research and education organization consisting of a worldwide community of researchers, educators, and related professionals.

## American Council on Science and Health (ACSH)

1995 Broadway, Suite 202
New York, NY 10023-5882
212-362-7044
✉: acsh@acsh.org
**www.acsh.org**
ACSH provides consumers with up-to-date scientifically sound information on the relationship between human health and chemicals, foods, lifestyles, and the environment. Booklets and special reports on a variety of topics are available.

## Center for Auto Safety (CAS)

1825 Connecticut Ave., NW, Suite 330
Washington, DC 20009-5708
202-328-7700
**www.autosafety.org**
CAS advocates on behalf of consumers in auto safety and quality, fuel efficiency, emissions, and related issues.

## Center for Science in the Public Interest (CSPI)

1220 L St., NW, Suite 300
Washington, DC 20005
202-332-9110
✉: cspi@cspinet.org
**www.cspinet.org**
CSPI conducts research, education, and advocacy on nutrition, health, food safety, and related issues. It also provides consumers with current information about their health and well being via their monthly *Nutrition Action Healthletter*.

---

### Contacting National Consumer Organizations

National Consumer Organizations are committed to assisting consumers and protecting their rights via advocacy, research, and outreach efforts. Some organizations assist individuals with problems, while others collect consumer complaints and statistics to better understand consumer trends and direct their advocacy efforts.

---

## Center for the Study of Services (CSS)

1625 K St., NW, 8th Floor
Washington, DC 20006
Toll free: 1-800-213-7283
**www.checkbook.org**
CSS publishes *Consumers CHECKBOOK* so that consumers can evaluate the quality and prices of service firms and stores in their local area.

## Coalition Against Insurance Fraud

1012 14th St., NW, Suite 200
Washington, DC 20005
202-393-7330
✉: info@insurancefraud.org
**www.insurancefraud.org**
The Coalition is an alliance of consumer groups, government agencies, and insurance companies dedicated to combating all forms of insurance fraud through advocacy and public information.

## Consumer Action

221 Main St., Suite 480
San Francisco, CA 94105
415-777-9635 (Consumer Complaints)
TTY: 415-777-9456
✉: info@consumer-action.org
**www.consumer-action.org**
Consumer Action is an education and advocacy organization specializing in credit, finance, and telecommunications issues. Consumer Action offers a multi-lingual consumer complaint hotline, and consumer education materials in several languages. Community-based organizations can receive these free publications in bulk.

## Consumer Federation of America (CFA)

1620 I St., NW, Suite 200
Washington, DC 20006
202-387-6121
✉: cfa@consumerfed.org
**www.consumerfed.org**
**www.idtheftinfo.org**
CFA is a consumer advocacy and education organization. It represents consumer interests on issues such as, telephone service, insurance and financial services, product safety, indoor air pollution, health care, product liability, and utility rates. It develops and distributes studies of various consumer issues, as well as printed consumer guides.

**Consumers Reports**
101 Truman Ave.
Yonkers, NY 10703-1057
914-378-2000
914-378-2455 (Consumer Policy Institute)
Toll free: 1-800-879-9848 (*Consumer Reports* magazine)
Toll free: 1-866-208-9427 (ConsumerReports.org)
**www.consumersunion.org**
**www.consumerreports.org**
Consumer Reports publishes a magazine of the same name. It is an independent, nonprofit testing and information organization serving only consumers. *Consumer Reports* is a comprehensive source for unbiased advice about products and services, personal finance, health and nutrition, and other categories based on their independent tests.

**Families USA**
1201 New York Ave., NW, Suite 1100
Washington, DC 20005
202-628-3030
✉: info@familiesusa.org
**www.familiesusa.org**
Families USA is a national, nonprofit membership organization committed to affordable, high quality health and long-term care. Families USA creates materials to educate and mobilize consumers on healthcare issues.

**Funeral Consumers Alliance (FCA)**
33 Patchen Rd.
South Burlington, VT 05403
802-865-8300
✉: fca@funerals.org
**www.funerals.org**
FCA protects a consumer's right to choose a dignified, meaningful, affordable funeral. In addition to informing the public about their available options and rights, FCA will assist in mediating complaints. The local affiliates around the country conduct funeral price surveys, and counsel the general public.

**Jump$tart Coalition for Personal Financial Literacy**
919 18th St., NW, Suite 300
Washington, DC 20006
202-466-8604
Toll free: 1-888-453-3822
✉: info@jumpstartcoalition.org
**www.jumpstart.org**
Jump$tart is a national coalition of organizations dedicated to improving the financial literacy of pre-kindergarten through college-age youth by providing advocacy, research standards, and educational resources. Jump$tart strives to prepare youth for life-long successful financial decision-making.

**Kids in Danger (KID)**
116 W. Illinois St., Suite 4E
Chicago, IL 60654
312-595-0649
✉: email@kidsindanger.org
**www.kidsindanger.org**
KID is dedicated to educating parents and caregivers about dangerous children's products.

**The Medicare Rights Center**
520 8th Ave., North Wing, 3rd Floor
New York City, NY 10018
Toll free: 1-800-333-4114 (Consumer Helpline)
✉: info@medicarerights.org
**www.medicarerights.org**
The Medicare Rights Center works to ensure access to affordable health care for older adults and people with disabilities through counseling, advocacy, and educational programs. It works with clients nationwide through a phone hotline, Internet services, a large volunteer network and community programs.

**National Community Reinvestment Coalition (NCRC)**
727 15th St., NW, Suite 900
Washington, DC 20005-2112
202-628-8866
**www.ncrc.org**
NCRC works to end discriminatory banking practices in underserved communities. It also offers a housing counseling network to help prospective and current homeowners.

**National Consumer Law Center (NCLC)**
Seven Winthrop Square
Boston, MA 02110-1245
617-542-8010
✉: consumerlaw@nclc.org
**www.consumerlaw.org**
NCLC is an advocacy and research organization focusing on the needs of low-income and other disadvantaged consumers. The NCLC works for fairness in financial services, ending predatory lending, and stopping consumer fraud. The NCLC doesn't work with individual consumers, but offers consumer brochures on their website.

**The National Consumer Protection Technical Resource Center**
Senior Medicare Patrol Resource Center (SMP)
PO Box 388
Waterloo, IA 50704-0388
Toll free: 1-877-808-2468
✉: info@smpresource.org
**www.smpresource.org**
The Center is funded by the U.S. Administration on Aging to support community based Senior Medicare Patrol Programs (SMP). The SMP projects help Medicare and Medicaid beneficiaries avoid, detect and prevent healthcare fraud and abuse.

**National Consumers League (NCL)**
1701 K St., NW, Suite 1200
Washington, DC 20006
202-835-3323
**www.nclnet.org**
**www.fakechecks.org**
**www.fraud.org**
**www.lifesmarts.org**
The NCL provides government, businesses, and other organizations with the consumers perspective on consumer issues and workplace concerns. The League sponsors the LifeSmarts competition, which is designed to develop consumer and marketplace knowledge of teenagers. NCL also works to provide consumers with the information they need to avoid becoming victims of telemarketing and Internet fraud and to help them get their complaints to law enforcement.

**National Council on the Aging (NCOA)**
1901 L St., NW, 4th Floor
Washington, DC 20036
202-479-1200
Toll free: 1-800-424-9046
TTY: 202-479-6674
✉: info@ncoa.org
**www.ncoa.org**
NCOA is a national voice for older adults — especially those who are vulnerable and disadvantaged — and the community organizations that serve them.

## Contacting Your Local Consumer Protection Offices

State, county, and city consumer protection offices offer a variety of important services. They might mediate complaints, conduct investigations, prosecute offenders of consumer laws, license and regulate professionals, provide educational materials, and advocate in the consumer interest.

An advantage of contacting a city or county government office is that it is familiar with local businesses, ordinances, and state laws.

Other local consumer and non-profit organizations may provide consumer assistance and work with the state consumer office. Be sure to contact your state consumer protection office to get more information about other local resources.

Before sending a written complaint, call the office to confirm that it handles the type of complaint you have and determine whether complaint forms are provided. Many offices distribute consumer materials specifically geared to state laws and local issues. Ask whether any information is available regarding your problem.

## Alabama

### State Offices

**Alabama Office of the Attorney General**
Consumer Affairs Section
501 Washington Ave.
Montgomery, AL 36104
334-242-7335
Toll free: 1-800-392-5658 (AL)
www.ago.state.al.us

## Alaska

### State Offices

**Office of the Attorney General**
Consumer Protection Unit
1031 W. 4th Ave., Suite 200
Anchorage, AK 99501-5903
907-269-5200
Toll free: 1-888-576-2529
✉: consumerprotection@alaska.gov
www.law.state.ak.us

## Arizona

### State Offices

**Arizona Office of the Attorney General-Phoenix**
Consumer Information and Complaints
1275 W. Washington St.
Phoenix, AZ 85007
602-542-5763
Toll free: 1-800-352-8431
(AZ, except Maricopa and Pima)
✉: consumerinfo@azag.gov
www.azag.gov

**Arizona Office of the Attorney General- Tucson**
Consumer Information and Complaints
400 W. Congress St.
South Bldg., Suite 315
Tucson, AZ 85701-1367
520-628-6504
Toll free: 1-800-352-8431
(AZ, except Maricopa and Pima)
✉: consumerinfo@azag.gov
www.azag.gov

## Arkansas

### State Offices

**Arkansas Office of the Attorney General**
Consumer Protection Division
323 Center St., Suite 200
Little Rock, AR 72201
501-682-2007
Toll free: 1-800-482-8982
(Consumer Hotline)
www.arkansasag.gov

## California

### State Offices

**California Bureau of Automotive Repair**
Department of Consumer Affairs
10949 N. Mather Blvd.
Rancho Cordova, CA 95670
Toll free: 1-800-952-5210
(Consumer Questions)
Toll free: 1-866-799-3811
(Complaint Intake)
✉: BAREditor@dca.ca.gov
www.autorepair.ca.gov

**California Department of Consumer Affairs**
Consumer Information Division
1625 N. Market Blvd., Suite N 112
Sacramento, CA 95834
916- 445-1254
Toll free: 1-800-952-5210
TTY: 916-928-1227, 1-800-326-2297
✉: dca@dca.ca.gov
www.dca.ca.gov

**California Office of the Attorney General**
Public Inquiry Unit
PO Box 944255
Sacramento, CA 94244-2550
916-322-3360
Toll free: 1-800-952-5225 (CA)
TTY: 1-800-735-2929
www.caag.state.ca.us

**Contractors State License Board**
9821 Business Park Dr.
Sacramento, CA 95827
916-255-3900 (Headquarters)
916-255-2924 (Northern CA)
562-345-7600 (Southern CA)
Toll free: 1-800-321-2752
www.cslb.ca.gov

### County Offices

**Contra Costa County District Attorney's Office**
Special Operations Division- Consumer Fraud
900 Ward St., 4th Floor
Martinez, CA 94553
925-957-8604
www.co.contra-costa.ca.us

**Fresno County District Attorney's Office**
Consumer & Environmental Protection Division
929 L St.
Fresno, CA 93721
559-600-3156
✉: damail@co.fresno.ca.us
www.co.fresno.ca.us

**Kern County District Attorney's Office**
Consumer Protection Unit
Justice Building
1215 Truxtun Ave., 4th Floor
Bakersfield, CA 93301
661-868-7600
✉: investigation@co.kern.ca.us
www.co.kern.ca.us/da

**Los Angeles County Department of Consumer Affairs**
500 W. Temple St., Room B-96
Los Angeles, CA 90012-2722
213-974-1452
Toll free: 1-800-593-8222 (L.A. County)
TTY: 213-626-0913
✉: dca@dca.lacounty.gov
dca.lacounty.gov

**Marin County District Attorney's Office**
Consumer Protection Unit
Hall of Justice, Room 130
3501 Civic Center Dr.
San Rafael, CA 94903
415-473-6450
✉: consumer@marincounty.org
www.co.marin.ca.us

**Monterey County District Attorney's Office**
Consumer Protection Division
1200 Aguajito Rd., Room 301
Monterey, CA 93940
831-755-5073 (Salinas)
831-647-7770 (Monterey)
831-385-8373 (King City)
www.co.monterey.ca.us

**Napa County District Attorney's Office**
Consumer/Environmental
Protection Division
931 Parkway Mall
Napa, CA 94559
707-253-4059 (Hotline)
✉: da@countyofnapa.org
www.countyofnapa.org

**Orange County District Attorney's Office**
Consumer Protection Unit
401 Civic Center Dr., W
Santa Ana, CA 92701
714-834-3600
✉: consumercomplaint@
da.ocgov.com
orangecountyda.com

**San Diego County District Attorney's Office**
Consumer Protection Unit
330 W. Broadway
San Diego, CA 92101
619-531-4040
619-531-3507 (Hotline)
www.sdcda.org

**San Francisco County District Attorney's Office**
Special Operations Division-
Consumer Protection Unit
732 Brannan St.
San Francisco, CA 94102
415-551-9595 (Hotline)
www.sfdistrictattorney.org

**San Luis Obispo County District Attorney's Office**
Economic Crime Unit
Consumer Advisory
County Courthouse Annex
1050 Monterey St., Room 223
San Luis Obispo, CA 93408
805-781-5856
www.slocounty.ca.gov

**San Mateo County District Attorney's Office**
Consumer and Environmental
Protection Unit
Hall of Justice and Records
400 County Center, 3rd Floor
Redwood City, CA 94063
650-363-4651
650-363-4636 (Complaints)
www.co.sanmateo.ca.us

**Santa Barbara County District Attorney's Office**
Consumer Mediation Services
1112 Santa Barbara St.
Santa Maria, CA 93101
805-568-2300
www.countyofsb.org/da

**Santa Clara County District Attorney's Office**
Consumer Protection Unit
70 W. Hedding St., West Wing
San Jose, CA 95110
408-792-2880
✉: consumer_mediation@
da.sccgov.org
www.santaclara-da.org

**Santa Cruz County District Attorney's Office**
Consumer Affairs Unit
701 Ocean St., Room 200
Santa Cruz, CA 95060
831-454-2050
TTY: 831-454-2123
✉: dao@co.santa-cruz.ca.us
www.co.santa-cruz.ca.us

**Solano County District Attorney's Office**
Consumer and Environmental Crimes
675 Texas St., Suite 5500
Fairfield, CA 94533
707-784-6859
✉: SolanoDA@solanocounty.com
www.co.solano.ca.us/depts/da

**Stanislaus County District Attorney's Office**
Consumer Protection Unit
832 12th St., Suite 300
Modesto, CA 95354
209-525-5550
www.stanislaus-da.org

**Ventura County District Attorney's Office**
Consumer Mediation Section
800 S. Victoria Ave.
Ventura, CA 93009
805-654-3110
Toll free: 1-800-660-5474 ext 3110
(Ventura)
da.countyofventura.org

**City Offices**

**Los Angeles City Attorney's Office**
Consumer Protection Unit
200 N. Main St., Room 800 CHE
Los Angeles, CA 90012
213-978-8080
TTY: 213-978-8310
www.atty.lacity.org

**San Diego City Attorney's Office**
Consumer and Environmental
Protection Unit
1200 3rd Ave., #1620
San Diego, CA 92101
619-533-5600
TTY: 619-702-7198
✉: cityattorney@sandiego.gov
www.sandiego.gov/cityattorney

**Santa Monica City Attorney's Office**
Consumer Protection Unit
1685 Main St., 3rd Floor
Santa Monica, CA 90401
310-458-8336
TTY: 310-458-8696
✉: consumer.mailbox@smgov.net
www.smgov.net/atty

## Colorado

### State Offices

**Colorado Office of the Attorney General**
Consumer Protection Section
1525 Sherman St., 7th Floor
Denver, CO 80203
303-866-5189
Toll free: 1-800-222-4444 (CO)
✉: stop.fraud@state.co.us
www.coloradoattorneygeneral.gov

### County Offices

**Fourth Judicial District Attorney's Office**
Economic Crimes Division
El Paso and Teller Counties
105 E. Vermijo Ave.
Colorado Springs, CO 80903
719-520-6000
www.4thjudicialda.com

**Pueblo County District Attorney's Office**
Economic Crimes Unit
215 W. 10th St.
Pueblo, CO 81003
719-583-6000
pueblo.org

**Weld County District Attorney's Office**
915 10th St.
PO Box 1167
Greeley, CO 80632-1167
970-356-4010
www.co.weld.co.us

### City Offices

**Denver District Attorney's Office**
Economic Crimes Unit
201 W. Colfax Ave.
Denver, CO 80202
720-913-9179
✉: stop.fraud@state.co.us
www.denverda.org

## Connecticut

### State Offices

**Connecticut Attorney General's Office**
55 Elm St.
Hartford, CT 06106
860-808-5318
www.ct.gov/ag

**Department of Consumer Protection**
165 Capitol Ave.
Hartford, CT 06106-1630
Toll free: 1-800-842-2649
TTY: 860-713-7240
✉: dcp.commisioner@ct.gov
www.ct.gov/dcp

### City Offices

**Middletown Office of Consumer Protection**
Director of Consumer Protection
245 deKoven Dr.
Middletown, CT 06457
860-344-3491
TTY: 860-344-3521
www.cityofmiddletown.com

## Delaware

### State Offices

**Delaware Department of Justice**
Consumer Protection Division
820 N. French St., 5th Floor
Wilmington, DE 19801
302-577-8600
Toll free: 1-800-220-5424
✉: consumer.protection@state.de.us
www.attorneygeneral.delaware.gov

## District Of Columbia

### City Offices

**Department of Consumer and Regulatory Affairs**
1100 4th St., SW
Washington, DC 20024
202-442-4400
TTY: 202-123-4567
✉: dcra@dc.gov
www.consumer.dc.gov
www.dcra.dc.gov

**Office of the Attorney General**
Consumer Protection and Antitrust
441 4th St., NW
Washington, DC 20001
202-442-9828 (Hotline)
✉: consumer.protection@dc.gov
www.consumer.dc.gov
www.oag.dc.gov

## Florida

### State Offices

**Florida Department of Agriculture and Consumer Services**
Division of Consumer Services
Terry Lee Rhodes Building
2005 Apalachee Pkwy.
Tallahassee, FL 32399-6500
850-410-3800
Toll free: 1-800-435-7352 (FL)
Toll free: 1-800-352-9832 (in Spanish)
www.800helpfla.com

**Florida Department of Financial Services**
Division of Consumer Services
200 E. Gaines St.
Tallahassee, FL 32399
850-413-3089
Toll free: 1-877-693-5236
www.myfloridacfo.com/Division/Consumers

**Florida Office of the Attorney General**
PL-01 The Capitol
Tallahassee, FL 32399-1050
850-414-3990
Toll free: 1-866-966-7226 (FL)
Toll free: 1-800-203-3099
TTY: 1-800-955-8771
myfloridalegal.com
www.seniorsvscrime.com

### Regional Offices

**Ft. Lauderdale Branch- Office of the Attorney General**
Economic Crimes Division
110 S.E. 6th St., 9th Floor
Fort Lauderdale, FL 33301-5000
954-712-4600
www.myfloridalegal.com

**Jacksonville Branch- Office of the Attorney General**
Economic Crimes Division
1300 Riverplace Blvd., Suite 405
Jacksonville, FL 32207
904-348-2720
www.myfloridalegal.com

**Orlando Branch- Office of the Attorney General**
Economic Crimes Division
135 W. Central Blvd., Suite 1000
Orlando, FL 32801
407-999-5588
www.myfloridalegal.com

**Tampa Branch- Office of the Attorney General**
Economic Crimes Division
Concourse Center 4
3507 E. Frontage Rd., Suite 325
Tampa, FL 33607-1795
813-287-7950
www.myfloridalegal.com

**West Palm Beach Branch- Office of the Attorney General**
Economic Crimes Division
1515 N. Flagler Dr., Suite 900
West Palm Beach, FL 33401
561-837-5000
myfloridalegal.com

**County Offices**

**Broward County Permitting, Licensing & Consumer Protection Division**
One N. University Dr., Mailbox 302
Plantation, FL 33324
954-765-4400
✉: consumer@broward.org
www.broward.org/
permittingandlicensing

**Hillsborough County Consumer Protection Agency**
1101 E. 139th Ave.
Tampa, FL 33613
813-903-3430
www.hillsboroughcounty.org/
consumerprotection

**Miami-Dade County Consumer Services Department**
Consumer Protection Section
140 W. Flagler St., Suites 902
Miami, FL 33130
305-375-3677
✉: consumer@miamidade.gov
www.miamidade.gov/csd

**Office of the State Attorney for Miami-Dade County**
Economic Crime Division
1350 N.W. 12th Ave.
Miami, FL 33136-2111
305-547-0671
www.miamisao.com

**Orange County Consumer Fraud Unit**
415 N. Orange Ave.
PO Box 1673
Orlando, FL 32802
407-836-2490
✉: fraudhelp@sao9.org
www.orangecountyfl.net

**Palm Beach County Consumer Affairs Division**
50 S. Military Tr., Suite 201
West Palm Beach, FL 33415
561-712-6600
Toll free: 1-888-852-7362
(Boca/Delray/Glades)
www.pbcgov.com/consumer

**Pinellas County Office of Consumer Services**
631 Chestnut St.
Clearwater, FL 33756
727-464-6200
TTY: 727-464-6088
✉: consumer@pinellascounty.org
www.pinellascounty.org/
consumer

## Georgia

**State Offices**

**Georgia Governors Office of Consumer Affairs**
Two Martin Luther King, Jr. Dr., SE
Suite 356
Atlanta, GA 30334-9077
404-651-8600
Toll free: 1-800-869-1123 (GA)
www.consumer.georgia.gov

## Hawaii

**State Offices**

**Hawaii Department of Commerce and Consumer Affairs - Hilo**
Office of Consumer Protection
345 Kekuanaoa St., Suite 12
Hilo, HI 96720
808-933-0910
808-587-3222
(Consumer Resource Center)
✉: ocp@dcca.hawaii.gov
www.hawaii.gov/dcca

**Hawaii Department of Commerce and Consumer Affairs - Honolulu (Main Location)**
Office of Consumer Protection
235 S. Beretania St., Suite 801
Honolulu, HI 96813
808-586-2630
808-587-3222
(Consumer Resource Center)
✉: ocp@dcca.hawaii.gov
www.hawaii.gov/dcca/ocp

**Hawaii Department of Commerce and Consumer Affairs - Wailuku**
Office of Consumer Protection
1063 Lower Main St., Suite C-216
Wailuku, HI 96793
808-984-8244
808-587-3222
(Consumer Resource Center)
✉: ocp@dcca.hawaii.gov
www.hawaii.gov/dcca/ocp

## Idaho

**State Offices**

**Idaho Attorney General's Office**
Consumer Protection Division
954 W. Jefferson, 2nd Floor
PO Box 83720
Boise, ID 83720
208-334-2424
Toll free: 1-800-432-3545 (ID)
www.ag.idaho.gov

## Illinois

**State Offices**

**Illinois Office of the Attorney General - Carbondale**
Consumer Fraud Bureau
601 S. University Ave.
Carbondale, IL 62901
618-529-6400
Toll free: 1-800-243-0607
(Fraud Hotline, IL)
Toll free: 1-866-310-8398 (in Spanish)
TTY: 1-877-675-9339 (IL)
www.illinoisattorneygeneral.gov

**Illinois Office of the Attorney General - Chicago**
Consumer Fraud Bureau
100 W. Randolph St.
Chicago, IL 60601
312-814-3000
Toll free: 1-800-386-5438
(Fraud Hotline, IL)
Toll free: 1-866-310-8398 (in Spanish)
TTY: 1-800-964-3013 (IL)
www.illinoisattorneygeneral.gov

**Illinois Office of the Attorney General - Springfield**
Consumer Fraud Bureau
500 S. 2nd St.
Springfield, IL 62706
217-782-1090
Toll free: 1-800-243-0618
(Fraud Hotline, IL)
Toll free: 1-866-310-8398 (in Spanish)
TTY: 1-877-844-5461 (IL)
www.illinoisattorneygeneral.gov

### Regional Offices

**Chicago South Regional Office of the Attorney General**
7906 S. Cottage Grove Ave.
Chicago, IL 60619
773-488-2600
TTY: 1-866-717-8798
www.illinoisattorneygeneral.gov

**Chicago West Regional Office of the Attorney General**
306 N. Pulaski Rd.
Chicago, IL 60624
773-265-8808
TTY: 1-866-717-8804
www.illinoisattorneygeneral.gov

**East Central Illinois Regional Office of the Attorney General**
1776 E. Washington St.
Urbana, IL 61802
217-278-3366
TTY: 217-278-3371
www.illinoisattorneygeneral.gov

**Metro East Illinois Regional Office of the Attorney General**
201 W. Pointe Dr., Suite 7
Belleville, IL 62226
618-236-8616
TTY: 618-236-8619
www.illinoisattorneygeneral.gov

**Northern Illinois Regional Office of the Attorney General**
Zeke Giorgi Center
200 S. Wyman St., Suite 307
Rockford, IL 61101
815-967-3883
TTY: 815-967-3891
www.illinoisattorneygeneral.gov

**West Central Illinois Regional Office of the Attorney General**
628 Maine St.
Quincy, IL 62301
217-223-2221
TTY: 217-223-2254
www.illinoisattorneygeneral.gov

### County Offices

**Cook County State Attorney's Office**
Consumer Fraud Unit
69 W. Washington St., Suite 3130
Chicago, IL 60602
312-603-8600
312-603-8700 (Consumer Line)
✉: consumer@cookcountygov.com
www.statesattorney.org/index2/consumer_fraud.html

### City Offices

**Des Plaines Consumer Protection Services**
1420 Miner St., 6th Floor
Des Plaines, IL 60016
847-391-5006
✉: consumerprotection@desplaines.org
www.desplaines.org

**Chicago Division of Business Affairs and Consumer Protection**
City Hall, 8th Floor
121 N. LaSalle St.
Chicago, IL 60602
312-744-6060
TTY: 312-744-0254
www.cityofchicago.org/ConsumerServices

## Indiana

### State Offices

**Office of the Attorney General**
Consumer Protection Division
Government Center South, 5th Floor
302 W. Washington St.
Indianapolis, IN 46204
317-232-6330
Toll free: 1-800-382-5516 (Consumer Hotline)
www.indianaconsumer.com

## Iowa

### State Offices

**Iowa Office of the Attorney General**
Consumer Protection Division
1305 E. Walnut St.
Des Moines, IA 50319
515-281-5926
Toll free: 1-888-777-4590 (IA)
✉: consumer@ag.state.ia.us
www.IowaAttorneyGeneral.org

## Kansas

### State Offices

**Office of Kansas Attorney**
Consumer Protection and Antitrust Division
120 S.W. 10th St., Suite 430
Topeka, KS 66612-1597
785-296-3751
Toll free: 1-800-432-2310 (KS)
www.ag.ks.gov

### County Offices

**Douglas County District Attorney's Office**
Consumer Protection Division
111 E. 11th St.
Lawrence, KS 66044
785-330-2849 (Consumer Hotline)
785-841-0211 (Main)
✉: districtattorney@douglas-county.com
www.douglas-county.com/depts/da/da_cpu.aspx

**Johnson County District Attorney's Office**
Consumer Protection Division
Consumer Fraud Unit
PO Box 728
Olathe, KS 66051
913-715-3003 (Consumer Hotline)
da.jocogov.org

**Sedgwick County District Attorney's Office**
Consumer Fraud and Economic Crime Unit
1900 E. Morris St.
Wichita, KS 67211
316-660-3600
Toll free: 1-800-432-6878 (KS)
✉: consumer@sedgwick.gov
www.sedgwickcounty.org/da

## Kentucky

### State Offices

**Kentucky Office of the Attorney General**
Consumer Protection Division
1024 Capital Center Dr.
Frankfort, KY 40601
502-696-5389
Toll free: 1-888-432-9257 (Hotline)
✉: consumer.protection@ag.ky.gov
www.ag.ky.gov/cp

**Kentucky Office of the Attorney General - Louisville**
Consumer Protection Division
310 Whittington Pkwy., Suite 101
Louisville, KY 40222
502-429-7134
Toll free: 1-888-432-9257 (Hotline)
✉: consumer.protection@ag.ky.gov
www.ag.ky.gov/cp

**Kentucky Office of the Attorney General - Prestonsburg**
361 N. Lake Dr.
Prestonsburg, KY 41653
606-889-1821
✉: consumer.protection@ag.ky.gov
www.ag.ky.gov/cp

## Louisiana

### State Offices

**Louisiana Office of the Attorney General**
Consumer Protection Section
1885 N. 3rd St.
Baton Rouge, LA 70802
225-326-6465
Toll free: 1-800-351-4889
✉: ConsumerInfo@ag.state.la.us
**www.ag.state.la.us**

### County Offices

**Jefferson Parish District Attorney's Office**
Economic Crime Unit
200 Derbigny St.
Gretna, LA 70053
504-361-2920
**www.jpda.us**

## Maine

### State Offices

**Bureau of Consumer Credit Protection**
35 State House Station
Augusta, ME 04333
207-624-8527
Toll free: 1-800-332-8529 (ME)
TTY: 1-888-577-6690
**www.credit.maine.gov**

**Maine Attorney General's Office**
Consumer Information and
Mediation Service
Six State House Station
Augusta, ME 04333
207-626-8849
Toll free: 1-800-436-2131
(Consumer Protection)
✉: consumer.mediation@maine.gov
**www.maine.gov/ag**

## Maryland

### State Offices

**Maryland Office of the Attorney General**
Consumer Protection Division
200 Saint Paul Pl.
Baltimore, MD 21202
410-528-8662 (Consumer Mediation)
410-576-6550 (Consumer Information)
410-528-1840 (Medical Billing
Complaints)
Toll free: 1-888-743-0023 (Switchboard)
Toll free: 1-877-261-8807
(Health Plan Decision Appeals)
TTY: 410-576-6372 (MD)
✉: consumer@oag.state.md.us
**www.oag.state.md.us/consumer**

### Regional Offices

**Maryland Attorney General's Office - Eastern Shore**
Consumer Protection Division
201 Baptist St.
Salisbury, MD 21801-4976
410-713-3620
Toll free: 1-888-743-0023
(Baltimore Office)
TTY: 410-576-6372
✉: consumer@oag.state.md.us
**www.oag.state.md.us/consumer**

**Maryland Attorney General's Office - Southern Maryland**
PO Box 745
Hughesville, MD 20637
301-274-4620
Toll free: 1-866-366-8343
TTY: 410-576-6372 (Baltimore Office)
✉: consumer@oag.state.md.us
**www.oag.state.md.us/Consumer**

**Maryland Attorney General's Office - Western Maryland**
Consumer Protection Division
44 N. Potomac St., Suite 104
Hagerstown, MD 21740
301-791-4780
TTY: 410-576-6372 (Baltimore Office)
✉: consumer@oag.state.md.us
**www.oag.state.md.us/consumer**

### County Offices

**Howard County Office of Consumer Affairs**
6751 Columbia Gateway Dr.
Columbia, MD 21046
410-313-6420
✉: consumer@howardcountymd.gov
**www.howardcountymd.gov**

**Montgomery County Office of Consumer Protection**
100 Maryland Ave., Suite 330
Rockville, MD 20850
240-777-3636
240-777-3681 (Anonymous Consumer
Tip Line)
TTY: 240-773-3556
✉: ConsumerProtection@
montgomerycountymd.gov
**www.montgomerycountymd.gov/consumer**

## Massachusetts

### State Offices

**Massachusetts Office of the Attorney General**
Consumer Protection Division
One Ashburton Pl.
Boston, MA 02108-1518
617-727-8400 (Consumer Hotline)
TTY: 617-727-4765
✉: ago@state.ma.us
**www.mass.gov/ago**

**Office of Consumer Affairs and Business Regulation**
10 Park Plaza, Suite 5170
Boston, MA 02116
617-973-8700 (General Information)
Toll free: 1-888-283-3757 (MA,
Consumer Hotline)
TTY: 1-800-720-3480
**www.mass.gov/Consumer**

### Regional Offices

**Office of the Attorney General-Central Massachusetts Region**
Consumer Protection Division
10 Mechanic St., Suite 301
Worcester, MA 01608
508-792-7600
TTY: 617-727-4765
✉: ago@state.ma.us
**mass.gov/ago**

**Office of the Attorney General-Southern Massachusetts Region**
Consumer Protection Division
105 William St., 1st Floor
New Bedford, MA 02740-6257
508-990-9700
TTY: 617-727-4765
✉: ago@state.ma.us
**mass.gov/ago**

**Office of the Attorney General-Western Massachusetts Region**
Consumer Protection Division
1350 Main St., 4th Floor
Springfield, MA 01103-1629
413-784-1240
TTY: 617-727-4765
✉: ago@state.ma.us
www.mass.gov/ago

## County Offices

**Norfolk District Attorney's Office**
Consumer Protection Division
45 Shawmut Rd.
Canton, MA 02021
781-830-4800 ext. 279
www.mass.gov/da/norfolk

**Northwestern District Attorney's Office - Franklin County**
Consumer Protection Division
13 Conway St.
Greenfield, MA 01301
413-774-3186
northwesternda.org

**Northwestern District Attorney's Office - Hampshire County**
Consumer Protection Division
One Gleason Plaza
Northampton, MA 01060
413-586-9225
northwesternda.org

## City Offices

**Boston Consumer Affairs and Licensing**
One City Hall Square, Room 817
Boston, MA 02201-2039
617-635-3834
✉: MOCAL@cityofboston.gov
www.cityofboston.gov/
consumeraffairs

**Cambridge Consumers Council**
831 Massachusetts Ave., 1st Floor
Cambridge, MA 02139
617-349-6150
TTY: 617-349-6112
✉: Consumer@cambridgema.gov
www.cambridgema.gov/
consumercouncil.aspx

**Newton-Brookline Consumer Office**
Newton City Hall
1000 Commonwealth Ave.
Newton Centre, MA 02459
617-796-1292
TTY: 617-796-1089
www.newtonma.gov

**Revere Consumer Affairs Office**
150 Beach St.
Revere, MA 02151
781-286-8114
www.revere.org

**Springfield Mayors Office of Consumer Information**
City Hall, Room 315
36 Court St.
Springfield, MA 01103
413-787-6437
TTY: 413-787-6154
✉: moci@springfieldcityhall.com
www.springfieldcityhall.com

## Michigan

### State Offices

**Michigan Department of Agriculture and Rural Development**
Consumer Protection Section
Weights & Measures
940 Venture Ln.
Williamston, MI 48895
517-655-8202
Toll free: 1-800-632-3835
www.michigan.gov/wminfo

**Office of the Attorney General**
Consumer Protection Division
PO Box 30213
Lansing, MI 48909-7713
517-373-1140
Toll free: 1-877-765-8388
www.michigan.gov/ag

### County Offices

**Macomb County Consumer Protection Unit**
Office of the Prosecuting Attorney
One S. Main St., 3rd Floor
Mt. Clemens, MI 48043
586-469-5600
www.macombcountymi.gov

### City Offices

**Detroit Consumer Advocacy Division**
18100 Meyers Rd.
Detroit, MI 48235
313-224-6995
www.ci.detroit.mi.us

## Minnesota

### State Offices

**Office of the Attorney General**
Consumer Services Division
1400 Bremer Tower
445 Minnesota St.
St. Paul, MN 55101
651-296-3353
Toll free: 1-800-657-3787
TTY: 651-297-7206, 1-800-366-4812
www.ag.state.mn.us

### City Offices

**Minneapolis Department of Regulatory Services**
Division of Licenses and Consumer Services
350 S. 5th St.
City Hall, Room 1C
Minneapolis, MN 55415
612-673-2080
TTY: 612-673-2157
www.ci.minneapolis.mn.us/
business-licensing

## Mississippi

### State Offices

**Mississippi Department of Agriculture and Commerce**
Bureau of Regulatory Services
Consumer Protection
PO Box 1609
Jackson, MS 39215
601-359-1148
www.mdac.state.ms.us

**Mississippi Office of the Attorney General**
Consumer Protection Division
PO Box 22947
Jackson, MS 39225-2947
601-359-4230
Toll free: 1-800-281-4418 (MS)
www.ago.state.ms.us

## Missouri

### State Offices

**Missouri Attorney General's Office**
Consumer Protection Unit
PO Box 899
Jefferson City, MO 65102
573-751-3321
Toll free: 1-800-392-8222 (MO, Hotline)
✉: consumer.help@ago.mo.gov
www.ago.mo.gov

## Regional Offices

**Missouri Attorney General's Office- St Louis**

Consumer Protection Division
Old Post Office Building
815 Olive St., Suite 200
St. Louis, MO 63101
314-340-6816
Toll free: 1-800-392-8222 (MO, Hotline)
✉: consumer.help@ago.mo.gov
**www.ago.mo.gov**

### Montana

## State Offices

**Montana Office of Consumer Protection**

Office of Consumer Protection
PO Box 200151
2225 11th Ave.
Helena, MT 59620-0151
406-444-4500
Toll free: 1-800-481-6896
✉: contactocp@mt.gov
**www.doj.mt.gov/consumer**

### Nebraska

## State Offices

**Nebraska Office of the Attorney General**

Consumer Protection Division
2115 State Capitol
Lincoln, NE 68509
402-471-2682
Toll free: 1-800-727-6432 (NE)
Toll free: 1-888-850-7555 (in Spanish)
✉: ago.consumer@nebraska.gov
**www.ago.ne.gov**

### Nevada

## State Offices

**Nevada Department of Business and Industry**

Fight Fraud Task Force
**www.fightfraud.nv.gov**

### New Hampshire

## State Offices

**New Hampshire Office of the Attorney General**

Consumer Protection and Antitrust Bureau
33 Capitol St.
Concord, NH 03301
603-271-3641
Toll free: 1-888-468-4454 (Consumer Protection Hotline)
TTY: 1-800-735-2964 (NH)
✉: DOJ-CPB@doj.nh.gov
**www.doj.nh.gov/consumer**

### New Jersey

## State Offices

**Department of Law and Public Safety**

Division of Consumer Affairs
124 Halsey St.
Newark, NJ 07102
973-504-6200
Toll free: 1-800-242-5846 (NJ)
TTY: 973-504-6588
✉: askconsumeraffairs@
lps.state.nj.us
**www.njconsumeraffairs.gov**

## County Offices

**Bergen County Office of Consumer Protection**

One Bergen County Plaza, 3rd Floor
Hackensack, NJ 07601-7076
201-336-6400
**www.co.bergen.nj.us**

**Burlington County Office of Consumer Affairs/Weights & Measures**

PO Box 6000
Mount Holly, NJ 08060-6000
609-265-5098 (Weights & Measures)
609-265-5054 (Consumer Affairs)
✉: consumer@co.burlington.nj.us
**www.co.burlington.nj.us**

**Cape May County Consumer Affairs**

Four Moore Rd., DN 310
Cape May Court House, NJ 08210-1601
609-886-2903
✉: consumer@co.cape-may.nj.us
**www.capemaycountygov.net**

**Cumberland County Department of Consumer Affairs**

788 E. Commerce St.
Bridgeton, NJ 08302
856-453-2203
**www.co.cumberland.nj.us**

**Essex County Division of Consumer Services**

50 S. Clinton St., Suite 3201
East Orange, NJ 07018
973-395-8350
**www.essex-countynj.org**

**Gloucester County Office of Consumer Affairs and Weights & Measures**

254 County House Rd.
Clarksboro, NJ 08020
856-384-6855
TTY: 856-681-6128
**www.co.gloucester.nj.us/depts/c/
cpwm/default.asp**

**Hudson County Division of Consumer Affairs**

583 Newark Ave.
Jersey City, NJ 07306
201-795-6295 (Hotline)
**www.hudsoncountynj.org**

**Hunterdon County Office of Consumer Affairs**

PO Box 2900
Flemington, NJ 08822
908-806-5174
**www.co.hunterdon.nj.us/
consumeraffairs.htm**

**Mercer County Office of Consumer Affairs**

640 S. Broad St.
PO Box 8068
Trenton, NJ 08650-0068
609-989-6671
**www.mercercounty.org**

**Middlesex County Consumer Affairs**

711 Jersey Ave.
New Brunswick, NJ 08901
732-745-3875
✉: consumer@co.middlesex.nj.us
**www.co.middlesex.nj.us/
consumeraffairs/index.asp**

**Monmouth County Department of Consumer Affairs**

Hall of Records Annex
One E. Main St.
Freehold, NJ 07728-1255
732-431-7900
✉: consumeraffairs@
co.monmouth.nj.us
**www.visitmonmouth.com**

**Ocean County Department of Consumer Affairs**
1027 Hooper Ave., Bldg. #2
Toms River, NJ 08754-2191
732-929-2105
✉: ConsumerAffairs@co.ocean.nj.us
www.co.ocean.nj.us

**Passaic County Department of Consumer Protection/Weights & Measures**
Department of Law
1310 Route 23 N
Wayne, NJ 07470
973-305-5881 (Consumer Protection)
973-305-5750 (Weights & Measures)
www.passaiccountynj.org

**Somerset County Division of Consumer Protection**
20 Grove St.
PO Box 3000
Somerville, NJ 08876-1262
908-203-6080
✉: consumerprotection@
co.somerset.nj.us
www.co.somerset.nj.us

**Union County Department of Public Safety**
Division of Consumer Affairs
300 North Ave., E
Westfield, NJ 07090
908-654-9840
www.ucnj.org

## City Offices

**Nutley Consumer Affairs**
c/o Department of Public Affairs
149 Chestnut St.
Nutley, NJ 07110
973-284-4976
www.nutleynj.org

**Plainfield Action Services**
City Hall Annex, 1st Floor
510 Watchung Ave.
Plainfield, NJ 07061
908-753-3519
www.cityofplainfield.net/
plainfieldactionservices.htm

**Secaucus Department of Consumer Affairs**
Municipal Government Center
1203 Patterson Plank Rd.
Secaucus, NJ 07094
201-330-2008
www.njconsumeraffairs.gov/ocp/
countyoff.htm

**Union Consumer Affairs Office**
1976 Morris Ave.
Union, NJ 07083
908-851-5458
www.uniontownship.com

## New Mexico

### State Offices

**Office of Attorney Genereal**
Consumer Protection Division
PO Drawer 1508
Santa Fe, NM 87504-1508
505-827-6060
Toll free: 1-800-678-1508
www.nmag.gov

## New York

### State Offices

**New York State Department of State**
Division of Consumer Protection
Consumer Assistance Unit
99 Washington Ave.
Albany, NY 12231
518-474-8583
Toll free: 1-800-697-1220
www.nysconsumer.gov

**Office of the Attorney General- Albany Office**
Bureau of Consumer Frauds and Protection
State Capitol
Albany, NY 12224-0341
518-474-5481
Toll free: 1-800-771-7755 (NY)
TTY: 1-800-788-9898
www.ag.ny.gov

**Office of the Attorney General- New York City Office**
Bureau of Consumer Frauds and Protection
120 Broadway, 3rd Floor
New York, NY 10271-0332
212-416-8000
Toll free: 1-800-771-7755 (Hotline)
TTY: 1-800-788-9898
www.ag.ny.gov

### Regional Offices

**Binghamton Regional Office of the Attorney General**
State Office Building, 17th Floor
44 Hawley St.
Binghamton, NY 13901
607-721-8771
Toll free: 1-800-771-7755
(Consumer Hotline)
TTY: 1-800-788-9898
www.ag.ny.gov

**Brooklyn Regional Office of the Attorney General**
55 Hanson Pl., Suite 1080
Brooklyn, NY 11217
718-722-3949
Toll free: 1-800-771-7755
(Consumer Hotline)
TTY: 1-800-788-9898
www.ag.ny.gov

**Buffalo Regional Office of the Attorney General**
Main Place Tower, Suite 300A
350 Main St.
Buffalo, NY 14202
716-853-8400
Toll free: 1-800-771-7755
(Consumer Hotline)
TTY: 1-800-788-9898
www.ag.ny.gov

**Harlem Regional Office of the Attorney General**
163 W. 125th St., Suite 1324
New York, NY 10027
212-961-4475
Toll free: 1-800-771-7755
(Consumer Hotline)
TTY: 1-800-788-9898
www.ag.ny.gov

**Nassau Regional Office of the Attorney General**
200 Old Country Rd., Suite 240
Mineola, NY 11501
516-248-3302
Toll free: 1-800-771-7755
(Consumer Hotline)
TTY: 1-800-788-9898
www.ag.ny.gov

**Plattsburgh Regional Office of the Attorney General**
43 Durkee St., Suite 700
Plattsburgh, NY 12901-2958
518-562-3288
Toll free: 1-800-771-7755 (Consumer Hotline)
TTY: 1-800-788-9898
www.ag.ny.gov

**Poughkeepsie Regional Office of the Attorney General**
One Civic Center Plaza, Suite 401
Poughkeepsie, NY 12601-3157
845-485-3900
Toll free: 1-800-771-7755
(Consumer Hotline)
TTY: 1-800-788-9898
www.ag.ny.gov

**Rochester Regional Office of the Attorney General**
144 Exchange Blvd., Suite 200
Rochester, NY 14614-2176
585-546-7430
Toll free: 1-800-771-7755
(Consumer Hotline)
TTY: 1-800-788-9898
www.ag.ny.gov

**Suffolk Regional Office of the Attorney General**
300 Motor Pkwy., Suite 205
Hauppauge, NY 11788
631-231-2424
Toll free: 1-800-771-7755
(Consumer Helpline)
TTY: 1-800-788-9898
www.ag.ny.gov

**Syracuse Regional Office of the Attorney General**
615 Erie Blvd. W, Suite 102
Syracuse, NY 13204
315-448-4800
Toll free: 1-800-771-7755
(Consumer Hotline)
TTY: 1-800-788-9898
www.ag.ny.gov

**Utica Regional Office of the Attorney General**
207 Genesee St., Room 508
Utica, NY 13501
315-793-2225
Toll free: 1-800-771-7755
(Consumer Hotline)
TTY: 1-800-788-9898
www.ag.ny.gov

**Watertown Regional Office of the Attorney General**
Dulles State Office Building
317 Washington St.
Watertown, NY 13601
315-785-2444
Toll free: 1-800-771-7755
(Consumer Hotline)
TTY: 1-800-788-9898
www.ag.ny.gov

**Westchester Regional Office of the Attorney General**
101 E. Post Rd.
White Plains, NY 10601-5008
914-422-8755
Toll free: 1-800-771-7755
(Consumer Helpline)
TTY: 1-800-788-9898
www.ag.ny.gov

**County Offices**

**Albany County Department of Consumer Affairs**
Consumer Affairs
112 State St., Suite 1207-08
Albany County Office Building
Albany, NY 12207
518-447-7581
✉: consumer_complaints@albanycounty.com
www.albanycounty.com

**Erie County District Attorney's Office**
Consumer Fraud Bureau
Main Place Tower
350 Main St., Suite 300A
Buffalo, NY 14202
716-853-8404
www.oag.state.ny.us

**Nassau County Office of Consumer Affairs**
200 County Seat Dr.
Mineola, NY 11501
516-571-2600
www.nassaucountyny.gov

**Orange County Department of Consumer Affairs**
99 Main St.
Goshen, NY 10924
845-360-6700
www.co.orange.ny.us

**Putnam County Department of Consumer Affairs**
110 Old Route 6, Bldg. 3
Carmel, NY 10512
845-808-1617
www.putnamcountyny.com

**Rockland County Office of Consumer Protection**
18 New Hempstead Rd., 6th Floor
New City, NY 10956
845-708-7600
www.rocklandgov.com

**Schenectady County Department of Consumer Affairs/Bureau of Weights & Measures**
64 Kellar Ave.
Schenectady, NY 12306
518-356-7473 (Consumer Affairs)
518-356-6795 (Weights & Measures)
www.schenectadycounty.com

**Ulster County Consumer Fraud Bureau**
Consumer Fraud Bureau
20 Lucas Ave.
Kingston, NY 12401-3708
845-340-3260
www.ulstercountyny.gov/consumerfraud

**Westchester County Department of Consumer Protection**
112 E. Post Rd., 4th Floor
White Plains, NY 10601
914-995-2155
✉: conpro@westchestergov.com
consumer.westchestergov.com

**City Offices**

**Town of Colonie Attorney**
Consumer Protection Board
Memorial Town Hall
534 Loudon Rd.
Newtonville, NY 12128
518-783-2787
www.colonie.org

**Mt. Vernon Office of Consumer Affairs**
City Hall
One Roosevelt Square
Mount Vernon, NY 10550
914-665-2433
www.cmvny.com

**New York City Department of Consumer Affairs**
42 Broadway
New York, NY 10004
212-639-9675
TTY: 212-487-2710
www.nyc.gov/consumers

**Yonkers Consumer Protection Bureau**
87 Nepperhan Ave., Room 212
Yonkers, NY 10701
914-377-6808
914-377-3000 (Helpline)
www.yonkersny.gov

## North Carolina

### State Offices

**North Carolina Department of Agriculture and Consumer Services**
1001 Mail Service Center
Raleigh, NC 27699-1001
919-707-3000
www.agr.state.nc.us/index.htm

**North Carolina Office of the Attorney General**
Consumer Protection Division
Mail Service Center 9001
Raleigh, NC 27699-9001
919-716-6000
919-716-0058 (in Spanish)
Toll free: 1-877-566-7226 (NC)
www.ncdoj.gov

## North Dakota

### State Offices

**Office of the Attorney General**
Consumer Protection and Antitrust Division
Gateway Professional Center
1050 E. Interstate Ave., Suite 200
Bismarck, ND 58503-5574
701-328-3404
Toll free: 1-800-472-2600
TTY: 1-800-366-6888
✉: ndag@nd.gov
www.ag.nd.gov

## Ohio

### State Offices

**Ohio Attorney General's Office**
Consumer Protection Section
30 E. Broad St., 14th Floor
Columbus, OH 43215-3400
614-466-4320
Toll free: 1-800-282-0515
www.ohioattorneygeneral.gov

### County Offices

**Summit County Office of Consumer Affairs**
175 S. Main St., Suite 209
Akron, OH 44308
330-643-2879
✉: consumeraffairs@summitoh.net
www.co.summit.oh.us/
consumeraffairs

## Oklahoma

### State Offices

**Oklahoma Department of Consumer Credit**
3613 N.W. 56th St., Suite 240
Oklahoma City, OK 73112-4512
405-521-3653
Toll free: 1-800-448-4904 (Consumer Hotline)
www.ok.gov/okdocc

**Oklahoma Attorney General**
Consumer Protection Unit
313 N.E. 21st St.
Oklahoma City, OK 73105
www.oag.ok.gov

## Oregon

### State Offices

**Oregon Department of Justice**
Financial Fraud/Consumer Protection Section
1162 Court St., NE
Salem, OR 97301-4096
503-378-4320 (Salem)
503-229-5576 (Portland)
Toll free: 1-877-877-9392 (OR)
TTY: 1-800-735-2900
✉: consumer.hotline@doj.state.or.us
www.doj.state.or.us

## Pennsylvania

### State Offices

**Office of the Attorney General**
Bureau of Consumer Protection
Strawberry Square, 14th Floor
Harrisburg, PA 17120
717-787-9707
Toll free: 1-800-441-2555 (PA)
Toll free: 1-888-520-6680 (Home Improvement)
www.attorneygeneral.gov

### Regional Offices

**Erie Regional Office - Office of the Attorney General**
Bureau of Consumer Protection
1001 State St., 10th Floor
Erie, PA 16501
814-871-4371
www.attorneygeneral.gov

**Philadelphia Regional Office - Office of the Attorney General**
Bureau of Consumer Protection
21 S. 12th St., 2nd Floor
Philadelphia, PA 19107
215-560-2414
www.attorneygeneral.gov

**Pittsburgh Regional Office - Bureau of Consumer Protection**
Bureau of Consumer Protection
Manor Complex, 6th Floor
564 Forbes Ave.
Pittsburgh, PA 15219
412-565-5135
www.attorneygeneral.gov

**Scranton Regional Office of the Attorney General**
Bureau of Consumer Protection
100 Samter Building
101 Penn Ave.
Scranton, PA 18503
570-963-4913
www.attorneygeneral.gov

**State College Regional Office of the Attorney General**
Bureau of Consumer Protection
444 E. College Ave., Suite 440
State College, PA 16801
814-863-3900
www.attorneygeneral.gov

### County Offices

**Bucks County Department of Consumer Protection**
50 N. Main St.
Doylestown, PA 18901
215-348-7442
Toll free: 1-800-942-2669
✉: consumerprotection@
co.bucks.pa.us
www.buckscounty.org

**Delaware County Consumer Affairs**
201 W. Front St.
Government Center Building
Media, PA 19063
610-891-4865
www.co.delaware.pa.us/
consumeraffairs

## Puerto Rico

### State Offices

**Department de Asuntos Del Consumidor**
Apartado 41059
Minillas Station
Santurce, PR 00940
787-722-7555
Toll free: 1-866-520-3226 (PR)
**www.daco.gobierno.pr**

## Rhode Island

### State Offices

**Rhode Island Department of the Attorney General**
Consumer Protection Unit
150 S. Main St.
Providence, RI 02903
401-274-4400
TTY: 401-453-0410
✉: contactus@riag.ri.gov
**www.riag.state.ri.us**

## South Carolina

### State Offices

**South Carolina Department of Consumer Affairs**
PO Box 5757
Columbia, SC 29250
803-734-4200
Toll free: 1-800-922-1594 (SC)
✉: scdca@scconsumer.gov
**www.scconsumer.gov**

## South Dakota

### State Offices

**South Dakota Office of the Attorney General**
Consumer Protection
1302 E. Hwy. 14, Suite 3
Pierre, SD 57501
605-773-4400
Toll free: 1-800-300-1986 (SD)
TTY: 605-773-6585
✉: consumerhelp@state.sd.us
**www.state.sd.us/atg**

## Tennessee

### State Offices

**Tennessee Department of Commerce and Insurance**
Division of Consumer Affairs
500 James Robertson Pkwy., 12th Floor
Nashville, TN 37243-0600
615-741-4737
Toll free: 1-800-342-8385 (TN)
✉: consumer.affairs@tn.gov
**www.tn.gov/consumer**

**Tennessee Office of the Attorney General**
Consumer Advocate and Protection Division
PO Box 20207
Nashville, TN 37202-0207
615-741-1671
**www.tn.gov/attorneygeneral**

## Texas

### State Offices

**Texas Office of the Attorney General**
Consumer Protection Division
PO Box 12548
Austin, TX 78711-2548
Toll free: 1-800-621-0508
**www.oag.state.tx.us**

### Regional Offices

**Office of the Attorney General - Dallas Region**
Consumer Protection Division
1412 Main St., Suite 810
Dallas, TX 75202
214-969-5310
Toll free: 1-800-621-0508 (TX)
**www.oag.state.tx.us**

**Office of the Attorney General - El Paso Region**
Consumer Protection Division
401 E. Franklin Ave., Suite 530
El Paso, TX 79901
915-834-5800
Toll free: 1-800-621-0508
**www.oag.state.tx.us**

**Office of the Attorney General - Houston Region**
Consumer Protection Division
808 Travis St., Suite 1520
Houston, TX 77002-1702
713-223-5886
Toll free: 1-800-621-0508
**www.oag.state.tx.us**

**Office of the Attorney General - McAllen Region**
Consumer Protection Division
3201 N. McColl Rd., Suite B
McAllen, TX 78501
956-682-4547
Toll free: 1-800-621-0508 (TX)
**www.oag.state.tx.us**

**Office of the Attorney General - San Antonio Region**
Consumer Protection Division
115 E. Travis St., Suite 925
San Antonio, TX 78205
210-225-4191
Toll free: 1-800-621-0508 (TX)
**www.oag.state.tx.us**

### County Offices

**Dallas County District Attorney's Office**
Check Division/ID Fraud
133 N. Industrial Blvd., LB 19
Dallas, TX 75207
214-653-3672
**www.dallascounty.org**

**Harris County District Attorney's Office**
Consumer Protection Section
1201 Franklin St., Suite 600
Houston, TX 77002-1923
713-755-5836
**app.dao.hctx.net**

## Utah

### State Offices

**Utah Department of Commerce**
Division of Consumer Protection
PO Box 146704
160 E. 300 S, 2nd Floor
Salt Lake City, UT 84114-6704
801-530-6601
Toll free: 1-800-721-7233
✉: consumerprotection@utah.gov
**www.consumerprotection.utah.gov**

## Vermont

### State Offices

**Vermont Agency of Agriculture, Food, and Markets**
Food Safety and Consumer Protection
116 State St.
Montpelier, VT 05620
802-828-2426
www.vermontagriculture.com

**Vermont Office of the Attorney General**
Consumer Assistance Program
146 University Pl.
Burlington, VT 05405
802-656-3183
Toll free: 1-800-649-2424 (VT)
✉: consumer@uvm.edu
www.atg.state.vt.us

## Virgin Islands

### State Offices

**Virgin Islands Department of Licensing and Consumer Affairs**
3000 Golden Rock Shopping Center, Suite 9
St. Croix, VI 00820
340-773-2226
www.dlca.gov.vi

**Virgin Islands Department of Licensing and Consumer Affairs**
Property and Procurement Bldg.
8201 Sub Base, Suite 1
St. Thomas, VI 00802
340-774-3130
www.dlca.gov.vi

## Virginia

### State Offices

**Virginia Office of the Attorney General**
Consumer Protection Section
900 E. Main St.
Richmond, VA 23219
804-786-2042
Toll free: 1-800-552-9963 (VA)
TTY: 1-800-828-1120
www.ag.virginia.gov

### Regional Offices

**Office of the Attorney General-Northern Virginia**
10555 Main St., Suite 350
Fairfax, VA 22030
703-277-3540
www.ag.virginia.gov

**Office of the Attorney General-Southwest Region**
204 Abingdon Pl.
Abingdon, VA 24211
276-628-2759
www.ag.virginia.gov

**Office of the Attorney General-Western Region**
3033 Peters Creek Rd.
Roanoke, VA 24019
540-562-3570
www.ag.virginia.gov

### County Offices

**Fairfax County Department of Cable Communications and Consumer Protection**
12000 Government Center Pkwy., Suite 433
Fairfax, VA 22035
703-222-8435
www.fairfaxcounty.gov/consumer.htm

### City Offices

**Office of Consumer Affairs**
301 King St.
City Hall, Room 1900
Alexandria, VA 22314
703-746-4800
www.alexandriava.gov/citizen

## Washington

### State Offices

**Washington Office of the Attorney General**
Consumer Protection Division
PO Box 40100
1125 Washington St., SE
Olympia, WA 98504-0100
Toll free: 1-800-551-4636 (WA)
TTY: 1-800-833-6384
www.atg.wa.gov

### Regional Offices

**Bellingham Office of the Attorney General**
Consumer Protection Division (Island, San Juan, Skagit, and Whatcom Counties)
103 E. Holly St., Suite 308
Bellingham, WA 98225-4728
360-676-2037
Toll free: 1-800-551-4636 (WA)
TTY: 1-800-833-6384
www.atg.wa.gov

**Seattle Office of the Attorney General**
Consumer Protection Division (N. King, Snohomish, Clallam and Jefferson Counties, and Bainbridge Island)
800 5th Ave., Suite 2000
Seattle, WA 98104
206-464-7744
Toll free: 1-800-551-4636 (WA)
TTY: 1-800-833-6384
www.atg.wa.gov

**Spokane Office of the Attorney General**
Consumer Protection Division (Eastern Washington)
1116 W. Riverside Ave.
Spokane, WA 99201-1194
509-456-3123
Toll free: 1-800-551-4636 (WA)
TTY: 1-800-833-6384
www.atg.wa.gov

**Tacoma Office of the Attorney General**
Consumer Protection Division (Pierce, Mason, Grays Harbor Kitsap, and South King Counties)
1250 Pacific Ave., Suite 105
Tacoma, WA 98402
253-593-5243
Toll free: 1-800-551-4636 (WA)
TTY: 1-800-833-6384
www.atg.wa.gov

**Vancouver Office of the Attorney General**

Consumer Protection Division
(Clark, Cowlitz, Pacific, Skamania, Wahkiakum, Lewis, and Thurston Counties)
1220 Main St., Suite 549
Vancouver, WA 98660-2964
360-759-2100
Toll free: 1-800-551-4636 (WA)
TTY: 1-800-833-6384
**www.atg.wa.gov/consumer**

## West Virginia

### State Offices

**Office of the Attorney General**

Consumer Protection Division
PO Box 1789
Charleston, WV 25326-1789
304-558-8986
Toll free: 1-800-368-8808 (WV)
✉: consumer@wvago.gov
**www.wvago.gov**

## Wisconsin

### State Offices

**Wisconsin Department of Agriculture, Trade and Consumer Protection**

Bureau of Consumer Protection
PO Box 8911
2811 Agriculture Dr.
Madison, WI 53708-8911
608-224-4953
Toll free: 1-800-422-7128 (WI)
TTY: 608-224-5058
✉: DATCPhotline@wi.gov
**www.datcp.state.wi.us**

## Wyoming

### State Offices

**Office of the Attorney General**

Consumer Protection Unit
123 State Capitol
200 W. 24th St.
Cheyenne, WY 82002
307-777-5833
TTY: 307-777-5351
**attorneygeneral.state.wy.us**

## Contacting Your Local Banking Authority

The officials listed below regulate and supervise state-chartered banks. Many of them handle or refer problems and complaints about other types of financial institutions as well. Some also answer general questions about banking and consumer credit. If you are dealing with a federally-chartered bank, check Federal Agencies on page 96. Also see the chart in the Banking section on page 7.

### Alabama

**State Banking Department**
PO Box 4600
Montgomery, AL 36103-4600
334-242-3452
Toll free: 1-866-465-2279
**www.banking.alabama.gov**

### Alaska

**Department of Commerce, Community and Economic Development**
Division of Banking and Securities
PO Box 110807
Juneau, AK 99811-0807
907-465-2521
Toll free: 1-888-925-2521
TTY: 907-465-5437
✉: dbsc@commerce.state.ak.us
**www.commerce.state.ak.us/bsc/home.htm**

### Arizona

**Department of Financial Institutions**
2910 N. 44th St., Suite 310
Phoenix, AZ 85018
602-771-2800
✉: consumeraffairs@azdfi.gov
**www.azdfi.gov**

### Arkansas

**State Bank Department**
400 Hardin Rd., Suite 100
Little Rock, AR 72211
501-324-9019
✉: asbd@banking.state.ar.us
**www.arkansas.gov/bank**

### California

**State Department of Financial Institutions**
45 Fremont St., Suite 1700
San Francisco, CA 94105-2219
415-263-8500
916-322-0622 (Consumer Services)
Toll free: 1-800-622-0620 (CA)
✉: consumer@dfi.ca.gov
**www.dfi.ca.gov**

**State Department of Financial Institutions- Los Angeles**
300 S. Spring St., Suite 15513
Los Angeles, CA 90013-1259
213-897-2085
916-322-0622 (Consumer Services)
Toll free: 1-800-622-0620 (CA)
✉: consumer@dfi.ca.gov
**www.dfi.ca.gov**

**State Department of Financial Institutions- Sacramento**
1810 13th St.
Sacramento, CA 95811
916-322-5966
916-322-0622 (Consumer Services)
Toll free: 1-800-622-0620 (CA)
✉: consumer@dfi.ca.gov
**www.dfi.ca.gov**

**State Department of Financial Institutions- San Diego**
7575 Metropolitan Dr., Suite 108
San Diego, CA 92108
619-682-7227
916-322-0622 (Consumer Services)
Toll free: 1-800-622-0620 (CA)
✉: consumer@dfi.ca.gov
**www.dfi.ca.gov**

### Colorado

**Department of Regulatory Agencies**
Division of Banking
1560 Broadway, Suite 975
Denver, CO 80202
303-894-7575
✉: banking@dora.state.co.us
**www.dora.state.co.us/banking**

### Connecticut

**Connecticut Department of Banking**
Financial Institutions Division
260 Constitution Plaza
Hartford, CT 06103
860-240-8180
Toll free: 1-800-831-7225
**www.state.ct.us/dob**

### Delaware

**Office of the State Bank Commissioner**
555 E. Loockerman St., Suite 210
Dover, DE 19901
302-739-4235
**www.banking.delaware.gov**

### District Of Columbia

**Department of Insurance, Securities and Banking**
Attn: Consumer Protection Advocate
810 1st St., NE, Suite 701
Washington, DC 20002
✉: disb@dc.gov
**www.disb.dc.gov**

### Florida

**Office of Financial Regulation**
Division of Financial Institutions
Consumer Assistance Group
200 E. Gaines St.
Tallahassee, FL 32399-0371
850-410-9800
Toll free: 1-800-848-3792 (FL)
**www.flofr.com**

### Georgia

**Department of Banking and Finance**
2990 Brandywine Rd., Suite 200
Atlanta, GA 30341-5565
770-986-1633
Toll free: 1-888-986-1633 (GA)
**www.dbf.georgia.gov**

## Hawaii

**Department of Commerce and Consumer Affairs**
Division of Financial Institutions
PO Box 2054
Honolulu, HI 96805
808-586-2820
808-274-3141 (Kauai)
808-984-2400, 6-2820# (Maui)
808-974-4000, 6-2820# (Hawaii)
Toll free: 1-800-468-4644
✉: dfi@dcca.hawaii.gov
**www.hawaii.gov/dcca/dfi**

## Idaho

**Department of Finance**
Financial Institutions Bureau
PO Box 83720
Boise, ID 83720-0031
208-332-8005
Toll free: 1-888-346-3378 (ID)
✉: finance@finance.idaho.gov
**www.finance.idaho.gov**

## Illinois

**Department of Financial and Professional Regulation**
Division of Banking
320 W. Washington St.
Springfield, IL 62786
217-782-3000
Toll free: 1-800-532-8785
TTY: 217-524-6644
**www.idfpr.com**

## Indiana

**Department of Financial Institutions**
30 S. Meridian St., Suite 300
Indianapolis, IN 46204
317-232-3955
Toll free: 1-800-382-4880 (IN)
**www.in.gov/dfi**

## Iowa

**Division of Banking**
200 E. Grand Ave., Suite 300
Des Moines, IA 50309-1827
515-281-4014
✉: IDOBcomplaints@idob.state.ia.us
**www.idob.state.ia.us**

## Kansas

**Office of the State Bank Commissioner**
700 S.W. Jackson St., Suite 300
Topeka, KS 66603-3714
785-296-2266
✉: complaints@osbckansas.org
**www.osbckansas.org**

## Kentucky

**Department of Financial Institutions**
1025 Capitol Center Dr., Suite 200
Frankfort, KY 40601
502-573-3390
Toll free: 1-800-223-2579
✉: kfi@ky.gov
**www.kfi.ky.gov**

## Louisiana

**Office of Financial Institutions**
PO Box 94095
Baton Rouge, LA 70804-9095
225-925-4660
✉: complaints@ofi.la.gov
**www.ofi.state.la.us**

## Maine

**Bureau of Financial Institutions**
Consumer Outreach Program
36 State House Station
Augusta, ME 04333-0036
207-624-8570
Toll free: 1-800-965-5235
✉: BFI.info@maine.gov
**www.maine.gov/pfr/ financialinstitutions**

## Maryland

**Department of Labor, Licensing and Regulation**
Commissioner of Financial Regulation
500 N. Calvert St., Suite 402
Baltimore, MD 21202
410-230-6077 (Consumer Services)
Toll free: 1-888-784-0136 (MD)
✉: CFRComplaints@dllr.state.md.us
**www.dllr.state.md.us/finance**

## Massachusetts

**Division of Banks**
1000 Washington St.
10th Floor
Boston, MA 02118-6400
617-956-1500
Toll free: 1-800-495-2265 (MA)
TTY: 617-956-1577
✉: dobconsumer.assistan@ state.ma.us
**www.mass.gov/dob**

## Michigan

**Office of Financial and Insurance Regulation**
PO Box 30220
Lansing, MI 48909-7720
517-373-0220
Toll free: 1-877-999-6442 (MI)
✉: ofir-fin-info@michigan.gov
**www.michigan.gov/ofir**

## Minnesota

**Department of Commerce**
Division of Financial Institutions
85 7th Pl. E, Suite 500
St. Paul, MN 55101
651-296-2135
TTY: 651-296-2860
✉: general.commerce@state.mn.us
**mn.gov/commerce**

## Mississippi

**Department of Banking and Consumer Finance**
901 Woolfolk Building, Suite A
501 N. West St.
Jackson, MS 39201
601-359-1031
Toll free: 1-800-844-2499 (MS)
**www.dbcf.state.ms.us**

## Missouri

**Department of Finance**
Harry S. Truman State Office Building
PO Box 716
Room 630
Jefferson City, MO 65102
573-751-3242
✉: finance@dof.mo.gov
**www.finance.mo.gov**

## Montana

**Division of Banking and Financial Institutions**
PO Box 200546
Helena, MT 59620
406-841-2920
TTY: 406-841-2974
www.banking.mt.gov

## Nebraska

**Department of Banking and Finance**
PO Box 95006
Lincoln, NE 68509-5006
402-471-2171
Toll free: 1-877-471-3445
www.ndbf.ne.gov

## Nevada

**Department of Business and Industry**
Financial Institutions Division
2785 E. Desert Inn Rd.
Las Vegas, NV 89121
702-486-4120
www.fid.state.nv.us

## New Hampshire

**State Banking Department**
53 Regional Dr., Suite 200
Concord, NH 03301
603-271-3561
Toll free: 1-800-437-5991
TTY: 1-800-735-2964
✉: NHBD@Banking.State.NH.US
www.nh.gov/banking

## New Jersey

**Department of Banking and Insurance**
Division of Banking
PO Box 471
Trenton, NJ 08625-0471
609-292-7272
Toll free: 1-800-446-7467
www.state.nj.us/dobi

## New Mexico

**Regulation and Licensing Department**
Financial Institutions Division
2550 Cerrillos Rd., 3rd Floor
Santa Fe, NM 87505
505-476-4885
✉: rld.fid@state.nm.us
www.rld.state.nm.us/
financialinstitutions

## New York

**Banking Department**
Consumer Help Unit
25 Beaver St.
New York, NY 10004-2319
212-709-3530
Toll free: 1-877-226-5697 (NY)
✉: consumer@banking.state.ny.us
www.banking.state.ny.us

## North Carolina

**Commissioner of Banks**
4309 Mail Service Center
Raleigh, NC 27699-4309
Toll free: 1-888-384-3811
www.nccob.org

## North Dakota

**Department of Financial Institutions**
2000 Schafer St., Suite G
Bismarck, ND 58501-1204
701-328-9933
TTY: 1-800-366-6888 (ND)
✉: dfi@nd.gov
www.nd.gov/dfi

## Ohio

**Department of Commerce**
Division of Financial Institutions
Consumer Complaints
77 S. High St., 21st Floor
Columbus, OH 43215-6120
614-728-8400
Toll free: 1-866-278-0003
TTY: 1-800-750-0750
✉: webdfi-cf@com.state.oh.us
www.com.ohio.gov/fiin

## Oklahoma

**State Banking Department**
2900 N. Lincoln Blvd.
Oklahoma City, OK 73105
405-521-2782
www.ok.gov/banking

## Oregon

**Department of Consumer and Business Services**
Division of Finance and Corporate Securities
PO Box 14480
Salem, OR 97309-0405
503-378-4140
Toll free: 1-866-814-9710 (OR)
✉: dcbs.dfcsmail@state.or.us
dfcs.oregon.gov

## Pennsylvania

**Department of Banking**
Consumer Services
17 N. 2nd St., Suite 1300
Harrisburg, PA 17101-2290
717-787-1854
Toll free: 1-800-722-2657
TTY: 1-800-679-5070
www.banking.state.pa.us

## Puerto Rico

**Oficina del Comisionado de Instituciones Financieras**
PO Box 11855
San Juan, PR 00910-3855
787-723-3131
www.ocif.gobierno.pr

## Rhode Island

**Department of Business Regulation**
Division of Banking
1511 Pontiac Ave., Bldg. 68-2
Cranston, RI 02920
401-462-9500
✉: bankinquiry@dbr.ri.gov
www.dbr.state.ri.us

## South Carolina

**Office of the Commissioner of Banking**
State Board of Financial Institutions
1205 Pendleton St., Suite 305
Columbia, SC 29201
803-734-2001
www.banking.sc.gov

### South Dakota

**Department of Labor and Regulation**
Division of Banking
217 1/2 W. Missouri Ave.
Pierre, SD 57501-4590
605-773-3421
✉: banking@state.sd.us
**www.dlr.sd.gov/reg/bank**

### Tennessee

**Department of Financial Institutions**
Consumer Resources Division
414 Union St., Suite 1000
Nashville, TN 37219
615-253-2023
Toll free: 1-800-778-4215 (TN)
✉: TDFI.ConsumerResources@tn.gov
**www.tennessee.gov/tdfi**

### Texas

**Department of Banking**
2601 N. Lamar Blvd., Suite 201
Austin, TX 78705
512-475-1300
Toll free: 1-877-276-5554 (Consumer Hotline)
✉: consumer.complaints@dob.texas.gov
**www.banking.state.tx.us**

### Utah

**Department of Financial Institutions**
PO Box 146800
Salt Lake City, UT 84114-6800
801-538-8830
**www.dfi.utah.gov**

### Vermont

**Department of Financial Regulation**
Banking Division
89 Main St.
Montpelier, VT 05620-3101
802-828-3307
Toll free: 1-888-568-4547 (VT)
✉: dfr.bnkconsumer@state.vt.us
**www.dfr.vermont.gov**

### Virgin Islands

**Office of the Lieutenant Governor**
Division of Banking and Insurance
5049 Kongens Gade
St. Thomas, VI 00802
340-774-7166
**www.ltg.gov.vi**

### Virginia

**State Corporation Commission**
Bureau of Financial Institutions
PO Box 640
Richmond, VA 23218
804-371-9657
804-371-9705 (Complaints)
Toll free: 1-800-552-7945 (VA)
TTY: 804-371-9206
**www.scc.virginia.gov**

### Washington

**Department of Financial Institutions**
Division of Banks
PO Box 41200
Olympia, WA 98504-1200
360-902-8704
Toll free: 1-877-746-4334
TTY: 360-664-8126
**www.dfi.wa.gov**

### West Virginia

**Division of Banking**
900 Pennsylvania Ave.
Suite 306
Charleston, WV 25302
304-558-2294
**www.wvdob.org**

### Wisconsin

**Department of Financial Institutions**
Bureau of Consumer Affairs
PO Box 8041
Madison, WI 53708-8041
608-264-7969
TTY: 608-266-8818
**www.wdfi.org**

### Wyoming

**Division of Banking**
Herschler Building, 3rd Floor, East
122 W. 25th St.
Cheyenne, WY 82002
307-777-7797
✉: doa-dob-web@wyo.gov
**audit.state.wy.us/banking**

## Contacting Your Local Insurance Regulator

The officials listed below enforce laws and regulations for each type of insurance. Many of these offices can also provide you with information to help you make informed insurance-buying decisions. See the the Insurance section in Part I of this *Handbook* for advice (p. 31).

If you have a question or complaint about your insurance company's policies, contact the company before you contact your state insurance regulator.

### Alabama

**Department of Insurance**
PO Box 303351
Montgomery, AL 36130-3351
334-241-4141 (Consumer Services)
334-269-3550
✉: ConsumerServices@
insurance.alabama.gov
**www.aldoi.gov**

### Alaska

**Division of Insurance**
Department of Commerce, Community and Economic Development
Robert B. Atwood Building
550 W. 7th Ave., Suite 1560
Anchorage, AK 99501-3567
907-269-7900
Toll free: 1-800-467-8725
TTY: 907-465-5437
✉: insurance@alaska.gov
**www.dced.state.ak.us/insurance**

### Arizona

**Department of Insurance**
Consumer Affairs Division
2910 N. 44th St., Suite 210
Phoenix, AZ 85018-7269
Toll free: 1-800-325-2548 (AZ)
✉: consumers@azinsurance.gov
**www.id.state.az.us**

### Arkansas

**Insurance Department**
Consumer Services Division
1200 W. 3rd St.
Little Rock, AR 72201-1904
✉: insurance.consumers@
arkansas.gov
**www.insurance.arkansas.gov**

### California

**Department of Insurance**
Consumer Services Division
300 S. Spring St., South Tower
Los Angeles, CA 90013
213-897-8921
Toll free: 1-800-927-4357 (CA)
TTY: 1-800-482-4833
**www.insurance.ca.gov**

**Department of Managed Health Care, California HMO Help Center**
980 9th St., Suite 500
Sacramento, CA 95814-2725
Toll free: 1-888-466-2219
TTY: 1-877-688-9891
**www.hmohelp.ca.gov**

### Colorado

**Division of Insurance**
1560 Broadway, Suite 850
Denver, CO 80202
Toll free: 1-800-930-3745 (CO)
TTY: 711
✉: insurance@dora.state.co.us
**www.dora.state.co.us/Insurance**

### Connecticut

**Insurance Department**
Consumer Affairs Division
PO Box 816
Hartford, CT 06142-0816
860-297-3900
Toll free: 1-800-203-3447 (CT)
✉: cid.ca@ct.gov
**www.ct.gov/cid**

### Delaware

**Insurance Department**
841 Silver Lake Blvd.
Dover, DE 19904
302-674-7310
Toll free: 1-800-282-8611
✉: consumer@state.de.us
**www.delawareinsurance.gov**

### District Of Columbia

**Department of Insurance, Securities and Banking**
Attn: Consumer Services Division
810 1st St., NE, Suite 701
Washington, DC 20002
✉: disb@dc.gov
**www.disb.dc.gov**

### Florida

**Office of Insurance Regulation**
200 E. Gaines St.
Tallahassee, FL 32399
850-413-3140
**www.floir.com**

### Georgia

**Insurance and Safety Fire Commissioner**
Two Martin Luther King, Jr. Dr.
West Tower, Suite 704
Atlanta, GA 30334
404-656-2070
Toll free: 1-800-656-2298 (GA)
✉: Consumer@oci.ga.gov
**www.gainsurance.org**

### Hawaii

**Department of Commerce and Consumer Affairs**
Insurance Division
PO Box 3614
Honolulu, HI 96811
808-586-2790
✉: insurance@dcca.hawaii.gov
**www.hawaii.gov/dcca/ins**

### Idaho

**Department of Insurance**
Consumer s Bureau
700 W. State St.
PO Box 83720
Boise, ID 83720-0043
208-334-4250
Toll free: 1-800-721-3272 (ID)
**www.doi.idaho.gov**

## Illinois

**Division of Insurance-Springfield**
320 W. Washington St.
Springfield, IL 62767-0001
217-782-4515
Toll free: 1-877-527-9431 (Office of
Consumer Health Insurance)
Toll free: 1-866-445-5364
(Consumer Assistance Hotline)
TTY: 217-524-4872
✉: doi.infodesk@illinois.gov
**www.insurance.illinois.gov**

## Indiana

**Department of Insurance
Consumer Services Division**
311 W. Washington St., Suite 300
Indianapolis, IN 46204
317-232-2395
Toll free: 1-800-622-4461 (IN)
✉: consumerservices@idoi.in.gov
**www.in.gov/idoi**

## Iowa

**Division of Insurance**
330 Maple St.
Des Moines, IA 50319-0065
515-281-6348
Toll free: 1-877-955-1212 (IA)
**www.iid.state.ia.us**

## Kansas

**Insurance Department**
Consumer Assistance Division
420 S.W. 9th St.
Topeka, KS 66612
785--296-7829
Toll free: 1-800-432-2484 (KS)
TTY: 1-877-235-3151
✉: commissioner@ksinsurance.org
**www.ksinsurance.org**

## Kentucky

**Department of Insurance**
Consumer Protection and
Education Division
PO Box 517
Frankfort, KY 40602-0517
502-564-6034
Toll free: 1-800-595-6053
TTY: 1-800-648-6056
**insurance.ky.gov**

## Louisiana

**Department of Insurance**
PO Box 94214
Baton Rouge, LA 70804-9214
225-342-5900
Toll free: 1-800-259-5300
✉: consumeradvocacy@ldi.la.gov
**www.ldi.state.la.us**

## Maine

**Bureau of Insurance**
34 State House Station
Augusta, ME 04333-0034
207-624-8475
Toll free: 1-800-300-5000 (ME)
TTY: 1-888-577-6690
✉: Insurance.PFR@maine.gov
**www.maine.gov/insurance**

## Maryland

**Insurance Administration**
Consumer Division
200 St. Paul Pl., Suite 2700
Baltimore, MD 21202
410-468-2000
Toll free: 1-800-492-6116
TTY: 1-800-735-2258
**www.mdinsurance.state.md.us**

## Massachusetts

**Division of Insurance**
1000 Washington St., Suite 810
Boston, MA 02118-6200
Toll free: 1-877-563-4467 (MA)
TTY: 617-521-7490
✉: doicss.mailbox@state.ma.us
**www.state.ma.us/doi**

## Michigan

**Office of Financial and Insurance
Regulation**
PO Box 30220
Lansing, MI 48909-7720
517-373-0220
Toll free: 1-877-999-6442
✉: ofir-ins-info@michigan.gov
**www.michigan.gov/ofir**

## Minnesota

**Department of Commerce**
Insurance Division
85 7th Pl. E, Suite 500
St. Paul, MN 55101
651-296-4026
Toll free: 1-800-657-3602 (MN)
✉: general.commerce@state.mn.us
**www.insurance.mn.gov**

## Mississippi

**Department of Insurance**
PO Box 79
Jackson, MS 39205-0079
601-359-3569
Toll free: 1-800-562-2957 (MS)
✉: consumer@mid.state.ms.us
**www.mid.state.ms.us**

## Missouri

**Department of Insurance, Financial,
and Professional Registration**
Consumer Affairs Division
PO Box 690
Jefferson City, MO 65102-0690
Toll free: 1-800-726-7390 (MO)
TTY: 573-526-4536
✉ consumeraffairs@
insurance.mo.gov
**www.insurance.mo.gov**

## Montana

**Commissioner of Securities
and Insurance**
Insurance Division
840 Helena Ave.
Helena, MT 59601
406-444-2040
Toll free: 1-800-332-6148 (MT)
TTY: 406-444-3246
**www.csi.mt.gov/consumers**

## Nebraska

**Department of Insurance**
PO Box 82089
941 O St., Suite 400
Lincoln, NE 68501-2089
402-471-2201
Toll free: 1-877-564-7323 (NE)
TTY: 1-800-833-7352
✉: DOI.ConsumerAffairs@
nebraska.gov
**www.doi.ne.gov**

STATE INSURANCE REGULATORS

# STATE INSURANCE REGULATORS

## Nevada

**Department of Business and Industry**
Division of Insurance
1818 E. College Pkwy.
Carson City, NV 89701
775-687-4270
Toll free: 1-888-872-3234
✉: cscc@doi.state.nv.us
www.doi.nv.gov

**Department of Business and Industry**
Division of Insurance
2501 E. Sahara Ave., #302
Las Vegas, NV 89104
702-486-4009
Toll free: 1-888-872-3234 (NV)
www.doi.nv.gov

## New Hampshire

**Department of Insurance**
21 S. Fruit St., Suite 14
Concord, NH 03301
603-271-2261
Toll free: 1-800-852-3416 (NH)
TTY: 1-800-735-2964 (NH)
✉: consumerservices@ins.nh.gov
www.nh.gov/insurance

## New Jersey

**Department of Banking and Insurance**
Consumer Inquiries and Complaints
PO Box 325
Trenton, NJ 08625
609-292-7272
Toll free: 1-800-446-7467
www.dobi.nv.gov

## New Mexico

**Public Regulation Commission**
Insurance Division
PO Box 1269
1120 Paseo De Peralta
Santa Fe, NM 87501
505-827-4601
Toll free: 1-888-427-5772 (NM)
www.nmprc.state.nm.us

## New York

**Department of Financial Services**
Insurance Department - Consumer Assistance Unit
One Commerce Plaza
Albany, NY 12257
518-474-6600
Toll free: 1-800-342-3736 (NY)
✉: consumers@ins.state.ny.us
www.dfs.ny.gov

**Insurance Department**
Insurance Division - Consumer Assistance Unit
25 Beaver St.
New York, NY 10004
212-480-6400
Toll free: 1-800-342-3736 (NY)
✉: consumers@ins.state.ny.us
www.ins.state.ny.us

## North Carolina

**Department of Insurance**
1201 Mail Service Center
Raleigh, NC 27699-1201
919-807-6750 (Consumer Services)
Toll free: 1-800-546-5664
(NC, Consumer Services)
www.ncdoi.com

## North Dakota

**Insurance Department**
State Capitol
600 E. Boulevard Ave., 5th Floor
Bismarck, ND 58505-0320
701-328-2440
Toll free: 1-800-247-0560 (ND)
TTY: 1-800-366-6888
✉: insurance@nd.gov
www.nd.gov/ndins

## Ohio

**Department of Insurance**
Office of Consumer Affairs
50 W. Town St., 3rd Floor, Suite 300
Columbus, OH 43215
614-644-2658
Toll free: 1-800-686-1526
(Consumer Hotline)
Toll free: 1-800-686-1527
(Fraud Hotline)
Toll free: 1-800-686-1578
(Senior Hotline)
TTY: 614-644-3745
www.insurance.ohio.gov

## Oklahoma

**Insurance Department**
Five Corporate Plaza
3625 N.W. 56th St., Suite 100
Oklahoma City, OK 73112
405-521-2991
Toll free: 1-800-522-0071 (OK)
www.ok.gov/oid

## Oregon

**Insurance Division**
PO Box 14480
Salem, OR 97309-0405
503-947-7984
Toll free: 1-888-877-4894 (OR)
✉: cp.ins@state.or.us
www.insurance.oregon.gov

## Pennsylvania

**Insurance Department**
Consumer Service
1209 Strawberry Square
Harrisburg, PA 17120
717-787-2317
Toll free: 1-877-881-6388 (PA)
TTY: 717-783-3898
✉: ra-in-consumer@pa.gov
www.insurance.state.pa.us

## Puerto Rico

**Office of the Commissioner of Insurance**
B5 Calle Tabonuco, Suite 216 PMB 356
Guaynabo, PR 00968-3029
Toll free: 1-888-722-8686
www.ocs.gobierno.pr

## Rhode Island

**Department of Business Regulation**
Insurance Division
1511 Pontiac Ave.
Cranston, RI 02920
401-462-9520
✉: InsuranceInquiry@dbr.ri.gov
www.dbr.state.ri.us

## South Carolina

**Department of Insurance**
Consumer Services
PO Box 100105
Columbia, SC 29202-3105
803-737-6180
Toll free: 1-800-768-3467 (SC)
✉: consumers@doi.sc.gov
www.doi.sc.gov

## South Dakota

**Department of Labor and Regulation**
Division of Insurance
445 E. Capital Ave.
Pierre, SD 57501
605-773-3563
✉: insurance@state.sd.us
**www.dlr.sd.gov/insurance**

## Tennessee

**Department of Commerce and Insurance**
Consumer Insurance Services
500 James Robertson Pkwy.
Nashville, TN 37243-0574
Toll free: 1-800-342-4029 (TN)
✉: CIS.complaints@state.tn.us
**www.tn.gov/commerce**

## Texas

**Department of Insurance**
Consumer Protection (111-1A)
PO Box 149091
Austin, TX 78714-9091
512-804-5140
Toll free: 1-800-252-3439
TTY: 512 322-4238
✉: onsumerprotection@
tdi.state.tx.us
**www.tdi.state.tx.us**

## Utah

**Department of Insurance**
State Office Building
450 N. State St., Room 3110
Salt Lake City, UT 84114-6901
801-538-3800
Toll free: 1-800-439-3805 (UT)
TTY: 801-538-3826
**www.insurance.utah.gov**

## Vermont

**Department of Financial Regulation**
Insurance Consumer Section
89 Main St.
Montpelier, VT 05620-3101
802-828-3302
Toll free: 1-800-964-1784(VT)
✉: dfr.insuranceinfo@state.vt.us
**www.dfr.vermont.gov**

## Virgin Islands

**Division of Banking and Insurance**
5049 Kongens Gade
St. Thomas, VI 00802
340-774-7166
**www.ltg.gov.vi**

## Virginia

**State Corporation Commission**
Bureau of Insurance
PO Box 1157
Richmond, VA 23218
804-371-9741
Toll free: 1-800-552-7945 (VA)
Toll free: 1-877-310-6560 (Nationwide)
TTY: 804-371-9206
✉: bureauofinsurance@
scc.virginia.gov
**www.scc.virginia.gov**

## Washington

**Office of the Insurance Commissioner**
Consumer Advocacy
PO Box 40256
Olympia, WA 98504-0256
360-725-7080
Toll free: 1-800-562-6900 (WA)
TTY: 360-586-0241
✉: cap@oic.wa.gov
**www.insurance.wa.gov**

## West Virginia

**Offices of the Insurance Commissioner**
PO Box 50540
Charleston, WV 25305-0540
304-558-3386
Toll free: 1-888-879-9842 (WV)
TTY: 1-800-435-7381
✉: consumer.service@
wvinsurance.gov
**www.wvinsurance.gov**

## Wisconsin

**Office of the Commissioner of Insurance**
PO Box 7873
Madison, WI 53707-7873
608-266-0103
Toll free: 1-800-236-8517 (WI)
TTY: Dial 711 and ask for 608-266-3586
✉: ocicomplaints@wisconsin.gov
**oci.wi.gov**

## Wyoming

**Department of Insurance**
Consumer Affairs Section
106 E. 6th Ave.
Cheyenne, WY 82002
307-777-7402
Toll free: 1-800-438-5768 (WY)
**insurance.state.wy.us**

## Contacting Your Local Securities Administrator

State securities regulators protect the investing public. Each state has its own laws and regulations for securities brokers and securities, including stocks, mutual funds, commodities, real estate, and more. The agencies listed below enforce these laws and regulations. They also license securities professionals, register securities, and investigate consumer complaints. While these agencies do not provide investment advice, many of them offer educational resources so investors can make informed investment decisions.

If you have a question or complaint about an investment, call the company or bank involved. If you are not satisfied with the response you get, call your state securities agency. See the Investing section in Part I of this *Handbook* for additional advice and sources of assistance (p. 35).

### Alabama

**Securities Commission**
PO Box 304700
Montgomery, AL 36130-4700
334-242-2984
Toll free: 1-800-222-1253 (AL)
✉: asc@asc.alabama.gov
**www.asc.state.al.us**

### Alaska

**Department of Commerce, Community and Economic Development**
Division of Banking and Securities
PO Box 110807
Juneau, AK 99811-0807
907-465-2521
Toll free: 1-888-925-2521 (AK)
TTY: 907-465-5437
✉: dbsc@alaska.gov
**www.commerce.state.ak.us**

### Arizona

**Arizona Corporation Commission**
Securities Division
1300 W. Washington St., 3rd Floor
Phoenix, AZ 85007
602-542-4242
Toll free: 1-866-837-4399 (AZ)
✉: info@azinvestor.gov
**www.azinvestor.gov**

### Arkansas

**Securities Department**
Heritage West Building
201 E. Markham St., Suite 300
Little Rock, AR 72201-1692
501-324-9260
Toll free: 1-800-981-4429
✉: info@securities.arkansas.gov
**www.securities.arkansas.gov**

### California

**Department of Corporations**
Consumer Services Office
1515 K St., Suite 200
Sacramento, CA 95814
Toll free: 1-866-275-2677
TTY: 1-800-735-2966
**www.corp.ca.gov**

### Colorado

**Department of Regulatory Agencies**
Division of Securities
1560 Broadway, Suite 900
Denver, CO 80202
303-894-2320
TTY: 1-800-659-2656
✉: securities@dora.state.co.us
**www.dora.state.co.us/securities**

### Connecticut

**Department of Banking**
Securities and Business Investments Division
260 Constitution Plaza
Hartford, CT 06103-1800
860-240-8230
Toll free: 1-800-831-7225
**www.ct.gov/dob**

### Delaware

**Division of Securities**
Carvel State Office Building
820 N. French St., 5th Floor
Wilmington, DE 19801
302-577-8424
TTY: 302-577-5783
**www.state.de.us/securities**

### District Of Columbia

**Department of Insurance, Securities and Banking**
810 1st St., NE, Suite 701
Attn: Consumer Protection Advocate
Washington, DC 20002
202-727-8000
✉: disb@dc.gov
**disb.dc.gov**

### Florida

**Office of Financial Regulation**
Division of Securities
Consumer Assistance Group
200 E. Gaines St.
Tallahassee, FL 32399-0375
850-410-9500
Toll free: 1-800-848-3792 (FL)
**www.flofr.com**

### Georgia

**Office of the Secretary of State**
Division of Securities and Business Regulation
237 Coliseum Dr.
Macon, GA 31217-3858
478-207-2440
**www.sos.ga.gov/securities**

### Hawaii

**Department of Commerce and Consumer Affairs**
Securities Enforcement Branch
Business Registration Division
PO Box 40
Honolulu, HI 96810
808-586-2744
Toll free: 1-877-477-2267
✉: seb@dcca.hawaii.gov
**www.hawaii.gov/dcca/sec**

### Idaho

**Department of Finance**
Securities Bureau
PO Box 83720
Boise, ID 83720-0031
208-332-8000
Toll free: 1-888-346-3378 (ID)
✉: finance@finance.idaho.gov
**www.finance.idaho.gov**

## Illinois

**Secretary of State**
Securities Department
Jefferson Terrace
300 W. Jefferson St., Suite 300A
Springfield, IL 62702
217-782-2256
Toll free: 1-800-628-7937 (IL)
**www.cyberdriveillinois.com**

## Indiana

**Office of the Secretary of State**
Securities Division
302 W. Washington St., Room E111
Indianapolis, IN 46204
317-232-6681
Toll free: 1-800-223-8791 (IN)
**www.in.gov/sos/securities/index.htm**

## Iowa

**Securities Bureau**
340 Maple St.
Des Moines, IA 50319
515-281-5705
Toll free: 1-877-955-1212 (IA)
**www.iid.state.ia.us/securities**

## Kansas

**Office of the Securities Commissioner**
109 S.W. 9th St., Suite 600
Topeka, KS 66612
785-296-3307
Toll free: 1-800-232-9580 (KS)
**www.ksc.ks.gov**

## Kentucky

**Department of Financial Institutions**
Division of Securities
1025 Capitol Center Dr., Suite 200
Frankfort, KY 40601-3868
502-573-3390
Toll free: 1-800-223-2579
✉: kfi@ky.gov
**www.kfi.ky.gov**

## Louisiana

**Office of Financial Institutions**
Securities Division
PO Box 94095
Baton Rouge, LA 70804-9095
225-925-4660
✉: ofila@ofi.louisiana.gov
**www.ofi.state.la.us**

## Maine

**Department of Professional and Financial Regulation**
Office of Securities
121 State House Station
Augusta, ME 04333-0121
207-624-8551
Toll free: 1-877-624-8551 (ME)
**www.maine.gov/pfr/securities**

## Maryland

**Office of the Attorney General**
Securities Division
200 Saint Paul Pl.
Baltimore, MD 21202-2020
410-576-6360
Toll free: 1-888-743-0023 (MD)
TTY: 410-576-6372
✉: securities@oag.state.md.us
**www.oag.state.md.us**

## Massachusetts

**Office of the Secretary of the Commonwealth**
Securities Division
One Ashburton Pl., 17th Floor
Room 1701
McCormack Building
Boston, MA 02108
617-727-3548
Toll free: 1-800-269-5428 (MA)
TTY: 617-878-3889
✉: securities@sec.state.ma.us
**www.sec.state.ma.us/sct/sctidx.htm**

## Michigan

**Office of Financial and Insurance Regulation**
Securities Division Consumer Services Division
PO Box 30220
Lansing, MI 48909
517-373-0220
Toll free: 1-877-999-6442
✉: ofir-sec-info@michigan.gov
**www.michigan.gov/ofirsecurities**

## Minnesota

**Department of Commerce**
Securities Division
Consumer Protection and Education
85 7th Pl. E, Suite 500
St. Paul, MN 55101
651-282-5064
Toll free: 1-800-657-3602 (MN)
TTY: 651-296-2860
✉: securities.commerce@state.mn.us
**www.mn.gov/commerce**

## Mississippi

**Secretary of State's Office**
Securities Division
Business Regulation and Enforcement
PO Box 136
Jackson, MS 39205-0136
601-359-1048
**www.sos.ms.gov**

## Missouri

**Office of the Secretary of State**
Securities Division
600 W. Main St.
Jefferson City, MO 65101-1276
573-751-4136
Toll free: 1-800-721-7996 (MO)
✉: securities@sos.mo.gov
**www.sos.mo.gov**

## Montana

**State Auditor's Office**
Securities Division
840 Helena Ave.
Helena, MT 59601
406-444-2040
Toll free: 1-800-332-6148 (MT)
✉: stateauditor@mt.gov
**www.csi.mt.gov/consumers**

# STATE SECURITIES ADMINISTRATORS

## Nebraska

**Department of Banking and Finance**
Bureau of Securities
PO Box 95006
Lincoln, NE 68509-5006
402-471-3445
Toll free: 1-877-471-3445
**www.ndbf.ne.gov**

## Nevada

**Office of the Secretary of State**
Securities Division
555 E. Washington Ave., Suite 5200
Las Vegas, NV 89101
702-486-2440
✉: nvsec@govmail.state.nv.us
**www.nvsos.gov**

## New Hampshire

**Bureau of Securities Regulation**
107 N. Main St., #204
Concord, NH 03301
603-271-1463
Toll free: 1-800-994-4200
✉: securities@sos.nh.gov
**sos.nh.gov/sec_reg.aspx**

## New Jersey

**Department of Law and Public Safety**
Bureau of Securities
PO Box 47029
Newark, NJ 07101
973-504-3600
Toll free: 1-866-446-8378 (NJ)
✉: Askbureauofsecurities@
dca.lps.state.nj.us
**www.njsecurities.gov**

## New Mexico

**Regulation and Licensing Department**
Securities Division
2550 Cerrillos Rd., 3rd Floor
Santa Fe, NM 87505
505-476-4580
Toll free: 1-800-704-5533 (NM)
**www.rld.state.nm.us/securities**

## New York

**Office of the Attorney General**
Investor Protection Bureau
120 Broadway, 23rd Floor
New York, NY 10271
212-416-8222
**www.oag.state.ny.us**

## North Carolina

**Secretary of State**
Securities Division
PO Box 29622
Raleigh, NC 27626-0622
919-733-3924
Toll free: 1-800-688-4507
(Investor Hotline)
✉: secdiv@sosnc.com
**www.secretary.state.nc.us/sec**

## North Dakota

**Securities Department**
State Capitol
600 E. Boulevard Ave., 5th Floor
Bismarck, ND 58505-0510
701-328-2910
Toll free: 1-800-297-5124 (ND)
✉: ndsecurities@nd.gov
**www.ndsecurities.com**

## Ohio

**Department of Commerce**
Division of Securities
77 S. High St., 22nd Floor
Columbus, OH 43215-6131
Toll free: 1-800-788-1194
(Investor Protection Hotline)
✉: securitiesgeneral.questions@
com.state.oh.us
**www.com.ohio.gov/secu**

## Oklahoma

**Department of Securities**
First National Center
120 N. Robinson Ave., Suite 860
Oklahoma City, OK 73102
405-280-7700
**www.securities.ok.gov**

## Oregon

**Department of Consumer and Business Services**
Division of Finance and Corporate Securities
PO Box 14480
Salem, OR 97309-0405
Toll free: 1-866-814-9710
TTY: 503-378-4100
✉: dcbs.dfcsmail@state.or.us
**dfcs.oregon.gov**

## Pennsylvania

**Securities Commission**
Eastgate Office Building, 2nd Floor
1010 N. 7th St.
Harrisburg, PA 17102-1410
717-787-8061
Toll free: 1-800-600-0007 (PA)
✉: pscwebmaster@pa.gov
**www.psc.state.pa.us**

## Puerto Rico

**Office of the Commissioner of Financial Institutions**
Securities Division
PO Box 11855
San Juan, PR 00910-3855
787-723-3131
TTY: 1-800-981-7711 (Consumers)
✉: valores@ocif.gobierno.pr
**www.ocif.gobierno.pr**

## Rhode Island

**Department of Business Regulation**
Securities Division
1511 Pontiac Ave.
Cranston, RI 02920
401-462-9527
✉: securitiesinquiry@dbr.ri.gov
**www.dbr.state.ri.us**

## South Carolina

**Office of the Attorney General**
Securities Division
PO Box 11549
Columbia, SC 29211-1549
**www.scag.gov/scsecurities**

## South Dakota

**Department of Labor and Regulation**
Division of Securities
445 E. Capitol Ave.
Pierre, SD 57501-3185
605-773-4823
✉: drr.securities@state.sd.us
**www.dlr.sd.gov/securities**

## Tennessee

**Department of Commerce and Insurance**
Securities Division
500 James Robertson Pkwy., Suite 680
Nashville, TN 37243-0575
615-741-2947
Toll free: 1-800-863-9117 (TN)
✉: Securities.1@tn.gov
**www.state.tn.us/commerce/securities**

## Texas

**State Securities Board**
PO Box 13167
Austin, TX 78711-3167
512-305-8300
**www.ssb.state.tx.us**

## Utah

**Department of Commerce**
Division of Securities
PO Box 146760
Salt Lake City, UT 84114-6760
801-530-6600
Toll free: 1-800-721-7233 (UT)
✉: securities@utah.gov
**www.securities.utah.gov**

## Vermont

**Department of Financial Regulation**
Securities Division
89 Main St.
Montpelier, VT 05620-3101
802-828-3421
✉: DFR.SecuritiesInfo@state.vt.us
**www.dfr.vermont.gov**

## Virginia

**State Corporation Commission**
Division of Securities and Retail Franchising
PO Box 1197
Richmond, VA 23218
Toll free: 1-800-552-7945 (VA)
TTY: 804-371-9206
✉: SRF_General@scc.virginia.gov
**www.scc.virginia.gov/srf**

## Washington

**Department of Financial Institutions**
Division of Securities
PO Box 41200
Olympia, WA 98504-1200
360-902-8760
Toll free: 1-877-746-4334
TTY: 360-664-8126
**www.dfi.wa.gov**

## West Virginia

**State Auditor's Office**
Securities Commission
1900 Kanawha Blvd., E
Building 1, Room W-100
Charleston, WV 25305
304-558-2251
Toll free: 1-877-982-9148
✉: securities@wvsao.gov
**www.wvsao.gov/securitiescommission**

## Wisconsin

**Department of Financial Institutions**
Division of Securities
PO Box 1768, 4th Floor
Madison, WI 53701-1768
608-266-1064
TTY: 608-266-8818
**www.wdfi.org**

## Wyoming

**Office of the Secretary of State**
Compliance Division
State Capitol Building
200 W. 24th St.
Cheyenne, WY 82002-0020
307-777-7370
✉: investing@wyo.gov
**soswy.state.wy.us**

**Contacting Your Local Utilities Commission**

State utilities commissions regulate services and rates for gas, electricity, and telephones in your state. In some states, the utility commissions regulate other services such as water, transportation, and the moving of household goods. Rates for utilities and services provided between states are regulated by the federal government.

Many utilities commissions handle consumer complaints. Sometimes, if they receive a number of complaints about the same utility matter, they will conduct investigations.

## Alabama

**Public Service Commission**
Consumer Services
PO Box 304260
Montgomery, AL 36130
334-242-5218
Toll free: 1-800-392-8050 (AL)
www.psc.state.al.us

## Alaska

**Regulatory Commission**
Consumer Protection and
Information Section
701 W. 8th Ave., Suite 300
Anchorage, AK 99501-3469
907-276-6222
Toll free: 1-800-390-2782
TTY: 907-276-4533
✉: cp.mail@alaska.gov
rca.alaska.gov

## Arizona

**Corporation Commission**
Utilities Division
Consumer Services Section
1200 W. Washington St.
Phoenix, AZ 85007
602-542-4251
Toll free: 1-800-222-7000 (AZ)
✉: mailmaster@azcc.gov
www.cc.state.az.us

## Arkansas

**Public Service Commission**
Consumer Services Division
PO Box 400
Little Rock, AR 72203-0400
Toll free: 1-800-482-1164 (AR)
TTY: 1-800-682-2698
www.arkansas.gov/psc

## California

**Public Utilities Commission**
Consumer Affairs Branch
505 Van Ness Ave.
San Francisco, CA 94102
415-703-2782
Toll free: 1-800-649-7570 (CA)
TTY: 1-800-229-6846
✉: public.advisor@cpuc.ca.go
www.cpuc.ca.gov

## Colorado

**Public Utilities Commission**
Consumer Protection Division
1560 Broadway, Suite 250
Denver, CO 80202
303-894-2070
Toll free: 1-800-456-0858 (CO)
✉: PUCConsumer.Complaints@
dora.state.co.us
www.dora.state.co.us/puc

## Connecticut

**Department of Energy and
Environmental Protection**
Public Utilities Regulatory Authority
Consumer Services Unit
10 Franklin Square
New Britain, CT 06051
860-827-1553
Toll free: 1-800-382-4586 (CT)
TTY: 860-827-2837
✉: dpuc.information@po.state.ct.us
www.state.ct.us/dpuc

## Delaware

**Public Service Commission**
Cannon Building, Suite 100
861 Silver Lake Blvd.
Dover, DE 19904
302-736-7500
Toll free: 1-800-282-8574 (DE)
www.depsc.delaware.gov

## District Of Columbia

**Public Service Commission**
Office of Consumer Services
1333 H St., NW, Suite 600
East Tower
Washington, DC 20005
202-626-5120
www.dcpsc.org

## Florida

**Public Service Commission**
2540 Shumard Oak Blvd.
Tallahassee, FL 32399-0850
850-413-6100
Toll free: 1-800-342-3552 (FL)
TTY: 1-800-955-8771
✉: contact@psc.state.fl.us
www.floridapsc.com

## Georgia

**Public Service Commission**
Consumer Affairs Division
244 Washington St., SW
Atlanta, GA 30334
404-656-4501
Toll free: 1-800-282-5813 (GA)
✉: gapsc@psc.state.ga.us
www.psc.state.ga.us

## Hawaii

**Public Utilities Commission**
465 S. King St., Room 103
Honolulu, HI 96813
808-586-2020
✉: Hawaii.puc@hawaii.gov
www.puc.hawaii.gov

## Idaho

**Public Utilities Commission**
Consumer Assistance Section
PO Box 83720
Boise, ID 83720-0074
Toll free: 1-800-432-0369 (ID)
www.puc.idaho.gov

## Illinois

**Commerce Commission**
Consumer Affairs
527 E. Capitol Ave.
Springfield, IL 62701
217-782-2024
Toll free: 1-800-524-0795 (IL)
TTY: 1-800-858-9277
www.icc.illinois.gov

## Indiana

**Utility Regulatory Commission**
Consumer Affairs Division
101 W. Washington St., Suite 1500E
Indianapolis, IN 46204
317-232-2712
Toll free: 1-800-851-4268 (IN)
TTY: 317-232-8556
www.in.gov/iurc

## Iowa

**Utilities Board**
Customer Service Group
1375 E. Court Ave., Room 69
Des Moines, IA 50319-0069
515-725-7321
Toll free: 1-877-565-4450 (IA)
✉: customer@iub.iowa.gov
www.state.ia.us/iub

## Kansas

**Corporation Commission**
Office of Consumer Protection
1500 S.W. Arrowhead Rd.
Topeka, KS 66604
785-271-3140
Toll free: 1-800-662-0027 (KS)
TTY: 1-800-766-3777
✉: public.affairs@kcc.ks.gov
www.kcc.state.ks.us

## Kentucky

**Public Service Commission**
211 Sower Blvd.
PO Box 615
Frankfort, KY 40602
502-564-3940
Toll free: 1-800-772-4636
TTY: 1-800-648-6056
✉: psc.consumer.inquiry@ky.gov
www.psc.state.ky.us

## Louisiana

**Public Service Commission**
Galvez Building, 12th Floor
602 N. 5th St.
PO Box 91154
Baton Rouge, LA 70821-9154
225-342-4404
Toll free: 1-800-256-2397 (LA)
www.lpsc.org

## Maine

**Public Utilities Commission**
Consumer Assistance Division
18 State House Station
Augusta, ME 04333-0018
207-287-3831
Toll free: 1-800-452-4699 (ME)
TTY: 1-800-437-1220
✉: maine.puc@maine.gov
www.state.me.us/mpuc/
index.shtml

## Maryland

**Public Service Commission**
Six St. Paul St., 16th Floor
Baltimore, MD 21202
410-767-8000
Toll free: 1-800-492-0474
TTY: 1-800-201-7165
www.psc.state.md.us

## Massachusetts

**Department of Public Utilities**
Consumer Division
One South Station, Suite 2
Boston, MA 02110
617-737-2836
Toll free: 1-877-886-5066
✉: DPUConsumer.Complaints@
state.ma.us
www.mass.gov/dpu

## Michigan

**Public Service Commission**
PO Box 30221
Lansing, MI 48909
517-241-6180
Toll free: 1-800-292-9555 (MI)
✉: mpsc_commissioners@
michigan.gov
www.michigan.gov/mpsc

## Minnesota

**Public Utilities Commission**
Consumer Affairs Office
121 7th Pl. E, Suite 350
St. Paul, MN 55101-2147
651-296-0406
Toll free: 1-800-657-3782
✉: consumer.puc@state.mn.us
www.puc.state.mn.us

## Mississippi

**Public Service Commission**
P.O. Box 1174
Jackson, MS 39215
601-961-5430 (Central District)
601-961-5450 (Northern District)
601-961-5440 (Southern District)
Toll free: 1-800-356-6430
(Central District)
Toll free: 1-800-356-6428
(Northern District)
Toll free: 1-800-356-6429
(Southern District)
www.psc.state.ms.us

## Missouri

**Public Service Commission**
Consumer Services Department
200 Madison St.
PO Box 360
Jefferson City, MO 65102-0360
573-751-3234
Toll free: 1-800-392-4211 (MO)
TTY: 573-522-9061
✉: pscinfo@psc.mo.gov
www.psc.mo.gov

## Montana

**Public Service Commission**
PO Box 202601
Helena, MT 59620-2601
406-444-6150
Toll free: 1-800-646-6150 (MT)
TTY: 406-444-4212
www.psc.mt.gov

## Nebraska

**Public Service Commission**
1200 N St., Suite 300
Lincoln, NE 68508
402-471-3101
Toll free: 1-800-526-0017 (NE)
TTY: 402-471-0213
www.psc.state.ne.us

## Nevada

**Public Utilities Commission**
Consumer Division
1150 E. William St.
Carson City, NV 89701-3109
775-684-6100
702-486-2600 (Las Vegas)
**pucweb1.state.nv.us/pucn/**
**PUCHome.aspx**

## New Hampshire

**Public Utilities Commission**
Consumer Affairs Division
21 S. Fruit St., Suite 10
Concord, NH 03301-2429
603-271-2431
Toll free: 1-800-852-3793 (NH)
TTY: 1-800-735-2964 (NH)
✉: puc@puc.nh.gov
**www.puc.state.nh.us**

## New Jersey

**Board of Public Utilities**
Division of Customer Assistance
44 S. Clinton Ave.
Trenton, NJ 08625
609-341-9188
Toll free: 1-800-624-0241 (NJ)
Toll free: 1-800-624-0331
(Cable Complaints)
**www.bpu.state.nj.us**

## New Mexico

**Public Regulation Commission**
Consumer Relations Division
Utilities Division
1120 Paseo de Peralta
PO Box 1269
Santa Fe, NM 87501
505-827-4592
Toll free: 1-888-427-5772
TTY: 505-827-6911
✉: crd.complaints@state.nm.us
**www.nmprc.state.nm.us**

## New York

**Department of Public Service**
Office of Consumer Services
3 Empire State Plaza
Albany, NY 12223
518-474-7080
Toll free: 1-800-342-3377
(NY - General Complaints)
Toll free: 1-888-342-3355 (Termination)
TTY: 1-800-662-1220
✉: csd@dps.ny.gov
**www.askpsc.com**

## North Carolina

**Utilities Commission**
Consumer Services
4325 Mail Service Center
Raleigh, NC 27699-4325
919-733-9277
Toll free: 1-866-380-9816
✉: consumer.services@
psncuc.nc.gov
**www.ncuc.commerce.state.nc.us**

## North Dakota

**Public Service Commission**
600 E. Boulevard Ave., Dept. 408
Bismarck, ND 58505-0480
701-328-2400
Toll free: 1-877-245-6685
TTY: 1-800-366-6888 (ND)
✉: ndpsc@nd.gov
**www.psc.state.nd.us**

## Ohio

**Consumers' Counsel**
10 W. Broad St., Suite 1800
Columbus, OH 43215-3485
614-466-8574 (Outside OH)
Toll free: 1-877-742-5622
✉: occ@occ.state.oh.us
**www.pickocc.org**

**Public Utilities Commission**
180 E. Broad St.
Columbus, OH 43215
614-466-3292
Toll free: 1-800-686-7826 (OH)
TTY: 1-800-686-1570 (OH)
**www.puco.ohio.gov**

## Oklahoma

**Corporation Commission**
Consumer Services Division
PO Box 52000
Oklahoma City, OK 73152-2000
405-522-0478
Toll free: 1-800-522-8154 (OK)
**www.occeweb.com**

## Oregon

**Public Utility Commission**
Consumer Services Division
550 Capitol St., NE, Suite 215
PO Box 2148
Salem, OR 97308-2148
Toll free: 1-800-522-2404
TTY: 1-800-648-3458 (OR)
✉: puc.consumer@state.or.us
**www.puc.state.or.us**

## Pennsylvania

**Pennsylvania Office of Consumer Advocate**
Office of the Attorney General
555 Walnut St., 5th Floor, Forum Place
Harrisburg, PA 17101-1923
717-783-5048
Toll free: 1-800-684-6560 (PA)
✉: consumer@paoca.org
**www.oca.state.pa.us**

**Public Utility Commission**
Bureau of Consumer Services
PO Box 3265
Harrisburg, PA 17105-3265
**www.puc.state.pa.us**

## Puerto Rico

**Public Service Commission**
PO Box 190870
San Juan, PR 00918
787-756-1919
**www.csp.gobierno.pr**

## Rhode Island

**Public Utilities Commission**
Consumer Section
89 Jefferson Blvd.
Warwick, RI 02888
401-780-9700
✉: consumer.section@ripuc.org
**www.ripuc.org**

## South Carolina

**Office of Regulatory Staff**
Consumer Services Division
1401 Main St., Suite 900
Columbia, SC 29201
803-737-5230
Toll free: 1-800-922-1531 (SC)
TTY: 1-800-334-2217 (SC)
**www.regulatorystaff.sc.gov**

## South Dakota

**Public Utilities Commission**
Consumer Affairs
500 E. Capitol Ave.
Pierre, SD 57501-5070
605-773-3201 (General)
Toll free: 1-800-332-1782
✉: PUCConsumerInfo@state.sd.us
**www.puc.sd.gov**

## Tennessee

**Regulatory Authority**
Consumer Services Division
460 James Robertson Pkwy.
Nashville, TN 37243-0505
615-741-2904
Toll free: 1-800-342-8359 (Consumer Services)
TTY: 1-888-276-0677
**www.state.tn.us/tra**

## Texas

**Public Utility Commission**
Customer Protection
1701 N. Congress Ave.
PO Box 13326
Austin, TX 78711-3326
512-936-7120
Toll free: 1-888-782-8477
TTY: 1-800-735-2988
✉: customer@puc.state.tx.us
**www.puc.state.tx.us**

## Utah

**Division of Public Utilities**
160 East 300 South
Salt Lake City, UT 84114-6751
Toll free: 1-800-874-0904 (UT)
TTY: 801-530-6769
✉: psc@utah.gov
**www.psc.utah.gov**

## Vermont

**Public Service Board**
112 State St., 4th Floor
Montpelier, VT 05620-2701
802-828-2358
TTY: 1-800-253-0191 (VT)
✉: psb.clerk@state.vt.us
**www.psb.vermont.gov**

## Virginia

**State Corporation Commission**
Division of Energy Regulation
PO Box 1197
Richmond, VA 23218
Toll free: 1-800-552-7945 (VA)
TTY: 804-371-9206
✉: EnergyReg@scc.virginia.gov
**www.scc.virginia.gov**

## Washington

**Utilities and Transportation Commission**
Consumer Protection
PO Box 47250
Olympia, WA 98504
360-664-1160
Toll free: 1-888-333-9882
TTY: 1-800-416-5289
✉: consumer@utc.wa.gov
**www.utc.wa.gov**

## West Virginia

**Consumer Advocate Division**
723 Kanawha Blvd., E
Union Building, Suite 700
Charleston, WV 25301
304-558-0526
**www.cad.state.wv.us**

**Public Service Commission**
Customer Assistance
PO Box 812
201 Brooks St.
Charleston, WV 25323
304-340-0300
Toll free: 1-800-642-8544
**www.psc.state.wv.us**

## Wisconsin

**Public Service Commission**
Consumer Affairs Unit
PO Box 7854
Madison, WI 53707-7854
608-266-2001
Toll free: 1-800-225-7729
TTY: 608-267-1479
**psc.wi.gov**

## Wyoming

**Public Service Commission**
2515 Warren Ave., Suite 300
Cheyenne, WY 82002
307-777-7427
Toll free: 1-888-570-9905 (WY)
✉: wyoming_psc@wyo.gov
**psc.state.wy.us**

## Contacting Trade & Professional Organizations

Companies that manufacture similar products or offer similar services often belong to an industry association. These associations help resolve problems between their member companies and consumers. Most also provide consumer information through publications and websites.

If you have a problem with a company and cannot resolve it by working directly with that firm, ask whether the company is a member of an association. Then check this section to see whether the association is listed. If the association is not included here, your local library has reference materials to help you find the appropriate contact.

### Advertising Self-Regulation Council (ASRC)
70 W. 36th St., 13th Floor
New York, NY 10018
Toll-free: 1-866-334-6272
**www.narcpartners.org**
**www.asrcreviews.org**
ASRC fosters truth and accuracy in national advertising through voluntary self-regulation. As an effort between the advertising industry and the Council of Better Business Bureaus, ASRC helps solve disputes over advertising claims.

### America's Health Insurance Plans (AHIP)
601 Pennsylvania Ave., NW, South Bldg., Suite 500
Washington, DC 20004
202-778-3200
✉: ahip@ahip.org
**www.ahip.org**
America's Health Insurance Plans (AHIP) is the national association representing companies that provide health insurance coverage to more than 200 million Americans. Member companies offer medical, long-term care, disability income, dental, supplemental, stop-loss insurance and reinsurance to consumers, employers and public purchasers.

### American Financial Services Association (AFSA) Education Foundation ♦
919 18th St., NW, Suite 300
Washington, DC 20006-5517
202-466-8611
✉: info@afsaef.org
**www.afsaef.org**
The AFSAEF mission is to educate consumers on personal finance concepts and to help consumers realize the benefits of responsible money management and understand the credit process. Their MoneySKILL® program educates young adults on personal finance concepts in the areas of income, expenses, assets, liabilities and risk management.

### American Arbitration Association
1633 Broadway, 10th Floor
New York, NY 10019
Toll-free: 1-800-778-7879
**www.adr.org**
This association is a not-for-profit public service organization committed to the resolution of disputes through arbitration, mediation, conciliation and other voluntary procedures.

### American Bankers Association (ABA)
1120 Connecticut Ave., NW
Washington, DC 20036
Toll-free: 1-800-226-5377
**www.aba.com**
ABA represents the concerns of banks and their employees. The ABA's Education Foundation offers personal finance resources to help consumers understand their financial choices.

### American Bar Association
321 N. Clark St.
Chicago, IL 60654
312-988-5000
✉: askaba@abanet.org
**www.americanbar.org**
The Bar Association is an association of lawyers. The ABA accredits law schools, and provides the public with information about the law, courts and guides for legal issues.

### American Cleaning Institute® (ACI) ♦
1331 L St., NW, Suite 650
Washington, DC 20005
202-347-2900
✉: info@cleaninginstitute.org
**www.cleaninginstitute.org**
ACI is the consumer source for free/low cost educational materials, designated to help individuals, families and communities stay clean, safe and healthy at home, work and school.

### American Council of Life Insurers
101 Constitution Ave., NW, Suite 700
Washington, DC 20001-2133
202-624-2000
✉: contact@acli.com
**www.acli.com**
The American Council of Life Insurers is a trade association of over 500 insurance companies that provide life insurance, pensions and annuities, long-term care, and disability income insurance.

### American Health Care Association (AHCA)
1201 L St., NW
Washington, DC 20005
202-842-4444
**www.ahcancal.org**
This federation of affiliated state health organizations advocates for quality care and services for frail, elderly and disabled Americans.

♦ Provided financial support for the publication of the Consumer Action Handbook.

**American Institute of Certified Public Accountants (AICPA)**
220 Leigh Farm Rd.
Durham, NC 27707
919-402-4500
Toll-free: 1-888-777-7077 (Ethics Hotline)
**www.aicpa.org**
AICPA works to ensures that the public remains confident in the integrity, competence and professionalism of CPAs.

**American Moving and Storage Association (AMSA)**
1611 Duke St.
Alexandria, VA 22314
703-683-7410
Toll-free: 1-888-849-2672
**www.moving.org**
AMSA offers a wealth of information on its consumer website, including a Mover Referral Service. It also sponsors a dispute settlement program to help consumers resolve loss and damage claims on interstate moves.

**American Pharmacists Association (APhA)**
2215 Constitution Ave., NW
Washington, DC 20037
202-628-4410
Toll-free: 1-800-237-2742
**www.pharmacist.com**
The APhA empowers its members to improve medication use and advance patient care through information, education, and advocacy.

**American Society of Travel Agents, Inc. (ASTA)**
1101 King St., Suite 200
Alexandria, VA 22314
703-739-2782
✉: consumeraffairs@asta.org
**www.astanet.com**
ASTA is an association of travel industry professionals. It provides training and education to professionals. They offer travel tips for consumers and accept consumer complaints about poor travel service.

**Assisted Living Federation of America (ALFA)**
1650 King St., Suite 602
Alexandria, VA 22314
703-894-1805
**www.alfa.org**
ALFA sets best practices for senior living. They also provide a directory of senior living communities and other materials to help consumers determine their assisted living needs.

**Association of Credit and Collection Professionals (ACA International)**
PO Box 390106
Minneapolis, MN 55439
952-926-6547
✉: aca@acainternational.org
**www.askdoctordebt.com**
ACA International's sets ethical standards for companies in the debt collection industry. They also use their website, askdoctordebt.org, to educate consumers about their rights.

**Association of Independent Consumer Credit Counseling Agencies (AICCCA)**
11350 Random Hills Rd., Suite 800
Fairfax, VA 22030
Toll-free: 1-866-703-8787
**www.aiccca.org**
AICCCA represents non-profit credit counseling companies. AICCCA sets industry standards to ensure that member companies provide quality service to consumers. The organization also provides information directly to consumers (budgeting tips and a searchable database to locate a credit counseling company) on their website.

**Automotive Recyclers Association (ARA)**
9113 Church St.
Manassas, VA 20110
571-208-0428
Toll-free: 1-888-385-1005
**www.a-r-a.org**
ARA member companies are dedicated to the efficient removal and reuse of automotive parts, and the safe disposal of inoperable motor vehicles.

**Cellular Telecommunications and Internet Association (CTIA)**
1400 16th St., NW, Suite 600
Washington, DC 20036
202-736-3200
**www.ctia.org**
CTIA oversees certification programs to ensure a high standard of quality for consumers of wireless devices.

**Certified Financial Planner Board of Standards**
1425 K St., NW, Suite 500
Washington, DC 20005
202-379-2200
Toll-free: 1-800-487-1497
✉: mail@cfpboard.org
**www.cfp.net**
The CFP Board works to ensure that the public benefits from competent financial planning. The CFP Board certifies financial planners who meet its requirements by granting use of their trademarks.

**Commission on the Accreditation of Rehabilitation Facilities (CARF)**
6951 E. Southpoint Rd.
Tucson, AZ 85756
Toll-free: 1-888-281-6531
**www.carf.org**
CARF is an independent accrediting body of rehabilitation, addiction, substance abuse, and retirement living services. The organization provides an online search tool to find services that match your rehabilitiation needs, as well as links to consumer resources.

### Consumer Electronics Association (CEA)
1919 S. Eads St.
Arlington, VA 22202
703-907-7600
Toll-free: 1-866-858-1555
✉: cea@ce.org
**www.ce.org**
CEA represents corporations involved in the design, development, manufacture and distribution consumer electronics. They offer free guides for buying electronics to consumers.

### Credit Union National Association (CUNA)
5710 Mineral Point Rd.
Madison, WI 53705-0431
Toll-free: 1-800-356-9655
**www.cuna.org**
CUNA serves more than 90% of credit unions through credit union leagues throughout the nation.

### Direct Marketing Association DMA)
1120 Avenue of the Americas
New York, NY 10036-6700
212-768-7277 ext. 1888
✉: consumer@the-dma.org
**www.dmachoice.org**
The DMA is the trade association for organizations involved in direct marketing. via direct mail, catalogs, the Internet, telemarketing, magazines, newspaper and TV ads. DMAs consumer website offers consumers options (free of charge) to better manage their mail.

### Direct Selling Association (DSA)
1667 K St., NW, Suite 1100
Washington, DC 20006
202-452-8866
✉: info@dsa.org
**www.dsa.org**
DSA is the trade association of firms that manufacture and distribute goods and services sold directly to consumers.

### Distance Education and Training Council (DETC)
1601 18th St., NW, Suite 2
Washington, DC 20009
202-234-5100
**www.detc.org**
The DETC is a voluntary, non-governmental, educational organization that accredits distance education institutions.

### Financial Industry Regulatory Authority (FINRA) ♦
1736 K St., NW
Washington, DC 20006
301-590-6500 (Call Center)
Toll-free: 1-800-289-9999 (Broker Check Hotline)
**www.finra.org**
FINRA is the largest independent regulator for all securities firms doing business in the US. The organization operates the largest dispute resolution forum in the securities industry for disputes between investors and securities firms. Consumers may check the background of individual investment professionals and firms using the BrokerCheck tool on the FINRA website.

### Financial Planning Association (FPA)
7535 E. Hampden Ave., Suite 600
Denver, CO 80231
Toll-free: 1-800-322-4237
✉: fpa@fpanet.org
**www.fpanet.org**
The Financial Planning Association is a leadership and advocacy organization connecting those who provide the services with consumers they serve. This organization is a resource for the public to find educational resources and a financial planner who will deliver advice using an ethical, objective, client-centered process.

### Food Marketing Institute (FMI)
2345 Crystal Dr., Suite 800
Arlington, VA 22202
202-452-8444
**www.fmi.org**
FMI conducts programs in research, education, industry relations and public affairs on behalf of grocery retailers and wholesalers.

### Grocery Manufacturers Association (GMA)
1350 I St. NW, Suite 300
Washington, DC 20005
202-639-5900
Toll-free: 1-800-355-0983
**www.gmaonline.org**
GMA represents food, beverage, and consumer products companies. The Association helps to ensure the safety and security of consumer packaged goods.

### Insurance Information Institute (III)
110 William St.
New York, NY 10038
212-346-5500
✉: info@iii.org
**www.iii.org**
The III is a nonprofit, communications organization supported by the property/casualty insurance industry that works to improve public understanding of insurance.

### International Association of Movers (IAM)
5904 Richmond Hwy., Suite 404
Alexandria, VA 22303
703-317-9950
✉: info@iamovers.org
**www.iamovers.org**
IAM is a global association of movers and forwarders committed to providing customers with the highest level of service available. IAM offers consumer tips for moving, domestically or internationally, on their website.

## International Cemetery, Cremation and Funeral Association (ICCFA)

107 Carpenter Dr., Suite 100
Sterling, VA 20164
703-391-8400
Toll-free: 1-800-645-7700
**www.iccfa.com**
ICCFA is the trade association dedicated to funerals, and final resting places. They provide management guidance to members and advocate for consumer choice and dispute resolution in circumstances surrounding final arrangements.

## Joint Commission

One Renaissance Blvd.
Oakbrook Terrace, IL 60181
630-792-5000
**www.jointcommission.org**
The Joint Commission accredits and certifies healthcare organizations and Programs.

## LeadingAge

2519 Connecticut Ave., NW
Washington, DC 20008
202-783-2242
✉: info@leadingage.org
**www.leadingage.org**
LeadingAge represents not-for-profit nursing homes, continuing care retirement communities, assisted living and senior housing facilities, and community service organizations. Consumers may search LeadingAge's online database for providers and facilities that fit their needs.

## Mortgage Bankers Association of America (MBA)

1717 Rhode Island Ave., NW, Suite 400
Washington, DC 20036
202-557-2700
**www.mortgagebankers.org**
The MBA is the national association representing the real estate finance industry, including mortgage banking firms, commercial banks, life insurance companies, title companies, and savings and loan associations.

## Mystery Shopping Providers Association (MSPA)

455 S. 4th St., Suite 650
Louisville, KY 40202
**www.mysteryshop.org**
The MSPA is dedicated to improving service quality using anonymous shoppers. MSPA does not hire mystery shoppers, but they do provide a voluntary certification program for mystery shoppers.

## National Association of Attorneys General (NAAG)

2030 M St., NW, 8th Floor
Washington, DC 20036
202-326-6000
**www.naag.org**
NAAG facilitates communication among attorneys general, who are responsible for enforcing civil laws in their respective states. The AG offices often oversee state government regulation agencies and represent the public interest.

## National Association of Home Builders (NAHB)

1201 15th St., NW
Washington, DC 20005
202-266-8200
Toll-free: 1-800-368-5242
**www.nahb.org**
NAHB works so that consumers have access to safe, decent, and affordable housing.

## National Association of Insurance Commissioners (NAIC)

1100 Walnut St., Suite 1500
Kansas City, MO 64106-2197
816-842-3600
Toll-free: 1-866-470-6242
✉: webpost@naic.org
**www.InsureUonline.org**
**www.naic.org**
NAIC is a national organization of insurance regulators. The organization helps insurance regulators facilitate the fair and equitable treatment of insurance consumers and promote competitive markets.

## National Association of Professional Insurance Agents (PIA)

400 N. Washington St.
Alexandria, VA 22314
703-836-9340
✉: piainfo@pianet.org
**www.pianet.com**
This association represents the interests and needs of insurance agents.

## National Association of Realtors (NAR)

430 N. Michigan Ave.
Chicago, IL 60611-4087
312-329-8200
Toll-free: 1-800-874-6500
**www.realtor.org**
NAR is the organization of real estate agents. It develops standards for effective and ethical real estate business practices.

## National Foundation for Credit Counseling (NFCC)

2000 M St., NW, Suite 505
Washington, DC 20036
Toll-free: 1-800-388-2227
**www.nfcc.org**
The NFCC promotes the national agenda for financially responsible behavior and builds capacity for its members to deliver the highest quality financial education and counseling services. Contact NFCC to locate an affiliated financial counseling agency in your area.

## National Funeral Directors Association (NFDA)

13625 Bishops Dr.
Brookfield, WI 53005-6607
262-789-1880
Toll-free: 1-800-228-6332
✉: nfda@nfda.org
**www.nfda.org**
NFDA helps consumers make informed decisions about funeral services and offers a third party dispute resolution program for complaints regarding funeral homes.

### National Futures Association (NFA) ♦
300 S. Riverside Plaza, Suite 1800
Chicago, IL 60606-6615
312-781-1300
✉: information@nfa.futures.org
**www.nfa.futures.org**
NFA is the industry-wide self-regulatory organization for the U.S. futures industry. NFA provides innovative and efficient regulatory programs and services that safeguard the integrity of the derivatives markets. Consumers should contact NFA regarding any firm or individual who solicits them for investments in futures, options on futures and foreign currency.

### National Institute for Automotive Service Excellence (ASE)
101 Blue Seal Dr. SE, Suite 101
Leesburg, VA 20175
703-669-6600
Toll-free: 1-888-273-8378
✉: webmaster@ase.com
**www.ase.com**
ASE is an independent organization that works to improve the quality of automotive service and repair through the voluntary testing and certification of automotive repair professionals.

### Network Branded Prepaid Card Association (NBPCA)
110 Chestnut Ridge Rd., Suite 111
Montvale, NJ 07645-1706
**www.nbpca.com**
NBPCA represents all companies involved in providing prepaid cards that carry a brand network logo (American Express, Discover, Mastercard, or Visa) that can be used at numerous retailers. You can contact the association to get tips on how to use and maintain your card, or ask experts your questions about your prepaid cards.

### North American Consumer Protection Investigators
✉: webmaster@nacpi.org
**www.nacpi.org**
NACPI provides training and support for consumer protection investigators in government agencies at all levels. NACPI does not investigate individual consumer complaints, but helps investigators share information of mutual concern.

### North American Securities Administrators Association, Inc. (NASAA)
750 1st St., NE, Suite 1140
Washington, DC 20002
202-737-0900
✉: info@nasaa.org
**www.nasaa.org**
NASAA is an international organization devoted to investor protection. NASAA is the voice of the 50 state securities agencies responsible for grass-roots investor protection, investor education and efficient capital formation.

### Society of Consumer Affairs Professionals International (SOCAP) ♦
625 N. Washington St., Suite 304
Alexandria, VA 22314
703-519-3700
✉: socap@socap.org
**www.socap.org**
SOCAP provides training, conferences and publications to encourage and promote effective communication and understanding among business, government and consumers; and to define and advance the consumer affairs profession.

### Tire Industry Association (TIA)
1532 Pointer Ridge Pl., Suite G
Bowie, MD 20716-1883
301-430-7280
Toll-free: 1-800-876-8372
✉: info@tireindustry.org
**www.tireindustry.org**
TIA represents all members of the tire industry, including companies that manufacture, sell, recycle, retread tires, along with their suppliers.

### Toy Industry Association, Inc. (TIA)
1115 Broadway, Suite 400
New York, NY 10010
212-675-1141
✉: info@toyassociation.org
**www.toyinfo.org**
**www.toy-tia.org**
TIA is the not-for-profit trade association for producers and importers of toys and youth entertainment products sold in North America.

### United States Tour Operators Association (USTOA)
345 7th Ave., Suite 1801
New York, NY 10001
212-599-6599
✉: information@ustoa.com
**www.ustoa.com**
USTOA is composed of companies whose tours and packages encompass the entire globe and who conduct business in the U.S.

# INDEX

# INDEX

Single copies of the current *Consumer Action Handbook* are available by writing *Handbook*, Federal Citizen Information Center, Pueblo, CO 81009. The *Handbook* can also be viewed and ordered online at USA.gov/consumer.

The *2013 Consumer Action Handbook* will be current through summer 2014. To place your name on a mailing list to receive the 2013 *Handbook*, please mail your request to the address listed above. For regularly updated consumer information, visit the Consumer Action website at USA.gov/consumer.

We need your help to keep the *Handbook* up-to-date. Please report any changes to *Handbook* Update, Office of Citizen Services and Innovative Technologies, Federal Citizen Information Center, 1800 F Street, NW, Washington, DC 20405 or e-mail action.handbook@gsa.gov.

www.ingramcontent.com/pod-product-compliance
Lightning Source LLC
Chambersburg PA
CBHW080946290526
45795CB00009B/2931